UNITIVE JUSTICE:
BENDING THE ARC OF JUSTICE TOWARD LOVE

SYLVIA CLUTE, JD, MPA

KWE PUBLISHING

Sylvia Clute, LLC.
Richmond, Va.
© 2024 by Sylvia Clute
All rights reserved.

First Edition, published February 2024

ISBNs: 978-0977971039 (paperback), 9781088248287 (ebook)

All rights reserved. No part of this book may be reproduced or utilized in any form or by any means, electronic or mechanical, including photocopying or recording, or by any information storage or retrieval system, without permission in writing from the copyright holder, except in the case of brief quotations embodied in critical articles and reviews.

*Dedicated to the Brave Hearts who will carry
Unitive Justice forward, pioneers creating a kinder, gentler world.*

Love is patient; love is kind. It does not envy. It does not boast. It is not proud. It is not rude; it is not self-seeking. It is not easily angered; it keeps no record of wrongs. Love does not delight in evil but rejoices with the truth. It always protects, always trusts; always hopes; always perseveres. Love never fails. And now these three things remain: faith, hope and love; but the greatest of these is love."

1 Corinthians 13: 4-8; 13 (NIV)

CONTENTS

CHAPTER ONE — 1
From There To Here

CHAPTER TWO — 10
From System Blindness to System Change

CHAPTER THREE — 15
Roots and Wrong Turns

CHAPTER FOUR — 30
Retribution and Revenge in the 20th and 21st Centuries

CHAPTER FIVE — 43
The Punishing Decades—A Manifestation of Our Dark Side

CHAPTER SIX — 59
Two Bridges from Punitive to Unitive Justice

CHAPTER SEVEN — 69
New Choices

CHAPTER EIGHT — 77
The 7 Arcs to Individual Transformation

Arc 1: Security/Order — 79
  From Rules to Values

Arc 2: Governance — 91
  From Control to Selfgovernance

Arc 3: Communication — 99
  From Deception to Honesty

Arc 4: Assessment — 108
  From Judgment to Insight

Arc 5: Interpersonal — 113
  From Distrust to Trust

Arc 6: Strength ... 118
    From Self-Doubt to Courage
Arc 7: Guiding Moral Principle ... 131
    From Proportional Revenge/Harm Answers Harm to Lovingkindness/Heal, Do No Harm

CHAPTER NINE ... 150
The 7 Arcs to Community Transformation
Arc 8: Benefit ... 152
    From Self-Interest to Community
Arc 9: Social Framework ... 158
    From Hierarchy/Top Down to Equality/Inclusion
Arc 10: Safety ... 172
    From Punishment to Connection
Arc 11: Goal ... 182
    From Compliance to Mutually Beneficial Action/Wholeness
Arc 12: Focus ... 188
    From Event to Context
Arc 13: Animation ... 200
    From Opposition/Confrontation to Synergy
Arc 14: Energy/Spirit ... 204
    From Fear to Love

CHAPTER TEN ... 220
New Information that Compels System Change

CHAPTER ELEVEN ... 229
Unitive Justice and Lovingkindness in Action

Acknowledgments ... 261
About the Author ... 263
Endnotes ... 265

CHAPTER ONE
FROM THERE TO HERE

Justice is essential to me and has been from an early age. That is why, in 1970, I entered law school—after surmounting the quotas designed to keep women and minorities out of the legal profession. I saw becoming an attorney as an opportunity to help, in my small way, to make the world a more just place.

Throughout my earlier education, I learned that our legal system was exceptionally fair and just—our guarantee of due process made it so. On my first day of law school, the new students were told that our (the U.S.) legal system is the best in the world. I now wonder why I didn't ask, "The best for whom?", when law school admissions had long barred or limited women and minorities from entering.

In the 1970s, discrimination against women and minorities was still prevalent and generally legal in many places. Upon graduation from law school, I met all the requirements for practicing law only to find that I could not get an interview in a law firm in Richmond, Virginia, where my husband and I settled down with our children. I was told on several occasions, "There is no need to interview you—our clients don't want to be represented by a woman." Fortunately, that has since changed, albeit women remain marginalized, often prevented from accessing more senior roles in private law firms and the judiciary, for example.[1] It is still a system that is best for some but not for others.

While a Richmond law firm would not hire me, there was one job open to a woman. I became the first female attorney ever hired at the Reynolds Metals Headquarters in Richmond. At the time, Reynolds did not hire women for their law department. Ironically, I was hired to work on compliance with federal affirmative action requirements in its Equal Opportunity Affairs Division. It was not long, however, before my desire to be a trial attorney prevailed. In 1975 I left Reynolds to hang out my shingle and become a solo practitioner.

It was now the height of the Women's Movement. One advantage of being out on my own was that there was no senior partner to tell me what I could or could not do, so I chose to become an activist for women's rights while also trying civil cases. The fact that women had to fight for their rights in the 1970s was another indication of bias in the system, but our fight was not as herculean as it was for those in the civil rights movement—women were not being lynched. Many people have been fighting for fairness in our justice system for a long time, yet many accept the punitive model as what is best.

Yet another early challenge to my trust in the justice system came when I read Nils Christie's description of the Western system of justice in his renowned article, "Conflicts as Property."[2] It was a counternarrative to what I learned in law school—but I knew it was true.

Christie, a Norwegian sociologist, and criminologist explains that the Western justice system is like a state-owned business. This state-owned system for addressing crime has enabled those in control (judges, lawyers, therapists, and criminologists, to name a few) to treat conflict as though it is an asset of their privately-owned business. While the people theoretically own the legal system—they might be compared to the shareholders of the business—their say in the process is even more limited than those who own stock certificates. Citizens cannot dispose of their interest in the system even if they find it dysfunctional and sometimes immoral, and they have little say in its operation.

Christie describes the role of lawyers in the business of justice as follows:

> Lawyers are particularly good at stealing conflicts. . . They are trained to prevent and solve conflicts. They are socialized into a subculture with a surprisingly high agreement concerning interpretation of norms, and regarding what sort of information can be accepted as relevant in each case. Many among us have, as laymen, experienced the sad moments of truth when our lawyers tell us that our best arguments in our fight against our neighbour are without any legal relevance whatsoever and that we for God's sake ought to keep quiet about them in court. Instead, they pick out arguments we might find irrelevant or even wrong to use.[3]

I had done enough trial work to recognize Christie's description of what lawyers often do in litigation. The attorney's winning theory of the case and the client's understanding of what happened can be worlds apart. Often, the client is not permitted to tell their story about what occurred, which may feel confusing, disempowering, and demoralizing to the client.

Treatment personnel, including criminologists, are another group Christie describes as using conflicts for their own self-interest. They benefit from ensuring the offender in a criminal case is seen not merely as a criminal, but as "a legitimate target for treatment."[4] Christie describes the role of criminologists (his profession) as:

> ... an auxiliary science for the professionals within the crime control system. We have focused on the offender, made her or him into an object for study, manipulation, and control. We have added to all those forces that have reduced the victim to a nonentity and the offender to a thing.[5]

In fact, our basic social structure according to Christie, tends to define each of us by our individual roles, not as total persons. Seeing our individual roles as disconnected silos forces us to be separate and segregated according to characteristics, such as gender, race, disability, sexual orientation or age.[6] These add to our depersonalization, lack of information, and lack of understanding of one another. It ignores our interconnectedness.

When a conflict arises, this compartmentalization renders us less able to cope with the situation ourselves, so we turn to the experts. That objectification never felt right to me, and as a female, I was directly impacted by it. But my system blindness (described in Chapter Two) kept me from realizing that it could be different.

In 1987, I had an even more profound revelation, one that changed my life forever. It was about ten years into my career as a trial attorney and perhaps fifteen years after setting upon my spiritual journey. I realized from my study of *A Course in Miracles* that there are two models of justice: *vengeance and love*. That changed everything. I knew what justice as vengeance was—that is the punitive model of justice found in our court system and that was all I could offer my clients. By then, I had already seen more than enough of the injustice that our legal system produces. I had no clue what Justice as Love looked like or how to implement it, but at that moment, I committed to finding out—a much longer journey than I ever expected.

As I delved deeper into this new insight I came to have a deeper understanding of what it meant. Not only is the traditional system hierarchical and so complex it forces people to rely on the experts, I encountered much that confirmed my assessment that punitive justice is a seriously flawed model. It uses punishment to maintain control, but it has no means of addressing the underlying causes of crime. In fact, it excludes that information from consideration by characterizing it as "collateral." As I traveled this journey, I also realized that Justice as Love is a reality.

It eventually became increasingly difficult to walk into a courtroom. The more I understood the true potential of a legal justice system with no punitive elements, the harder it was for me to accept retribution and revenge as justice. I felt like Alice attending the Mad Hatter's birthday party—more and more surreal. I was expected to participate in the insanity and pretend this is reality.

In 2003, after twenty-eight years as a trial attorney, I stopped practicing law. The first two years I spent back in graduate school and healing from my years in the trial attorney gladiator pit. I had learned how to gird myself against the pain I was present to as a trial attorney and the cases I handled. I had learned to live with dishonesty by people I knew were inherently honest when not in this win-lose system, including some of the lawyers. When I ceased being a part of that system, I welcomed the opportunity to turn my focus to what I now call "Unitive Justice," or "Justice as Love." This model has no punitive elements. It is grounded in lovingkindness and sees our connection to one another as paramount.

For clarity, I would like to share my definitions of some of the terms I use in this book. I intentionally capitalize Unitive Justice and Love to designate them as key terms.

justice: one's foundational belief in what is right and just.

punitive justice: a system of proportional revenge that answers harm with more harm. When the counter harm is proportional (in equal measure) to the original harm being answered, it is deemed moral and just in the punitive system. Punitive justice is sometimes called "retributive justice" because it uses punishment as retribution for a wrong or criminal act—or as a threat, if someone does not comply.

Unitive Justice: a system that builds on our interconnectedness and our shared humanity to create a model of justice that achieves individual and community wellbeing and safety; it has no punitive elements. Unitive Justice recognizes that beneath all the complexity of our conflicts, separation is the problem, and so it follows that connection is the solution. As Unitive Justice progressively dismantles our barriers to connection, we grow stronger individually, as a community and as a culture.

Unitive Justice is not just a modification of the traditional justice system; it represents an entirely different understanding of justice. How we can implement Justice as Love with intention, where justice as vengeance now prevails, is what I seek to demonstrate throughout this book.

Love: the benevolent feeling for others that embodies connection beyond judgment and separation; Oneness. The term will be capitalized hereafter when it refers to the emotion in its most valid form; to be distinguished from when we use the term "love" to mean feelings or activities such as personal intimacy, sexual relations, or affection for material objects.

shared humanity: the bond created by simultaneously recognizing the inestimable worth of one's self and the inestimable worth of one's neighbor. At the level of our shared humanity, we are equal; anything that appears to be less is mere judgment and separation.

JUSTICE AS LOVE

Justice as Love has roots that are at least as old as the roots of retributive justice. We find evidence of justice with no punitive elements in various places if we know what to look for and where. For instance, the ancient system of Ubuntu in Africa was a way to organize an orderly society that did not rely on penal institutions, such as jails or prisons. In the 1600s, the Quakers organized themselves in a non-hierarchical, non-judgmental, and non-punitive system that has held reasonably steady for centuries. Quakerism is a pacifist religion, as are the Amish.

From time to time, we see compelling, humbling examples of Justice as Love, which for many of us are difficult to comprehend. On October 2, 2006, in a small Amish enclave in Lancaster County, Pennsylvania, a man murdered five young schoolgirls, wounded others, and then killed himself in a planned attack. The people of this quiet Amish community sought no revenge. Instead, some of the elders visited the widow of the killer to offer forgiveness.

Nearly a decade later in 2015, a twenty-one-year-old young man with an automatic weapon murdered nine people during a Bible study session at the historic Emanuel Church in Charleston, South Carolina, hoping to incite racial violence. The family members of those who were murdered did not seek the expected revenge. One said, "We have no room for hating, so we have to forgive."[7]

One of the most remarkable applications of Justice as Love that I am aware of was created by two men, Paul Taylor and Weldon "Prince" Bunn, during their twenty-plus years of incarceration in Virginia prisons. They transformed themselves and the prison culture by transcending the ultra-punitive prison system *while they were in it*. They had not heard of Ubuntu or attended a Quaker meeting, yet they intuitively found *within themselves* what was required; guided by our internal moral compass, it springs from the heart.

While Paul Taylor is his birth name, I will refer to him as "Taylor Paul," the name he took for himself while he was incarcerated. This was his way of letting those in "free society" know that he was the complete opposite of who they described him to be.

Taylor and Prince had a determination not to die in prison, despite life-plus-26 and life-plus-80-year sentences. They knew that the path that got them into prison was not the path to their release. Although they were confined to prison, they had everything they needed to achieve transformation. First, *they had to give up their retribution and revenge thinking— that was the key to bringing their inherent goodness to the fore.* In essence, they transcended duality consciousness, enabling them to experience Unitive Consciousness.

duality consciousness: the mistaken belief that separation is real. In duality, only fragmentation is universal, nothing is whole; it is the lower order of reality. It is a mental state of sustained opposition, for example, good versus evil, us versus them. Fear of the "other" fuels sustained chaos and conflict, an uncreative use of one's mind. Only in duality consciousness can retribution and revenge be understood as justice.

Unitive Consciousness: the state of being interconnected in wholeness; the non-dual nature of self and all of creation; the higher order of reality. In this mental state, Love and justice are one. When we *awaken to Unitive Consciousness, we discover who we truly are—the embodiment of lovingkindness*. When we extend Love to another, the receiver has more Love but we also increase the Love within our self, reversing the physical law that says your gain is my loss.

While in duality thinking, the concept of Unitive Consciousness may be difficult to understand. I hope that changes as readers delve further into the book. For those who are interested in an even deeper conversation about Unitive Consciousness, I recommend Elena Mustakova's book, *Global Unitive Healing: Integral Skills for Personal and Collective Transformation*. Elena describes our evolution toward Unitive Consciousness as follows. Unitive healing starts with us listening inward, overcoming inner fragmentation, and allowing ourselves to become whole. We learn how to use our minds mindfully so that we do not fall into mental traps, we learn the role of heart and become more aware of the role of language. This enables us to expand into community and national healing, and even global healing.

What we need to achieve Unitive Consciousness lies within. When Taylor and Prince escaped the dualistic thinking that mired them in separation and the us-versus-them worldview, they were able to draw on the wisdom they had within themselves to guide their paths to transformation. This was how they came to create a process of Justice as Love that changed not only themselves but the prison culture as well. Throughout this book, I will share more about the inspiration and insight into Unitive Justice that I received from both Taylor and Prince.

In part, as a result of what I have learned from Taylor and Prince, and despite the ubiquitous nature of our punitive structures, culture and institutions, I am convinced that Justice as Love is inherent in who we are. This is why Justice as Love continues to show up in random acts of kindness that manifest unexpectedly, even in a prison pod.

Some might fear that this book supports an idealistic approach, such as the release of all inmates in jails and prisons because those institutions violate the principles of Unitive Justice. As you will learn, that is far from what I support. I note later in the book that jails and prisons may be a good place to start as we begin to create Unitive Justice communities. Transformation takes time, and inmates have time. Time provides the opportunity to learn about transformation that benefits them and will benefit their communities upon their release—if they are given the necessary tools needed to take this path. Taylor and Prince prove this is possible.

Unitive Justice is not a "quick fix" for the brokenness in our world, but it is a start. A small Unitive Justice community would not have stopped Hitler when he was ravaging Europe and exterminating millions of people. But the fact that grave injustices on that scale have existed and can happen again is a compelling reason to begin to create our small pockets of Unitive Justice wherever we can and to nurture them with all the Love we can muster.

The promise that Justice as Love holds for transforming our justice system (and our world) is at once both idealistic and practical. It may take many lifetimes to transform a world tethered to dualistic thinking, and yet it can be implemented by one person, in one prison pod, in one family, in one relationship as soon as right now. To the extent that you can suspend dualistic thinking while reading this book, the possibilities and opportunities for applying Unitive Justice will more easily be seen and understood.

Justice remains as important to me as it ever was, but I now reject retribution—answering one harm with another—as worthy of being called justice. I also now know that true justice can be achieved; I am more certain of this than I have ever been. "The arc of history is long, but it bends toward justice," said Martin Luther King, Jr. in 1968. This may be truer now than at any time in human history, providing we change our thoughts, words and actions from a dualistic lens to a unitive one, seeing Justice as Love, not as retribution.

This book comes with an urgent message. If we hope to create peace, save our environment, end systemic racism and other debilitating prejudices, address deep pockets of poverty and achieve lasting positive change, we must transform our understanding of justice. It took me decades to realize this and years to see an alternate path. I hope this book helps my readers recognize Justice as Love, not only as a realistic possibility but as an imperative.

The invitation for you to join this journey includes some questions at the end of each chapter for you to consider. If you are so inclined, please keep a Unitive Justice journal nearby to record your reflections. Before you begin reading Chapter Two, I invite you to write your answers to the following questions in your journal. Hopefully, comparing what you write now and your understanding after reading the book will strengthen any seeds of change that are planted in the process.

* * *

Invitation to Journal. Consider these questions:

   a. What is your present definition of "justice"?
   b. Why is justice important to you?
   c. What would your ideal system of justice look like?

CHAPTER TWO
FROM SYSTEM BLINDNESS TO SYSTEM CHANGE

Justice system change is no small undertaking. First of all, justice is not limited to the courts—it is all-encompassing and exists to a large extent in our minds. The dualistic thinking that now prevails manifests in punitive and repressive social systems across diverse environments. I will often write about system change in the area of criminal justice, but this book addresses a whole system change—a shift from duality to Unitive Consciousness throughout all human endeavors.

In this chapter, we will consider one of the significant hurdles to achieving justice system change, wherever it exists—system blindness. This means being immersed in a system but not fully understanding how the system works or your role in sustaining it.

System blindness is a little like asking a fish how the water is today, and the fish responds: "What water?" Fish have no concept of what it is like to exist in something other than water, so they have nothing with which water can be compared.

Like fish in water, most of us live in a punitive culture that we do not even realize we are in—a culture that embraces the concept of retributive justice as the norm without knowing there are better, more just, alternatives. This model is the substance of many schools' disciplinary rules, corporate personnel policies, and even church rules. It has been practiced in many households for generations. The old adage, "spare the rod, spoil the child," implicitly tells us retributive justice is the best way to raise/educate our children. And punitive justice provides the rationale for every war that is fought.

However, the comparison to fish fails because the punitive system is less real than the water fish live in. Punitive justice is a social construct; it is neither natural nor inevitable. Our traditional system of justice was made up over time and it exists only because humans tacitly consent to its legitimacy. From birth, most of us are conditioned to believe that justice and vengeance go hand in hand. My hope is that this book will help some escape that misguided mindset.

Many of us have little direct contact with our legal system. We might personally experience how traffic violations or civil actions are handled in court and some of us have served on juries. But what most of us know about the legal system comes from television, radio, movies and the Internet, where the "good people" usually win in an adversarial system, leaving the "bad people" facing punitive justice. In my experience as a trial attorney, it is not clear that the "good people" are the winners in our punitive system of justice, in part because the difference between winning and losing is more complex than the clearly drawn line found in the punitive narrative.

Even when a client wins the case, victory in this adversarial arena has limitations. Many lawsuits are brought among people with long-standing relationships—spouses, family members, business partners, employees and employers, doctors and patients, and neighbors. Our traditional legal system does not include the goal of repairing the underlying relationships among the litigants and, in fact, relationships may be damaged even further by the litigation. A win in court may still be accompanied by a feeling of deep loss. Presenting the facts about who did what in one event or another provides no opportunity to address the root causes, yet the facts in the case are nearly always symptoms of deeper brokenness in need of healing. An adversarial process is not designed to get at this deeper truth.

Sometimes it is not clear-cut who the "good people" are. Each competing side tends to see themselves as the "good people," so there is no agreement there. On top of that, during the latter half of the 20th century, U.S. policymakers went on an incarceration binge (see Chapter Five) that cast the net of our criminal law system ever wider. A growing number of our citizens who consider themselves to be "good people" have family members, friends, and some even found themselves in jail or prison. Our flawed theory of retributive justice made the U.S. the biggest jailer in the world, but retributive justice is not limited to the courts.

In a culture immersed in punitive justice, retribution and revenge largely appear as the only type of justice available for most of us to learn or apply. Textbooks and media sources teach us—explicitly and implicitly —that the punitive model is how justice operates, suggesting that there is no other choice. These messages are reinforced by a multitude of teachings, both religious and secular, that bestow legitimacy on the punitive system. We overlook the mental gymnastics required to de-emphasize the spiritual teachings found in all major religions that are based on lovingkindness, such as the Golden Rule and "love your enemies," and then we disregard the resulting hypocrisy.

We are conditioned to accept our laws, those who enforce them, and what our courts do as "normal." Often repeated and over-simplified narratives about how the justice system works, such as, "equal justice for all," "justice is blind," and "the punishment fits the crime" tend to obscure the complexity of the justice system and its inner workings. As a result, we often fail to realize what is being done in our name, with our tacit consent, under the general rubric of "justice."

System blindness keeps us from being aware of how embedded we are in the punitive system, how little we understand about how it operates, and how we may be directly or indirectly facilitating its operation without realizing how that happens. In our society, we are led to believe that the justice system operates fairly, but when we understand the multitude of weaknesses that plague a punitive system of justice, we discover that the opposite is often true.

The failures of our traditional system of justice are well known, especially by those operating within it. Over the years, there have been many efforts to correct flaws, but without truly understanding how the system functions, we are sometimes blind to how new solutions impact the rest of the system. For example, major penal reforms have fallen short because the punitive system manages to adapt stealthily to those reforms and the system continues much the same. This pattern is found in the penitentiary itself, the adult reformatory, the juvenile court, parole, and community corrections. There is now some concern that Restorative Justice may fall prey to this same transgression.[1]

Some reform efforts undertaken with the intention of alleviating punitive measures have the reverse effect, enabling the punitive justice system to get bigger, not better. Parole was intended to shorten prison sentences by providing an early release for good behavior. In fact, the penalties for parole violations after release often add more time to sentences, making them longer than serving the original sentence in full.

Another example of how a change resulted in unexpected consequences is the misguided reform that arose from our assumption that punishment is the most effective way to enforce compliance among noncompliant youth. The reform policy of zero-tolerance discipline in schools that began in the 1990s led to many first-time youth offenders being labeled as "non-compliant" and funneled into the school-to-prison pipeline[2]. Our schools became institutions that fed our incarceration binge (*see* Chapter Five), often with tragic results. As Martin Luther King, Jr. said, "The prescription for the cure rests with the accurate diagnosis of the disease."[3] We failed that test.

Our system blindness is further obscured by the fact there is a good argument in support of the system that we now have, namely, it could be much worse. Our existing legal and enforcement agencies do create a degree of order and justice. We are encouraged to see law-breaking as an offense against public order, a frame in which we can see ourselves as potential victims. This frame encourages us to see the legal system as beneficial to us, necessary for our protection, whether or not we understand or agree with how adjudication and punishment actually work. The enormous cost that inflicting revenge repeatedly has on the population as a whole and the damage it causes to individuals is largely out of sight and out of mind.

Just talking about what is broken is not enough. We must simultaneously have a viable, actionable alternative that we can choose to implement instead—a system that is rational, morally consistent, and one that makes our individual lives better. To be sustainable, it must also strengthen the fabric of our communities. The information provided in this book shows how Unitive Justice meets all of these criteria.

* * *

Invitation to Journal. Consider these questions:

> a. Have you been harmed (perhaps punished) by someone who told you it was for your own good? If so, did this strengthen or weaken your relationship? If it caused you harm, was the harm eventually healed? If so, how?
> b. Have you caused someone harm, thinking it was the best thing to do in the circumstances, but later realized that it made things worse for that person and/or your relationship with them? If so, what happened?

c. What experience of retribution and revenge do you most regret in your life? It may have been your direct experience of retribution and revenge, or it may have been an indirect experience, perhaps an event that you witnessed happening to someone else, but it impacted you. What happened and what was the outcome?

CHAPTER THREE
ROOTS AND WRONG TURNS

It was not preordained that justice in Western culture would be retributive; there are parts of the world that did not take that route. When we ask why we have the punitive justice system that we have, the answer is replete with echoes of the past and hidden determinants from long ago that still shape our beliefs and institutions. In order to overcome our system blindness, we need to better understand how our system of justice came to be and how it operates. Not just what is taught in law school, but how we got in the circumstances that now exist.

This is not a complete history, but in this chapter, we will consider a few of the major forks in the road that got us here. It is important to lay this foundation, because the cure rests with the accurate diagnosis of the disease. We cannot diagnose the disease until we can identify its roots, recognize wrong turns, how symptoms manifest and impact our lives, and how *we* unwittingly participate in keeping these punitive structures in place.

THE CODE OF HAMMURABI

We begin with an ancient legal development that is foundational in Western justice, the Code of Hammurabi, a collection of Babylonian laws developed during the reign of Hammurabi (ending circa 1750 BCE). This set of statutes institutionalized many earlier traditions, such as the brutal trial by ordeal. It was, nonetheless, an advance over earlier tribal custom as it outlawed crude practices like the blood feud, private revenge, and marriage by capture.[1]

Perhaps its most important contribution to the modern era is that the Code of Hammurabi codified "an eye for an eye, a tooth for a tooth" justice in what was called the *lex talionis* (the law of retaliation). This part of the code provides that one who causes harm is to receive as punishment precisely those injuries and damages they inflicted upon their victim.[2] This provision reflected state governance of justice in one of its earliest forms.[3]

Requiring retribution to be equal to the harm being answered (i.e., proportional) no doubt reflected a desire on the ruler's part that wrongdoers be "fairly" punished. This limitation curtailed more brutal reactions, such as slaughtering an entire village in retaliation for a single death. Seen as "fair punishment," justice as proportional revenge took root.

The importance of the Code of Hammurabi to our modern justice system is that it made inflicting more harm as a way to stop harm both legal and moral. When a wrong was committed, answering that harm with a harm of equal measure became the accepted understanding of justice. As we shall see, this model of justice proved to be extremely useful to those in control. They could write a law and punish those who failed to comply—whether the law was just or not. Punitive justice affirms that "might makes right."

Our traditional Western justice system is still a system of proportional revenge. Our criminal codes are filled with the measure of revenge (punishment) needed to balance the harm being answered. Even today, many see this as the only viable model of justice and anything else as idealistic and unrealistic. Moreover, we fail to see how we pass this system on to our youth when our own behavior models punishment and revenge as the means to compliance.

THE DOCTRINE OF DISCOVERY AND CORPORATIONS

From a historical perspective, retributive justice is central to how the modern world developed. With its laws written by those in control and compliance enforced with punishment, nations with this system were able to conquer foreign lands using force, violence, and deception. They then claimed their domination and control was "legal" because they adopted laws that said it was. Punitive justice provides a system that can enable might to prevail over morality. How was this dominance achieved?

When the opportunity arose to colonize lands around the globe, including in North America, this punitive model of justice in which the king wrote the rules and then enforced them with punishment proved to be an effective legal vehicle for taking land and resources from indigenous peoples. An example of how this played out is found in a series of papal bulls, i.e., public decrees issued by the pope or the Vatican, to the kings of Portugal and Spain in the 15th century. The following section on the Doctrine of Discovery is based on the writings of John Montgomery,[4] a corporate law reformer. He describes the doctrine's function and impacts as follows:

> These [papal] bulls split the New World between Portugal and Spain and authorized their kings to conquer any non-Christian peoples in these territories and exploit them and their lands and resources. The Doctrine of Discovery established that white, European, male, Christians were the superior humans. The Doctrine of Discovery became the moral and legal justification for European nations to seize foreign lands, vanquish their indigenous peoples and exploit them and their lands and resources for the benefit of the crown.

The Doctrine of Discovery was of monumental consequence. It gave legitimacy to colonial empires and the practices of white supremacy, slavery, and genocide. This doctrine negates any notion of love for each other or concern for our shared planetary home. Our global civilization and economic system that is based on the domination and exploitation of people and the planet can be traced directly to the Doctrine of Discovery. It paved the way for the doctrine of Manifest Destiny that propelled the expansion of the U.S. from the Atlantic Ocean to the Pacific Ocean, and the melding of white supremacy with Christianity that is re-emerging today.

Understanding how the Doctrine of Discovery functioned during what is now called the Age of Discovery requires that we consider how corporations, one of the principal actors in our economic system, served then and now as the agents of empire. Corporations serve as the cornerstone of domination over people and the planet. The original corporations that enabled this domination were the Dutch and British East India Companies, legal entities that were used to conquer foreign territories and exploit their peoples and resources for the crown. The corporation's basic design works so well that it has changed little in 500 years. Corporations still conquer markets and exploit them for their owners. It is notable that Pope Francis recently repudiated the Doctrine of Discovery, after European colonial powers used it for centuries to legitimize the seizure and exploitation of Indigenous lands in Africa, the Americas, and beyond.[5] It's at least a start.

By law or custom, traditional corporations are designed to serve one purpose – to maximize stockholder welfare. Under this doctrine, they need not assume responsibility for the negative consequences of their corporate behavior on society or the environment. As a result, we have a global economic system dominated by multinational corporations that cause much harm at little cost to the institutions.

Montgomery describes corporations as amoral actors acting in an amoral economic system. This gives rise to conflict with the moral compass of many individual citizens around the world, and especially their particular spiritual traditions' equivalent of the Golden Rule—do unto others as you would have them do unto you. However, this conflict often goes unnoticed until it is too late because the decisions regarding what is done within the corporate structure are made behind closed doors in the boardroom. Montgomery calls this "the golden rule vs. the rule of gold."

While there is a movement to create a "benefit corporation" category that attempts to balance shareholder interest and public benefit, these efforts are dwarfed by more potent actions that have enhanced corporations' disproportionate control. For example, their control is magnified by U.S. Supreme Court decisions like *Santa Clara County v. Southern Pacific Railroad Company*, 118 U.S. 394 (1886), that established the legal principle that corporations have "corporate personhood" that entitles them to some of the constitutional rights accorded to human beings.

The finding that corporations are persons goes back to William Blackstone, an 18th-century English jurist (1723-1780) who wrote the tome called *Commentaries on the Laws of England*. Blackstone basically made up the rule that "[p]ersons are divided by the law into either natural persons or artificial. Natural persons are such as the God of nature formed us; artificial are such as are created and devised by human laws for the purposes of society and government, which are called corporations or bodies politic."[6] This legal fiction is used to contort the law to serve corporate interests, as a number of key legal decisions have done.

The 14th Amendment to the U.S. Constitution was written to guarantee the rights of citizens to the freed slaves; it states, "no state shall deny to any person within its jurisdiction the equal protection of the laws

. . ." It referred only to persons without specifying that it was to apply to "natural persons," not "artificial persons." The intent that it applied only to natural persons was so clear that it was disingenuous to argue that it applied to "artificial persons," but no matter. Indeed, since the *Santa Clara* case, Supreme Court justices, some of whom professed to be committed to the "original intent" of the constitution when it was written, have extended the application of constitutional rights clearly intended for human beings to corporations in a series of cases.

A particularly harmful application of corporate personhood's legal fiction is found in *Citizens United v. Federal Election Commission*, 558 U.S. 310 (2010). It overturned a prior ruling that prevented "the corrosive and distorting effects of immense aggregations of wealth that are accumulated with the help of the corporate form . . ." when it comes to political speech.[7] The court justified its new ruling saying the prior decision "interferes with the 'open marketplace of ideas' protected by the First Amendment."

Citizens United extended the First Amendment right of free speech to corporations and held that the government cannot restrict independent expenditures for political campaigns made by corporations, including nonprofit corporations, labor unions, and other associations. These monetary expenditures were held to be an exercise of corporations' constitutional right of free speech. Jimmy Carter described the decision as "unlimited political bribery."

This decision requires that we accept the notion that how much money you have is a legitimate measure of your access to free speech and the legal fallacy that corporations are people—evidence that laws can be written to protect the continuity of the system the lawmakers believe in,[8] and that can trump any requirement that the laws be fair. Fortunately, a nationwide campaign to circumvent *Citizens United* by creating a National Popular Vote Interstate Compact, state law by state law, is gaining momentum. (See www.NationalPopularVote.com for details.)

This ruling permits corporations to buy political influence far beyond what most individuals will ever have. With time, it is clear that this ruling is resulting in the concentration of control over our three branches of government—legislative, judicial and executive—in the hands of fewer and fewer people of wealth. A collateral impact of *Citizens United* is to weaken majority rule as corporate control becomes more broadly entrenched.

While corporations now have many of the same constitutional rights as people, they will never have the same responsibilities or limits that people have. A corporation is a legal fiction established by state law that bears no resemblance to being a person. A corporation does not physically die, so its existence can be in perpetuity—it never has to pay inheritance taxes. A corporation cannot be incarcerated for wrongdoing.

If a corporation gets a tarnished image, those running it can merely re-incorporate under a different name and market this new identity as though it has nothing to do with its past activities. Corporations can be used to hide the identity and activities of individuals so those individuals can act in secrecy. Laws and court decisions interpreting them can be skewed to favor one side and corporations are often the beneficiaries. This favoritism is sometimes due to the fact that some legislators are beholden to corporations for campaign donations and many conservative judges have been groomed by organizations like the Federalist Society to favor the corporate perspective.

The *Citizens United* case is a good example of what I experienced when I was trying cases. I concluded that judges, if they so choose, are able to find within a vast array of precedents a justification for the outcome they want to achieve. This is not considered abuse–it is within the scope of the authority we vest in them. If the ruling is in a lower court, perhaps a higher court will find a different justification to achieve a different outcome. Sometimes court rulings can, with great grassroots effort, be trumped by legislation and constitutional amendments supported by the majority of voters, but this is not common.

Perhaps the best protection we have against corporate abuse is to select our legislators with great care, doing what we can to ensure they are people of integrity. We can cultivate and support political candidates who understand the difference between how a punitive system functions and what we can do instead, namely, apply unitive principles to our systems. (More about that in Chapter Eleven, page 246.)

HOW PUNITIVE JUSTICE ACQUIRED MORAL LEGITIMACY

After considering the Doctrine of Discovery that was used to justify colonization in the name of Christianity, I would like to consider the relationship between religion and systems that are organized around punitive justice. The entwining of established religion and punitive justice began long ago and they became interdependent. I believe that our punitive system of justice has endured with the potency it has, at least in part, because of the moral legitimacy that organized religion provides it. Religious lessons about a vengeful god whose wrath is to be feared tacitly teach that retributive justice is moral.

Over time, many religious traditions came to embrace the Code of Hammurabi's principle that revenge is moral if it is proportional. This prepares us to be taught that it is moral to inflict harm upon law-breakers —as long as the punishment is deemed to be equal to the crime.

What is important to our discussion of Unitive Justice is that some religious traditions simultaneously teach that proportional revenge— answering harm with more harm—is *not* moral, so we have a choice about which lesson to emphasize. This includes at least the religions of Judaism, Christianity, and Islam.[9] A widely known example in the Christian world is the contradiction between the Sermon on the Mount and the Just War Doctrine.

In the Sermon on the Mount, Jesus admonished His followers to abandon "an eye for an eye" justice. Jesus brought a new covenant that says do not resist violence; love your enemies; pray for those who persecute you; when slapped on one cheek, turn the other cheek. To many, these are radical concepts, but they are vital for consistency in the morality taught by Jesus. Jesus never said, "be a little nonviolent." It was not long after Jesus' death that this moral consistency gave way to the expediency of might makes right. Ingenious ways were found to make violence seem legitimate and moral, despite what Jesus taught.

The structures found in a punitive justice system include proportional revenge, hierarchy, judgment, punishment, self-interest, deception and others that we explore when we consider Unitive Justice Theory in Chapters Eight and Nine. These punitive structures are necessary to maintain a monarchy. When Constantine (ca., 306 AD to 337 AD) became the first Roman emperor to legalize Christianity, it began the fusing of Christianity and state control. This fusion gave rise to a significant moral conflict: the nonviolence taught by Jesus versus maintaining the emperor's Roman Army. Proportional revenge justifies raising armies and using them to attack one's enemies, a rule Constantine was unwilling to abandon. This inconsistency between a punitive system and the teachings of Jesus was eventually "resolved" with a rule that made violating the teachings of Jesus "moral."

St. Augustine, a renowned Christian theologian of the 5th century, offered a solution called the "Just War Doctrine." This doctrine provides that the emperor and his armies can go to war and still be good Christians if certain conditions[10] are met:

1. The damage inflicted by the aggressor on the nation or community of nations must be lasting, grave, and certain (just cause);
2. All other means of ending the conflict must have been shown to be impractical or ineffective (last resort);
3. There must be serious prospects of success (likely success);
4. The use of arms must not produce evils and disorders graver than the evil to be eliminated (proportional revenge).

Who decides when the required conditions are met? The ruler—he is the decider.[11] As each measure is subjective, any ruler can claim to have met each test, even if the war is unjust. This applies not only to damage done to one individual or several; it also provides essential cover used to legitimize mass killings, such as the bombing of entire cities, done in times of war.[12]

Perhaps the Just War Doctrine is being reconsidered. When Patriarch Kirill, the leader of the Russian Orthodox Church and a close ally of President Vladimir Putin, used the Christian cross to justify Russia's war against Ukraine, Pope Frances reportedly told Kirill, "Once upon a time, there was also talk in our churches of holy war or just war. Today we cannot speak like this."[13] The Vatican quoted Pope Francis as adding, "Christian awareness of the importance of peace has developed."[14]

That inner whisper that tells us to do what's right has been there from the beginning, gently calling us to a higher standard. But so far, the loud voice of proportional revenge seems to be winning, despite the fact that all major religious traditions have a form of the Golden Rule among their teachings.[15] While many already do so, perhaps even more organized religions will consider shifting their emphasis to the lessons about Love contained in their doctrines as their part in creating system change.

ENGLISH COMMON LAW

When the U.S. legal system was established, it happened on a stage already populated with many established legal traditions. The proportional revenge that was made legal in the Code of Hammurabi was firmly entrenched in law. It provided one of the foundations for the primary source of U.S. justice—English Common Law. It was a particular English formulation of an eye-for-an-eye justice that was brought to U.S. shores by the colonists that still defines how we administer justice today. To understand the context, let's look at English history.

After Roman domination of the British Isles (CE 43 to CE 410), the British Isles were left to fend for themselves.[16] With no centralized authority to maintain order, justice became a local matter. Local officials met periodically to adjudicate disputes, not pursuant to an established procedure, but in various ways that fit the situation.[17] However, in the 12th and 13th centuries, this local autonomy was lost.

After the Norman Conquest of England in 1066, medieval kings began to consolidate their control and institutionalize royal authority over the delivery of justice. New forms of legal action were established using a system of "writs," or royal orders, each of which provided a specific remedy for a particular wrong.[18] Eventually, English "common law" was established, this being law that was common to all of England, and the administration of justice became the domain of the king. Thus, justice became a centralized system.

Previously, conflicts at the local level were treated as a matter between the individuals involved. When justice came to be administered by the king a decision of major consequence was made, a decision that solidified the punitive approach to justice in what became the hierarchical, centralized British court system. In essence, if the king had a law making a particular act a crime, *breaking the king's law was the crime and thus the king was now the victim.* The crime was no longer the harm done to the actual victim. For example, the killing of a person was not "the crime," it was breaking the king's law against murder. Violating the king's law against larceny became the crime, not the loss to the person whose property was taken.

We must refer to "an eye for an eye, a tooth for a tooth" justice to understand the structural shift that this represented. The Code of Hammurabi codified the principle that when a victim is harmed, the victim has a right to inflict retribution on the offender. So long as it is equal to the harm the victim suffered, *this harm is just and moral.* The key concept here is that the right of retribution belongs to the victim. English law transferred the victim's right to retribution to the king. *Atonement for the wrong was now due to the king, not the person harmed, as both a legal and a moral right.* The person harmed is reduced to a mere witness for the state, providing testimony, if needed, to prove that the offender violated the king's law.

The king's role became that of the victim with the right of revenge, in addition to being the judge, jury, and executioner. When the king has the authority to write any law he wants, and then enforce compliance with that law using his regime of punishment, even the penalty of death, what guardrails are there against abuse?

JUSTICE IN THE NEWLY FORMED UNITED STATES

When the British legal system came to the American colonies, it stood in contrast to what many of the indigenous peoples who had lived here for thousands of years practiced. Many native peoples looked at what was going on in the offender's life as more important than the particular nature of the crime; they saw the *relationship* among things as more important than the things themselves.[19] In the mind of the British colonists, however, the unwritten practices of indigenous people (who were also non-Christian) constituted the absence of a system of justice, presenting the opportunity to impose the king's system on these "primitive" people who had successfully lived without jails or prisons for centuries.

However, the American colonists eventually decided they didn't like how the oppressive and unfair British rule impacted them, leading to the American Revolution. After successfully overthrowing the king's authority, former colonists faced another challenge; how to structure a government without a monarch. To whom would the authority that the king traditionally exercised be allocated? Who would exercise control in their new nation?

When the American colonies declared their independence from the King of England, our Founding Fathers also had to decide who will govern and how they are selected. In England, who would be king was determined by birth. In the new system, they delegated the duties of running the government to three separate but purportedly equal branches of government. The authority to write the laws is delegated to the legislative branch of government. The authority to execute and carry out the laws passed by the legislators is delegated to the executive branch of government. Interpretation of the laws is delegated to the judicial branch of government, as well as the prosecution of lawbreakers and the adjudication of conflicts.

The most significant change in the British system that was made by the U.S. Founding Fathers was in *giving the right to choose who runs the government to those who are entitled to vote*. Initially, the right to vote was narrowly restricted, but the seeds of democracy were sewn. As the right to vote was extended to more citizens, majority rule became the new norm. Our votes are how the power of our voices is made manifest. Who will write our laws, who will administer those laws? We the people decide.

It is difficult to overemphasize the significance of this *rearrangement in the allocation of control,* one that now constitutes the heart of our democratic process. The right to vote empowers citizens to choose their representatives. This is foundational to the modern democratic form of government; it is what distinguished our form of government from an autocracy, a system in which one person makes the decisions for everyone. The right to vote and the importance of majority rule is seriously underappreciated by many eligible voters. This is the backbone of our democracy. Unfortunately, beyond who chooses the decision-makers, many other aspects of government remained much as they had been before the revolution.

Because the system remains grounded in duality consciousness, once they are elected, legislators become part of a top-down system that has many of the flaws found in a monarchy. Legislators have the authority to pass laws, but their laws may or may not result in fairness or reflect what the public desires. Legislators may even pass laws that serve their own self-interest or their personal desire for retribution at the expense of community wellbeing. Gerrymandering is a prime example of a self-serving law.[20] Either the voters are not attentive enough in selecting representatives who are people of integrity, or the system is such that it taints the integrity of those who would otherwise be honorable—and maybe a combination of both is at play.

Likewise, in the executive branch of government, the concentration of control in the president or a governor can be used to serve the best interests of the people, but that is not always the case. Who we elect to serve in these positions is of critical importance. So long as they remain in office, those in control can use their position to serve their self-interest or perhaps to serve the interests of their high-dollar donors—corporations using money as speech or other donors buying influence. Hopefully we are approaching a time when voters have the opportunity to vote for leaders who understand Unitive Justice.

While our Founding Fathers made important changes in who exercises control and how they are chosen, they did not fundamentally change the way justice was administered in the courts. Justice is still grounded on the measure of proportional revenge that we first saw in the Code of Hammurabi 1700 years before the era of Christ. Even without a monarch at the top, the state retains the role of victim when the state's law is broken. Even in states where judges are elected, the basic framework of the old system of justice remains intact.

Today, the fact the victim's right to retribution now belongs to the state is why, in criminal courts, cases are styled as the "Commonwealth of Virginia versus John Doe," or "The People of the State of Colorado versus Jane Doe." If the defendant pleads guilty or takes a plea bargain (an agreement between the defendants and prosecutor for the defendant to plead guilty to some of the charges in exchange for a shorter sentence) a trial is unnecessary. In this case, the real victim's testimony is not needed, making them even less relevant. Victim advocates have long fought the consequences of this diminishment of the role of victims in criminal court proceedings, but without system change, this is how the system is set up. The victim's need for answers and the community's desire for reconciliation is less important than the state's right to retribution.

Nor is the need for healing addressed in a civil suit—even a civil action is about proportional revenge, not healing individuals or the community. In a civil action, the person harmed seeks redress, usually in the form of monetary damages. If the plaintiff prevails, the court orders the defendant to pay money to their victim as their punishment. As a civil trial attorney, I often saw how money is a poor substitute for healing and restoration of the broken relationship that brought them to court.

As you might expect, our convoluted legal system has many weaknesses. In criminal cases, making the federal or state government the victim with the right to seek retribution resulted in a significant imbalance of resources between the accuser (the state) and the accused (the individual citizen). This imbalance can give rise to unfairness in the proceedings. The provisions in the U.S. Bill of Rights (the first ten amendments to the U.S. Constitution) were written primarily to address these concerns and curb potential government abuse. These amendments constrain the might of the state in its roles as accuser, prosecutor, judge, and punisher, but they can also make court proceedings complicated and expensive.

Specific constitutional rights designed to protect the individual against abuses by the state in criminal proceedings include the following:

- The right against unreasonable searches and seizures and the right to be charged only upon probable cause (Fourth Amendment);
- Citizens shall not be subject to double jeopardy or self-incrimination or be deprived of life, liberty, or property without due process of law (Fifth Amendment applies to the federal government and Fourteenth Amendment applies to state government);
- The right to a speedy and public trial by an impartial jury in the location where the crime was committed, the right to be informed of the nature and cause of the accusation, to be confronted by the witnesses, and to compel witnesses on one's behalf, and the right to counsel (Sixth Amendment); and
- The right to be free from excessive bail, fines, and cruel or unusual punishment (Eighth Amendment);

These rights are intended to ensure justice, but justice can actually be impeded by the manner in which they are applied. How these rights complicate the implementation of justice is especially evident in the Fifth Amendment right against self-incrimination. This right attempts to correct the imbalance between the accused and the might of the state by forcing the state to prove the defendant is guilty without the defendant having to admit guilt. To achieve this, the accused is presumed innocent and gets to plead not guilty, even when one is guilty.

While the right against self-incrimination helps protect individuals against the state's greater might or force, it comes at the expense of truthfulness. In this instance, the need to shift the burden of proof to the state is deemed *more important* than encouraging honesty. I recognized the significance of this distortion only when I discovered how a unitive system *requires* honesty. When I experienced what a profound difference honesty makes for those involved, and in the outcome, I no longer accepted the complex rules around self-incrimination as a way to achieve justice. They are a band-aid on a deeply flawed system.

Another serious flaw in the traditional system is that it is designed to *exclude* consideration of why the crime happened in the first place; there is no process for getting to the root cause of the problem. Not only does harm to the victim go unaddressed, our legal system also disregards any harm experienced by the community where the crime occurred. The current system does little to help the victim or the community heal, and crime continues.

While there are protections intended to help prevent abuse of the system by those in government and attempts to help balance the playing field, they are band-aids on the king's inherently flawed system of justice. The protections only address symptoms, not causes. The punitive system of justice often lacks substantive justice because it is not a system that addresses the root causes of crime, broken relationships, or finds lasting solutions. *The deeper we look, the more compelling the need for system change becomes.*

* * *

Invitation to Journal. Consider these questions:

a. Does the information in this chapter change how you see the justice system? If so, how?

b. Will it make any difference in how you go forward? If so, in what way?

c. If you could change something about our justice system, what would your priority for change be? Why do you want this particular change?

d. Do you see similarities between how punitive justice works and how institutions you are associated with work, be they secular or religious, educational or business? If so, what are the primary similarities? What are the primary differences?

CHAPTER FOUR
RETRIBUTION AND REVENGE IN THE 20th AND 21st CENTURIES

In the last chapter, we considered our ancestors' roots and wrong turns. In this chapter, we look at how well we have done regarding justice in modern times. This includes the decisions made by some who are alive today and no doubt even some who participated in the defining events.

So long as the majority of people are immersed in duality consciousness—the mistaken belief that separation is real—the outcome is predictable. The deep divides and chaos that result defined the 20th century, and continue into the 21st. The evidence is clear.

History provides many examples of how punitive justice is flawed, but it peaked in the 20th century when one war after another was fought to get even for one wrong or another. World War I, World War II, and Communist oppression alone may account for more than 130 million deaths. If we include the Korean War, the Vietnam War, and the many atrocities committed by various dictators and autocrats, the 20th century is easily the bloodiest in history—a time we ironically call the "modern era." With the invention of nuclear weapons, continuing to solve our disputes using mass killing could end life as we know it.

What about the second half of the 20th century, the time many of us who are alive today participated in? This is deemed to be a period of "peace," as there were no world wars and post-WWII alliances held strong.

Yet when we look deeper, the punitive model of justice continued and remains pervasive and unquestioned, as the structures and practices of punitive justice are found across the culture. The silence of the masses is testimony to how well we are conditioned to see a punitive system, not as the social construct that it is, but as a natural or inevitable process over which we have little control.

PUNITIVE SYSTEMS ARE NOT LIMITED TO THE CRIMINAL LAW SYSTEM

Perhaps the criminal law system is the most easily recognized punitive system, but this system is not limited to the legal arena. The structures that maintain a punitive system are the building blocks of all of our systems that impose control in one way or another and serve the interests of the few, not the many. This has long been the case.

Punitive structures are not limited to the criminal law system. They manifest wherever dualistic thinking prevails.

Unitive and dualistic thinking both played roles in the founding of the United States, and continue as themes throughout its history. The wars of conquest against the people who were already living here when European explorers and settlers arrived and the compromises to democratic ideals required by chattel slavery were grounded in dualistic thinking. Despite our self-image as a welcoming and inclusive nation, violence and fear have shaped our politics from the beginning.

Even what we think of as more progressive times, like the New Deal Era under Franklin Delano Roosevelt, were characterized by compromises with racist and xenophobic forces. Throughout U.S. history, there are many examples of duality consciousness dominating our politics and government institutions. There are periods, however, when dualistic thinking is more dominant than others. Unfortunately, the present era has a large measure of duality's us-versus-them dogma.

Here, I offer two examples of political movements grounded in dualistic thinking that significantly impact our current institutions, the Republican Southern Strategy and neoliberalism. They demonstrate how duality works at the institutional level through deception, disinformation and by playing on our fear of "the other." These two examples show us what to look for and what to avoid. Our best defense is to overcome our system blindness by understanding the forces at play.

THE REPUBLICAN SOUTHERN STRATEGY

Many threads are woven into the fabric of our troubled times. Because politics and government are where our public policies are formulated, when they are captured by dualistic thinking, the impact is especially destructive and widespread. That's where we begin.

A particularly illuminating example is the Republican Southern Strategy because it has now been around for over 50 years, long enough for us to see where such a dualistic strategy leads long term. Seeing where this flawed plan led over the course of half a century holds important lessons about how, and how not, to proceed as we go forward.

The Southern Strategy came into existence in the 1960s. Its genesis was in large part due to the fact that, although Dwight Eisenhower won two terms as President in the post-war 1950s, John F. Kennedy Jr. and Lyndon B. Johnson then won back to back victories for the Democratic Party. This, combined with the successes of the Black-led civil rights movement of the 1960s and the increasing political mobilization of young people put Republicans on the defensive. Although Nixon, a Republican, narrowly won the 1968 presidential election, Republicans feared that the political mobilization of Blacks and young people would prevent them from future wins.

This crisis coincided with the growing presence of television in many American homes. This gave politicians a new tool for manipulating public opinion using fear-mongering tactics. One of the first instances of politicians using modern media to manipulate the fears of voters was the Nixon-Humphrey presidential campaign in 1968. This major political race used advertising agencies to "package" the candidate[1] and turn out the vote using television ads.

The following year, Kevin Phillips a 28-year-old staffer in the Nixon White House, responded to the sense of a Republican crisis by publishing a book titled *The Emerging Republican Majority*. At the time, the South was dominated by "Dixiecrats," people registered as Democrats but that was due in large part to their rejection of the Republican Party because Abraham Lincoln, a Republican, had freed the slaves.

Phillips offered a strategy to turn the South from blue (Democratic) to red (Republican) by intentionally mobilizing racial animosity among voters—the epitome of dualistic thinking. He argued that the GOP (Republican Party) needed to move beyond its traditional base and reach out to white voters in the South and Southwest who were registered as Democrats but were not closely aligned with the Democratic Party on many issues. He saw an opportunity to do this using polarizing appeals that targeted and deepened the racial divide. Because it was-focused on the South, this became known as the Republican "Southern Strategy."

Phillips overtly asserted that the best hope for the Republican Party's future was pitting racial and ethnic groups against one another and capitalizing politically on the competitions and resentments that followed. "The whole secret of politics," he told the journalist Garry Wills during the 1968 presidential campaign, "is knowing who hates who."[2] Phillips seized the opportunity to exploit our fear to love by fueling our love to hate.

While race had always played a role in the criminal legal system, especially in the South, by the late 1960s, the civil rights movement was beginning to challenge those structures. Many hoped this was a turning point. It took a while, but the Republican Southern Strategy, coupled with political turmoil around the War in Vietnam, dimmed hopes that we might be able to turn away from our punitive system. It worked just as Phillips predicted. This political theory says, "win elections at any cost and by any means."

Phillip's game plan was tied to the fact U.S. presidents are not elected by the majority of votes cast, they are elected by counting the votes in the Electoral College. In most instances, if the candidate wins a majority of the votes cast in a given state, they are awarded *all* of that states' electoral votes. Winning the electoral college votes of a majority of the southern states can give a presidential candidate enough votes to win a presidential election even if they lose the popular vote.

Before adopting their Southern Strategy, some Republicans had joined Democrats in supporting the expansion of civil and voting rights and improving equal opportunity for minorities. In fact, President Richard Nixon championed the rights of minorities with an executive order that mandated affirmative action in companies that received federal contracts. My first job as an attorney was at the Reynolds Metals Headquarters in Richmond, Va,. in 1974 where I helped to implement this affirmative action mandate at Reynolds' aluminum plants around the country.

Even limited Republican support for affirmative action came to an end with the Southern Strategy. Instead, Republicans and conservative Democrats began to use affirmative action as another cultural wedge intended to drive us apart. It worked. I recall a white male manager in a

Reynolds plant in the South telling me he opposed affirmative action because "Negroes are lazy and unreliable." That racist generalization is untrue, but he bought into the race-bating message.

Republicans garnered the votes of white racist "Dixiecrats"[3] by opposing the 1964 Civil Rights Act, the 1965 Voting Rights Acts and the enforcement of desegregation statutes that the Democrats championed. As duality requires, deception was part of the playbook. When racism emerged as the winning political strategy, overt racism was made unnecessary by coded language that was easy for most to decipher. A presidential candidate's promise to support "states' rights" meant if he were elected president, the federal government would not intervene in how a state dealt with its race problem, so segregation could continue. Another coded term, "get tough on crime" was understood by many to mean Blacks would be more harshly punished in our criminal courts than whites to help keep them in their place.

While there were other factors at play, it was largely by politicizing racial animosity that the Republicans turned the South from blue to red, enabling them to win seven of the ten presidential elections between 1968 and 2004. Playing on our prejudices proved to be such an effective political weapon that it did not stop with race.

In the U.S., women's rights had long been curtailed by old common law practices that made women far less than equal, limitations that continued well into the 20th century. Inspired by the fight for civil rights on behalf of racial minorities, in the 1960s and 1970s women launched their own movement for equality. Republicans quickly targeted the women's movement as another opportunity to gain supporters by stoking long-standing prejudices, this time against women. This impacted me personally.

When I began practicing law in Virginia in the 1970s, old English Common law still limited many rights of women and children. Early in my practice, when there were few women attorneys in Richmond, I joined the effort to bring Virginia's laws relating to women and children into the 20th century. I also supported Virginia's ratification of the Equal Rights Amendment to the U.S. Constitution. I remember well the attacks upon those of us working for equality for not staying home to take care of our husband and children, led by Phyllis Schlafly, a busy activist attorney with six children. Hypocrisy has deep roots in every dualistic system. We were called names intended to be pejorative, like "feminists" and "women's libbers." The divides in the nation deepened.

What they perhaps did not foresee was that by the time we entered the 21st century, supporters of the Republican Party were disproportionately fearful, angry, prejudiced and willing to tear the system down. It provided a platform for white nationalists and anti-Semitism. Fear and anger became the Republican brand. This harmed not only the Republican party, but American politics as a whole.

The introduction of the Internet about thirty years ago added to the depth of our cultural separation. It is now easy to play on a multitude of prejudices against marginalized groups by stoking fears that are often manufactured by false conspiracy theories promulgated on a multitude of websites. The algorithms used by social media platforms not only direct users to sites that reinforce their existing views and feed them information that may be detached from reality, they also feed the separation and fear that pervades our belief systems.

Rob Enderle, principal analyst at the business consulting firm, the Enderle Group,[4] points out:

> This approach is pretty much how a con artist works; they use your perceptions against you to act against your self-interest. If you believe the world is flat, you get a ton of support for that belief. [Y]ou don't trust the government. Social media supports that as well; it pushes you down the path you are already on . . . while avoiding the pain of questioning if your path is the right one.[5]

Our nation eventually came to a point where any legitimate disagreement over a public policy became a means to deepen the chasm between opposing points of view. In subsequent decades, the political strategy of stoking hate and animosity was extended to social divides based on issues, such as religious beliefs, abortion, sexual orientation, gun rights, and eventually, even COVID vaccines and the books in school libraries. Our ability to use legitimate disagreement over a public policy to explore common ground seems now to be a forgotten, and sometimes a forbidden, skill.

If we only consider the short-term, the Southern Strategy that began in the late 1960s may appear to be a successful strategy—if you believe the means justify the end. When we expand our view to the 2016 presidential election and beyond, we learn what this fear-based approach has to teach us—the means and the end are inseparable. Using hatemongering as a political strategy gave Donald Trump a block of voters willing to sacrifice democracy rather than share control with the diversity of people who are becoming the American majority. At this point in time, the future of democracy in the U.S. is uncertain.

NEOLIBERALISM

In the last chapter, we considered the Doctrine of Discovery that was set in motion in the 15th century. Neoliberalism provides a modern version of the corporate dominance fostered by the Discovery Doctrine. This theory asserts that democracy is not the answer because it results in the tyranny of the *majority*. The most significant change in the British system made by the U.S. Founding Fathers and the one that underpins our democracy was in *giving the right to choose who runs the government to the people.* Neoliberalism will undo this, if it can.

In his book, *A Brief History of Neoliberalism*, David Harvey describes neoliberalism as

> a theory of political economic practices proposing that human well-being can best be advanced by the maximization of entrepreneurial freedoms within an institutional framework characterized by private property rights, individual liberty, unencumbered markets and free trade.[6]

An ideal neoliberal system gives unfettered rights to corporations, all obligations to governments when deregulation runs amuck and few rights to citizens.[7]

> Since the days of [President Ronald] Reagan, Republicans have argued that people who believe that the government should regulate business, provide a basic social safety net, protect civil rights, and promote infrastructure are destroying the country by trying

to redistribute wealth from hard working white Americans to undeserving minorities and women.[8]

There is a subtext. The minorities complain about are becoming the majority. Specific marginalized groups—Blacks, Indigenous people, those of non-heterosexual orientation, immigrants, Muslims, Jews and even women—are blamed for "destroying" our nation. The coded meaning is that they are to be feared because they challenge the long-standing dominance of cisgender heterosexual Christian white men. This has become a sort of Republican "political theology."

Neoliberalism was birthed in the 1940s by several thought leaders from the U.S. and Europe who feared that the rise of totalitarianism in the U.S.S.R. and elsewhere posed a threat to the values of Western civilization and to the protection of property rights. They met in Mont Pelerin, Switzerland, to design a free global market regulated by the rule of law and the moral standards of the West. However, with the end of the Cold War, the threat of totalitarianism diminished, and they shifted their focus to bringing about a global free-market economic system with corporations as a major beneficiary. Eventually neoliberalism became associated with politicians and policymakers such as Margaret Thatcher, Ronald Reagan and Alan Greenspan, public officials who used their positions to champion neoliberal public policies.[9]

Neoliberalism elevates individual and corporate property rights over all competing values. The result is a system that uses both politics and economics as the means to favor private enterprise, eliminate government regulation, and to promote private sector control of economic policies. Also known as free market capitalism, neoliberalism is designed to counter the government regulations and market control adopted to reverse the market failures of the 1930s during the Great Depression. The post-Depression economic safety net created by President Franklin Roosevelt's New Deal to shelter many Americans against economic hardship is disparaged as the "welfare state" by neoliberals.

Among the policies neoliberals support to maximize economic liberty and market efficiency include: deregulation of industry and commerce, free trade, curbing labor unions, privatization (the transfer of public assets to private hands because anything public is "inefficient"), fiscal austerity, low taxes with lax enforcement, corporate monopolies, globalization and reduced government spending for the social safety net. These policies have resulted in increased inequality in both wealth and income. Author and social scientist Susan George reports,

> If you are, roughly, in the top 20 percent of the income scale, you are likely to gain something from neo-liberalism and the higher you are up the ladder, the more you gain. Conversely, the bottom 80 percent all lose and the lower they are to begin with, the more they lose proportionally.[10]

The structural injustices inherent in neoliberalism are masked by myths. We are to accept competition as a means to weed out the unfit. We are told the system is fair because individual responsibility provides those at the bottom of the hierarchy a potential path to opportunity and a ladder to the top. What happens to the poorly educated and impoverished who don't make it is their own fault, never the fault of structural injustices. Myths such as these condition people to live with high levels of economic insecurity, competition over limited resources, as well as the stress and emotional and physical ailments that ensue.

Beginning in the 1970s, neoliberals, neoconservatives, and the religious right forged an alliance to combat the liberation movements of the 1960s.[11] Libertarian thinker James McGill Buchanan, who played a central role in designing the guiding principles of the neoliberal movement,

> [broke] with the most basic ethical principles of the classical liberalism he claimed to revere, of the market order as a quest for mutual advantage based on mutual respect. Instead, he was mapping a social contract based on "unremitting coercive bargaining" in which individuals treated one another as instruments toward their own ends, not fellow beings of intrinsic value. He was outlining a world in which the chronic domination of the wealthiest and most powerful over all others appeared the ultimate desideratum...[12]

Over the next fifty years, billionaire donors funded right-wing academics and institutions to promote libertarian ideology and build political control to advance their preferred neoliberal policies. Their cause

> was never really about freedom as most people would define it. It was about the promotion of crippling division among the people so as to end any interference with what those who held vast power over others believed should be their prerogatives. Its leaders had no scruples about enlisting white supremacy to achieve capital supremacy. And today, knowing that the majority does not share their goals and would stop them if they understood the endgame, the team of paid operatives seeks to win by stealth. Now, as then, the leaders seek Calhoun-style liberty for the few – the liberty to concentrate vast wealth, so as to deny elementary fairness and freedom to the many.[13]

In consequence, by 2012, the Republican party

> had evolved into an entity split into two overlapping parts: establishment conservatives who railed against taxes, government spending, and regulations, and Tea Party conservatives who railed against taxes, government spending, and regulations *and* who embraced various forms of extremism, political paranoia, and conspiracy theory.[14]

A tone of indifference to the needs and wellbeing of individuals is a hallmark of neoliberalism. Individuals provide the labor that makes the neoliberal economic system run, but labor is reduced to a cost of production and to be eliminated whenever possible. When this free market approach is applied to public services, such as health and education, it is a means of transferring public assets and tax dollars to the private sector for the purpose of generating profit from them. When public services are driven by a profit motive, it negates public services as a right.

Neoliberals seek to end government intervention, but not when it benefits them. They support-government intervention when it is needed to protect corporations and wealthy individuals from market failures that regulations could have prevented. Capital deregulation that resulted in increased financial instability and the Great Recession of 2007 to 2009 is one example.

The recession that arose at the end of the George W. Bush administration was largely caused by a lack of government regulation of a shadow banking industry that maximized profits using unregulated mortgage-backed securities. When this scheme imploded, it caused a housing bubble collapse that negatively impacted individual home owners across the nation. The homeowners got limited help but the banking industry got nearly $500 billion in industry bailouts[15] between 2008-2009 from the Obama administration. One of the big winners: private equity funds that use borrowed capital to buy viable enterprises, load them up with debt, and then drive them into bankruptcy after the private equity funds have recouped their initial stake.[16]

Neoliberalism is now rooted in an international network of "free market" think tanks that continue to frame the economic debate in a way that benefits corporations and shareholders above other stakeholders —*i.e.*, the general public and our home, the Earth. Neoliberal economics disregards the system's need for balance and wholeness. The criticism of neoliberal economics includes the threat it poses to democracy as it supports the dismantling of majority rule in favor of rule by property holders, something it must accomplish in order to advance its inequitable economic policies.

Neoliberalism turns the concept of voters choosing their leaders into the concept of voters rubber-stamping the leaders they are manipulated into backing.

> In order to realize (their goals), businesses needed a political class instrument and a popular base. They therefore actively sought to capture the Republican Party as their own instrument. . .
> The Republican Party needed, however, a solid electoral base if it was to colonize power effectively. . . [From the late 1970s on], the unholy alliance between big business and conservative Christians backed by the neoconservatives steadily consolidated, eventually eradicating all liberal elements . . . from the Republican Party, particularly after 1990, and turning it into the relatively homogeneous right-wing electoral force of present times. Not for the first, nor it is to be feared, for the last time in history *has a social group*

been persuaded to vote against its material, economic and class interests for cultural, nationalist, and religious reasons.[17] (Emphasis added.)

The Trump presidency gave full expression to the effort to dismantle majority rule, overtly using fear and division as Trump's 2020 reelection strategy. On election night after it became evident he would lose, Trump "launched his latest and most dangerous conspiracy theory. He declared the election was a 'fraud.'"[18]

The depth of our social and political divides was evident in the violent insurrection at the U.S. Capitol on Jan. 6, 2021. Those who see government as bad and those who see government as the bulwark of democracy cannot agree on what constitutes the common good. It seems we are now at a point when no opportunity is missed to, in some way, bludgeon legitimate political debate into political warfare.

The depth of the national divide was especially evident in February 2022 when the Republican National Committee described the violent insurrection at the nation's capital on January 6, 2021, as "legitimate political discourse." This denies what millions of us saw unfold, even as the violence occurred. Steve Schmidt is a former Republican presidential campaign strategist and co-founder of the Lincoln Project, a political action committee (PAC) formed in 2019 by former and current Republicans. Schmidt had this reaction to the RNC's description of January 6:

> We'll lose the country over this. This is an enormous deal. No political leader in America from either of the two political parties has ever made such a declaration. You have the institution, the third oldest political party in the world [the Republican Party], sanctioning fascistic violence. That is what this election is about. We will lose this country. At the end of the day, these next elections are going to be different than what 2020 was about, which was entirely, in my view, about Trump and his unfitness. The next elections are going to be about the American people. We have to decide if we're going to throw into the dustbin of history, put on the trash heap, the American experiment. . .[19]

The book *The Paradox of Democracy* traces the long history of democracies growing susceptible to would-be authoritarians. Co-author Sean

Illing warns that "[t]he history of democratic decline is a history of demagogues and autocrats exploiting the openness of democratic cultures to mobilize people against the very institutions that sustain democracy itself."[20] He cautions that the only way to fend off autocracy is to persuade more people to resist it.

Development economist Kate Raworth argues in her book, *Doughnut Economics*, that neoliberal economics have led civilization to the brink of collapse, and credits it with a significant portion of the responsibility for global warming and the resulting climate change. Raworth writes:

> On a planet with intricately structured ecosystems and a delicately balanced climate, this begs a now obvious question: how big can the global economy's throughflow of matter and energy [i.e., the system's "waste"] be in relation to the biosphere before it disrupts the very planetary life-support systems on which our well-being depends?

This is a question that neoliberal economics cannot answer without acknowledging its contribution to the problem.

* * *

Invitation to Journal. Consider these questions:

> a. Were you previously aware of the Republican Southern Strategy? If so, how would you describe it?
> b. Did you participate in or were you impacted by this strategy? If so, how?
> c. Were you previously aware of the dynamics of neo-liberalism? If so, how would you describe it?
> d. Are you concerned about the impact of neo-liberalism? If so, briefly describe.

CHAPTER FIVE
THE PUNISHING DECADES—A MANIFESTATION OF OUR DARK SIDE

A VISION OF REFORM DENIED

In 1971, before mass incarceration took hold, the National Advisory Commission on Criminal Justice Standards and Goals was appointed by the Administrator of the Law Enforcement Assistance Administration (LEAA). Its mission was to develop "national goals, standards, and priorities for reducing crime in America and for upgrading law enforcement, courts, corrections, and other systems related to reducing crime." Membership in the Commission was drawn from the three branches of state and local government and from industry and citizen groups. It also included police chiefs, judges, corrections leaders, and prosecutors.

These early statements in the Report give a sense of the hope and vision of its authors.

> The Commission hopes that its standards and recommendations will influence the shape of the criminal justice system in the nation for many years to come. And it believes that the adoption of those standards and recommendations will contribute to a measurable reduction in the amount of crime in America. [1]
> The changes must not be made out of sympathy for the criminal or disregard of the threat of crime to society. They must be made precisely because that threat is too serious to be countered by ineffective methods. [2]

When the Report was written, the political winds were already blowing in the opposite direction.

In its final report published in 1973,[3] the Commission provided politicians and policy makers with compelling reasons to reduce the nation's rate of incarceration. It concluded that incarceration failed to reduce crime and recidivism rates, and the number of people who return to jail and prison is notoriously high.

Institutions do succeed in punishing, but they do not deter. They protect the community, but that protection is only temporary. They relieve the community of responsibility by removing the offender, but they make successful reintegration into the community unlikely. They change the committed offender, but the change is more likely to be negative than positive.[4]

The Commission found evidence that reformatories, jails, and prisons cause more crime than they prevent. "Their very nature insures failure. Mass living and bureaucratic management of large numbers of human beings are counterproductive to the goals of positive behavior change and reintegration."[5]

The Commission recommended that the scope of corrections be narrowed, not enlarged, by excluding many juveniles, minor offenders, and sociomedical cases, and that the emphasis of corrections shift from institutions to community programs. While the Commission acknowledged that some institutions would be necessary for the incarceration of adults who cannot be supervised in the community without endangering public safety, it concluded that there were more than enough facilities to serve this need. It recommended that states refrain from building more state institutions for adults for the next ten years, except when total system planning shows that the need for them is imperative, and that juvenile detention facilities be closed within five years.[6] It recommended placing jurisdiction over juveniles in a family court, which should be a division of the general trial court.

The Commission further recommended that each state enact legislation repealing all mandatory provisions depriving persons convicted of criminal offenses of civil rights or other attributes of citizenship. "Actions necessary for maintaining social order do not require suspension of basic rights. Since criminal sanctions impinge on the most basic right—liberty—it is imperative that other restrictions be used sparingly, fairly, and only for cause."[7] After a sentence was served, the advisory group recommended that punishment stop and reintegration back into the community be the priority. That vision was resoundly denied.

THE CHOICE TO GET TOUGH ON CRIME

When the National Advisory Commission report was issued in 1973, playing on the voter's fears of crime was already proving to be the trump card in getting elected and re-elected, despite the deeply flawed nature of the policy. The Commission report was ignored. Instead, President Nixon (1969-1974) shifted the policy toward "get-tough-on-crime," and subsequent political leaders followed suit. Our penchant for retribution and revenge not only prevailed, the incarceration rate escalated to historic levels, and it is far from over.

The latter decades of the 20th century became a particularly dark time in the history of the criminal law system in the U.S. By the 1970s, enough people had televisions in their homes for it to be an effective political tool. Much to our detriment, modern media amplifies our ability to extract retribution and revenge. In the 1980s, politicians began using 30-second sound bites in ads on TV to mobilize voters. Whether the rate of crime was going up or down, the news media made it possible for politicians to launch "get-tough-on-crime" election campaigns designed to play on our fear of crime. Slogans like "the war on drugs," "abolish parole," "three strikes, you're out," "truth in sentencing," "mandatory minimums," "try juveniles as adults," and "zero tolerance" became ingrained in the collective mindset.

Because they were effective, both Republicans and Democrats engaged in these tactics. The media's sensationalized stories about violent crimes added to the public's appetite for retribution and revenge. Once elected, tough-on-crime politicians quickly turned their campaign slogans into law, but this had little to do with sound public policy. What it produced can be called "the punishing decades." The following chart sets out the results.

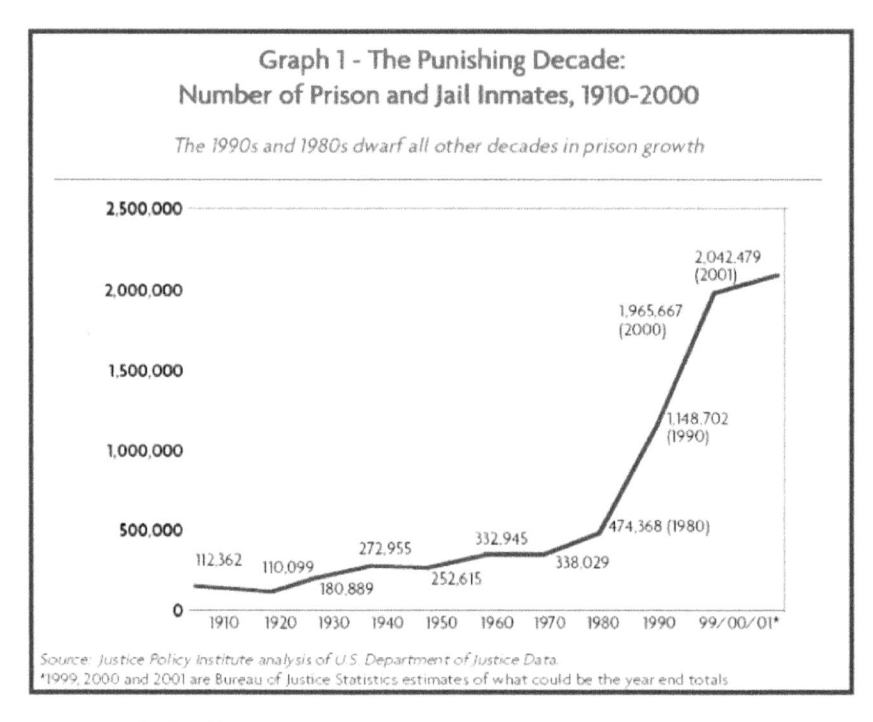

**Graph 1 - The Punishing Decade:
Number of Prison and Jail Inmates, 1910-2000**

The 1990s and 1980s dwarf all other decades in prison growth

- 112,362 (1910)
- 110,099 (1920)
- 180,889 (1930)
- 272,955 (1940)
- 252,615 (1950)
- 332,945 (1960)
- 338,029 (1970)
- 474,368 (1980)
- 1,148,702 (1990)
- 1,965,667 (2000)
- 2,042,479 (2001)

Source: Justice Policy Institute analysis of U.S. Department of Justice Data.
*1999, 2000 and 2001 are Bureau of Justice Statistics estimates of what could be the year end totals.

"The Punishing Decade: Prison and Jail Estimates at the Millennium," Justice Policy Institute, May, 2000, Washington, D.C., page 1. Reprinted with permission from the Justice Policy Institute.

The rate at which incarceration escalated in the U.S. during the punishing decades is astonishing. Between the 1980s to the early 2000s, the number of inmates in prisons and jails went from fewer than 500,000 to over 2.3 million.[8] By early in the 21st century, the U.S. corrections system incarcerated one out of every 100 adults in the U.S. If those on parole or probation are included, one adult in thirty-one was under "correctional" supervision.[9] With 5% of the world's population, the U.S. now has about 25% of the world's prisoners,[10] the highest rate of incarceration in the industrialized world.[11]

During this period, we cast aside rehabilitation as a goal of incarceration. Instead, the language of blame, judgment and retribution became the order of the day, driven by fear, anger and the promise that harsher punishment would achieve compliance and make us safe. There was little evidence to support this claim.

As a result of these get-tough-on-crime policies, more behaviors were criminalized and many prison sentences became mandatory and longer.

Early release for good conduct was all but eliminated. Judges were generally prevented from being lenient, even when the circumstances were compelling. This led some defense attorneys to advise their clients to plead guilty to crimes they didn't commit. They reasoned that a short sentence for a lesser crime they didn't do is better than a long sentence for a more serious offense that they didn't do. Rehabilitation programs, education, and training were targeted as "soft on crime," and scorned as treating criminals better than those not involved in crime.

As life sentences and sentences that spanned decades became common, prisons became plagued with a growing and expensive elderly prison population. Although criminal activity generally decreases dramatically with age,

> [b]etween 2009 and 2019, as the total population of individuals detained in state and federal prison systems decreased by 11.4%, the number of people over age 55 incarcerated in state and federal correctional institutions more than doubled from 75,300 to 180,836. This is often attributed to the large number of detained individuals who are aging in place due to long sentences and restrictive parole practices.[12]

Geriatric care and hospice care are now essential services in our prisons. When funding is not available, these services are not delivered.

RACE AND INCARCERATION

It may come as no surprise that mass incarceration disproportionately targeted racialized and marginalized groups—African Americans, immigrants, refugees, ethnic minorities and socially marginalized populations. This is easy to do because the perceived "otherness" of these groups that already exists in our culture is both relied upon and reinforced by casting them as criminals. Donald Trump fed such misinformation with tweets like this one on June 5, 2013, "Sadly, the overwhelming amount of violent crime in our major cities is committed by blacks and hispanics. . ."

The Republican Southern Strategy's use of race as a political weapon, as described in Chapter Four, also helps explain why racial minorities suffered the greatest impact from mass incarceration. Throughout the second half of the 20th century, the disparate impact on minorities, particularly Blacks, was very high.

The U.S. Department of Justice data for incarceration rates in 2006 shows that, while one in 30 men between the ages of 20 and 34 was behind bars, the figure was one in nine for Black males in that age group.[13] Legalized segregation was banned by the Civil Rights Act of 1964, but the expansion of the criminal code in a way that disproportionately impacted Black Americans provided another form of legalized race discrimination. Thus, mass incarceration is sometimes called "the new Jim Crow."[14] Indeed, with such a disparate impact arising in what is supposed to be an impartial process, one must wonder if some criminal trials are persecution for being a young Black man and not prosecution for crime.

The Sentencing Project notes that the targeting of African Americans began to escalate after the Brown v. Board of Education decision. It reports that "[i]n historical perspective, the 910,000 African Americans incarcerated today are more than nine times the number of 98,000 in 1954, the year of the Brown v. Board of Education decision."[15] As I described earlier, the politicization of race was the primary tactic used in the Republican Southern Strategy to win elections after the Civil Rights Movement began and passage of the Civil Rights Act of 1964. This strategy intentionally fueled white resentment and rage and the escalating rate of incarceration of African Americans provided a political end run around desegregation that white racists supported. It was not good public policy.

Too often, we fail to see that convicting the criminal is little more than a band-aid on a gaping social wound. We accept punishment of the offender as a satisfactory resolution without thinking about the deeper problems that continue to fester. When drugs and drug addiction escalated in the 1980s, we again failed to examine the whole or look for underlying causes. Instead, it provided another opportunity to politicize race.

While powder cocaine was more often the drug of choice in white neighborhoods, crack cocaine was prevalent in Black communities, and it was crack cocaine that was sensationalized by the media. The high-profile death of Black athlete Len Bias from a cocaine overdose in 1986 sent lawmakers on a punitive spree seeking more retribution. When Ronald Reagan signed the Anti-Drug Abuse Act of 1986 into law, it established mandatory minimum sentences for specific quantities of cocaine. Distribution of five grams of crack cocaine got a compulsory five-year sentence in federal prison, while one had to distribute 500 grams of powder cocaine to get the same mandatory sentence—a one to 100 difference.[16] The racial disparity was blatant.

In 1986, before the enactment of federal mandatory minimum sentencing for crack cocaine offenses, the average federal drug sentence for African Americans was 11% higher than for whites. Four years later, African Americans' average federal drug sentence was 49% higher.[17] When I first visited a prison in Virginia in the 1990s, I was startled to see that the inmate population was a sea of primarily Black men—another red flag that indicated system change was needed.[18]

MENTAL HEALTH AND INCARCERATION

In the strange world of incarceration, many see a connection between the state and county hospitals that released millions of people with mental health conditions between the 1950s and 1980s without providing a viable alternative and the high rate of incarcerated people with mental illness. By 2021, "nearly half the people in U.S. jails and more than a third of those in U.S. prisons have been diagnosed with a mental illness, compared to about a fifth in the general population."[19] A curious feature of these two systems, mental health and corrections, is that while "laws intended to protect civil liberties make it exceedingly difficult to hospitalize people against their will, it is remarkably easy to arrest them."[20] We failed to consider the whole or consider underlying causes. Now, our jails and prisons serve as asylums for many people with mental illnesses.

Our present knowledge about ACEs and PCEs, discussed in Chapter Ten, has important ramifications not only for schools but for jails and prisons, as well. According to a News Medical report,

> [t]rauma is almost ubiquitous among a male prison population, with rates of exposure to violence or traumatic events being reported as anywhere between about 62% to 100% - roughly double that in a community-based male population. This includes

physical assault and sexual abuse, the latter affecting almost 15-16% of male prisoners in sharp contrast to the 1-3% in the general male population.[21]

Post-traumatic stress disorder (PTSD) is a mental health condition caused by extremely traumatic events. It manifests as flashbacks of intrusive and frequent thoughts, images, sounds, smells, and feelings of a particular traumatic incident, as well as frequent nightmares. PTSD is known to be experienced by both female and male inmates in large numbers. Still, it is widely underdiagnosed and not well-researched. Also, little is known about the impact of imprisonment itself on one's mental health. We know that many inmates experience traumatic events in correctional facilities.

The traumatic effect of a prison environment is not limited to the inmates. The average life expectancy of law enforcement and correctional officers was shown to be 12 years shorter than the general population in a study conducted in Florida. Deaths among members of this group between 2000 and 2010 were nearly 19% higher.[22] PTSD and trauma that is experienced by the officers are contributing factors.

Fortunately, there are programs that address risk factors and support resiliency and recovery. One designed specifically for the officers is the Correctional Officer Trauma-responsive Training to address the toxic prison environment, a program offered by the Compassion Prison Project. Their goal is for all prisons to become trauma-informed environments where both prison residents and correctional officers feel safe and seen, and everyone is treated humanely.[23]

THE REST OF THE STORY—THE CONTEXT

A criminal trial answers three questions: "what law was broken, who broke it and how are they to be punished?" You will note that these questions deal only with the event—what happened and who did it, ignoring the context out of which the crime arose. This narrow focus permits the person accused of the crime to be cast as the object of the court process —the violator of code section x-y-z, the robber, the murderer, the felon and the criminal. Dehumanizing the accused in this way serves to sever their connection to the rest of us and deepens the perception of separation and our fear of them, too often an illusion that helps justify the punitive system, as described below.

If the story was told from the perspective of the accused, often it would be quite different. We would discover the context of the crime, which might include systemic injustices that are not defined as crimes in our law books. These injustices are nonetheless seen by many as immoral and sometimes equally as wrong as the crime that was committed. One reason the Broadway play, Les Miserables, is so moving is because, among other things, it portrays in human terms the injustice of extended incarceration for the crime of stealing bread needed for a family to survive.

Learning the offender's story may reveal a complex set of facts, layers of stories entangled in a larger whole. Ultimately, on a deeper level, that story inevitably reflects ourselves and a collective expression of our values. The interwoven threads tell the story of how interconnected we are. It may even reveal our shared responsibility for the systemic brokenness that a particular crime forces us to acknowledge. As a result, considering the context can have a significant impact on the outcome of criminal trials, as demonstrated in death penalty cases.

For a period of time, the death sentence was held to be cruel and unusual punishment. When the U.S. Supreme Court allowed executions to resume in 1976, it mandated two phases for death penalty trials: a phase to establish guilt, and a penalty phase to consider if the defendant should be sentenced to death. In the penalty phase, states are now required to define aggravating factors that juries are to consider, such as whether the murder was especially cruel or heinous.

But the defendant may also present evidence of mitigating factors. These might include the absence of a prior criminal record, positive things the defendant has done, the defendant's mental illness or a history of adverse childhood experiences that might include severe physical and mental abuse. It might also include evidence of how the institutions that are supposed to help repeatedly failed to do so for one bureaucratic reason or another. It is in such details that we discover the context in which the crime was committed.

This procedural change led to the new profession of "mitigation specialists," experts who present the offender's story in humanizing terms. Following a carefully scripted way to present a portrait of the defendant, these specialists develop the defendant's life story for the jury to consider. Family members and experts are called to testify about the hardships and difficulties, but also the positive aspects, of the defendant's life.

Danalynn Recer, a mitigation specialist in Houston, Texas, explains, "We insist on seeing their humanity, despite what they've done. That's what mitigation is all about. I'm not motivated just to make the system fair. I'm motivated to help these broken and despised people. I'm in it to stand up for them."[24] Recer is given a lot of credit for the fact that Houston used to be called the death-penalty capital of the world, but, thanks to Recer's work, Houston no longer holds this dubious distinction.

When the offender's humanity is revealed, execution becomes a more difficult choice.

When we examine the context, we are confronted with the ways that the criminal law system itself contributes to systemic brokenness. One example is incarcerating a family's breadwinner for life while leaving the other family members with no safety net. This often condemns other family members to a life of poverty, leading to an increased propensity to commit crime. Another example is sending people to prison and then denying them anything of value, such as education, in order to make their punishment harsher. Treating them as less than human feeds their negative attributes, and the result is that they do not improve; they may get worse. This failure fosters more crime.

We may forget that not everyone in the system is locked up for a long time. Here's how a Department of Health and Human Services report described how shortsighted the public policy that produced the punishing decades was:

> Each year, more than 600,000 individuals are released from state and federal prisons. Another 9 million cycle through local jails. More than two-thirds of prisoners are rearrested within three years of their release and half are reincarcerated. When reentry fails, the costs are high — more crime, more victims, and more pressure on already-strained state and municipal budgets. There is also more family distress and community instability. Roughly one in twenty-eight children currently has a parent behind bars.

Mass incarceration has been a major driver of poverty. Without mass incarceration, it is estimated that 5 million fewer Americans would have been poor between 1980 and 2014.[25]

Those who recycle through our jails and prisons bring the lessons they learn, the diseases they contract and the trauma they experience back to our communities. While we like to think former inmates are the "other," there is no wall that separates us. We are all in this together.

DOES MASS INCARCERATION KEEP US SAFE?

The national crime rate peaked in 1991 and has since had a downturn. According to the National Crime Victimization Survey, since 1993, the rate of violent crime has declined from 79.8 to 23.2 victimizations per 1,000 people.[26] In 2013, the violent crime rate and unreported crimes were the lowest since 1970. Did mass incarceration cause this steep decline?

The U.S. Department of Justice, National Institute of Corrections (NIC), reports a 2015 study that examined "one of the nation's least understood recent phenomena – the dramatic decline in crime nationwide over the past two decades – and analyzes various theories for why it occurred."[27] Based on an empirical analysis of more than 40 years of data from all 50 states and the 50 largest cities, the study found that harsh criminal justice policies, particularly increased incarceration that rose dramatically over the same period, were not the main drivers of the decline in crime. For more than 30 years, increased incarceration has been declining in its effectiveness as a crime control tactic; its effect on crime rates since 1990 has been limited and was non-existent since 2000.

The experience of mass incarceration in Kentucky is one specific example that supports this conclusion. In 2009, Kentucky had the highest incarceration rate in the nation, its corrections budget increased from $30 million in 1980 to nearly $470 million in 2010, and its prison population rose almost 80% between 1997 and 2009. Despite the dramatic increase in cost and rate of incarceration, Kentucky's crime rate remained about the same.[28]

Marc Mauer at the Sentencing Project estimated that 88% of the increase in incarceration in the U.S. between 1980 and 1996 was due to changes in sentencing policy adopted by legislators, not an increase in crime.[29] As the incarceration rate was escalating, the negative impact on other aspects of U.S. policy and the distribution of public resources received little attention—our system blindness at work. For example, housing an inmate for a year often costs approximately one teacher's annual salary; inevitably, we saw education budgets shrink as funding for corrections mushroomed.[30] The investment proved to be a poor one.

Mass incarceration involves immense social, fiscal, and economic costs. The National Institute of Corrections report mentioned at the beginning of this chapter recommended that programs that improve economic opportunities, modernize policing practices, and expand treatment and rehabilitation programs could be a more productive public safety investment than mass incarceration. The Sentencing Project concurs.[31] This remains good advice but may be hard to achieve because of the continued political and media hype around crime.

COST TO TAXPAYERS

And what did we, the taxpayers, get out of the punishing decades? "From 1979–80 to 2012–13, public PK–12 expenditures increased by 107 percent (from $258 to $534 billion), while total state and local corrections expenditures increased by 324 percent (from $17 to $71 billion) — triple the rate of increase in education spending."[32] From a policy perspective, investing more on getting our challenged youth through high school may have lowered the rate of incarceration.

> Linkages exist between educational attainment and incarceration. For example, two-thirds of state prison inmates have not completed high school. Young black men between the ages of 20 and 24 who do not have a high school diploma (or an equivalent credential) have a greater chance of being incarcerated than of being employed. At the same time, researchers have estimated that a 10 percent increase in high school graduation rates may result in a 9 percent decline in criminal arrest rates. (Citations omitted.)[33]

Nationally, by 2000 the cost of prison construction and housing totaled nearly $40 billion annually.[34] Some political candidates recognized the escalating costs and low returns, but those who openly opposed the get-tough approach were disparaged as "soft on crime." Some candidates who recognized the facts nonetheless presented themselves as tough-on-crime candidates. That reflects a widespread mistaken belief that the ends justify the means, in fact, the means and the ends are inseparable.

Our punitive law system is supposed to impose order by punishing those found guilty of violating the established laws and rules and deterring others through the threat of punishment. "Get-tough-on-crime" policies filled a growing number of prisons and "zero tolerance" in schools fueled the school-to-prison pipeline, a system that paves a path for youth to move first to detention centers and then to jails and prisons. But the evidence is irrefutable: our punitive law system has a high failure rate.

Based on 2005 figures, the U.S. Bureau of Justice Statistics (Department of Justice) reported that about two-thirds (67.8%) of released prisoners were arrested for a new crime within three years, and three-quarters (76.6%) were arrested within five years.[35] A study of these inmates that extended nine years beyond their original conviction showed that violations continued to be high. Five in six (83%) of the state prisoners released in 2005 across thirty states were arrested at least once during the nine years following their release. Extending the follow-up period to nine years captured more than twice as many post-release arrests as were captured during a three-year study.[36] A business with this extraordinary rate of failure would be short lived. How is our criminal law system sustained and maintained despite its failure to achieve its basic objective—corrections?

THE CRIMINAL LAW SYSTEM—BEHIND THE VEIL

Perhaps an even darker aspect of the criminal law system is revealed if we look behind the veil at the inner workings of this system. There we discover how the narrow focus on the event in a criminal trial is an essential, but largely invisible, element in sustaining the criminal law system over time, despite its consistent record of failure.

When the context in which crime occurs is not considered, those convicted of a crime are not only seen as the wrongdoers who commit specific acts of crime, they can also be targeted as scapegoats for the larger system's dysfunctions, including problems that are rooted in bad policy and systemic failures. Without more information, we tend to buy into excuses for why the system perpetually fails, such as "we need more prisons," "sentences are too short," or "they are so bad they cannot change."

Those accused of and convicted of crime are made out to be social dangers, threats to the "body politic," an alien presence that demands societal condemnation.[37] This displaced blame is made possible by excluding evidence of the context, as that is where the systemic failures become clear. There we might see the role that structures such as hierarchy, judgment, punishment and separation play in perpetuating systemic injustice, and how they contribute to the very problems the criminal law system is supposed to address.

Another aspect of this particular systemic dysfunction is that the U.S. does more than punish its criminals; it demonizes them, leading the public to see them as monsters. Andrew Cohen writes, "We see it on our airwaves. We read it online. We hear it from elected officials and from the police, and it's all sanctified by our courts of law."[38]

Perhaps demonizing people convicted of crime makes some citizens feel better about the harsh punishments our system inflicts on them—unless, or until, it impacts them or someone they love.[39] All the while, the systemic dysfunction, including the manufactured social divide between citizens and those convicted of crime, remains hidden from view by our system blindness.

Anastasia Chamberlen and Henrique Carvalho, members of the Criminal Justice Center at the Warwick University School of Law, explain how this scapegoating ritual sets up a hostile form of solidarity in which individuals are bonded together by their feeling of vulnerability and their antagonism towards criminals. Branding those convicted of crime as the "bad parts" is a way to preserve and reinforce a false sense of social integrity.[40]

Scapegoating is also a useful political tool, as it fuels our fear and makes us more easily subject to manipulation. The punishing decades graph on page 46, reflects how finely tuned the scapegoating ritual became in the "get tough on crime" political era of the late 20th century.

One factor that keeps the scapegoating tactic hidden is the widely held belief that it is legitimate—the general public has been conditioned to see the person or group being blamed as guilty, violent and immoral—"those people," and the discussion often ends there. It is a fragile ploy because if those directing their wrath on the accused realize they are not the cause of the underlying systemic brokenness, they would see the injustice of this narrow focus, not to mention the waste of resources. The tactic only works so long as those attacking the scapegoats are not aware that their system blindness keeps them from seeing the larger truth.

Chamberlen and Carvalho explain that when we focus on immediate and quick solutions to alleviate our feelings of insecurity we only target the manifestation of these problems, and not the problems themselves. As a result, we get solutions that are temporary at best and ineffective at worst. They compare this quick-fix solution to a painkiller used by someone suffering from a chronic condition—we find ourselves continuously reaching out for hostile justice, seeking stronger doses that can numb us before we eventually have to go back for more.[41] They contend this "illusion of order" gives the punitive system a compulsive, addictive quality. This illusion allows individuals "to experience an idealized world with just resolutions" where that world does not exist.[42]

A TURNING POINT?

The good news is that the get-tough-on-crime rhetoric is becoming less effective. Eventually, the high costs of incarceration, the work of activists from across the political spectrum pushing for a rollback of the toughest punishments, and the unexpected impact of COVID-19,[43] incarceration rates are down. Between 2000 and 2020, imprisonment rates for Black people fell by 47%, and the imprisonment rates for white people declined by 11%.

[44]The disparate impact on minorities also diminished. Over the first two decades of the 21st century, the ratio of Black to white state imprisonment rates fell by 40%. In 2000 Black adults were imprisoned at 8.2 times the rate of white adults, but in 2020 they were imprisoned at 4.9 times the rate of white adults.[45] Disparity in drug imprisonment rates dropped by 75%, accounting for about half of the overall decrease in the imprisonment rate gap between white and Black people. The disparity for parole violations disappeared.[46] If enough of us make our support of

criminal law reform known, outcomes will continue to become more equitable—that's how the system works.

IS GENUINE SYSTEM CHANGE POSSIBLE?

We will never achieve genuine system change in our punitive law system so long as we continue to function in duality consciousness. Contrary to how it may appear, reality is not a binary system, good versus bad. We are inherently good people, and it is also true that we make mistakes. To one degree or another, we are all both good and have the capacity to do harm. This reflects the complexity of the human condition. It was never a case of one side being perfect and the other not. When we feel separated and devoid of Love, we all cry for Love, often in ways that are harmful.

The Unitive Justice theory and practices described in Chapters Eight and Nine provide useful tools for looking at structural issues found in politicized racism, neoliberalism, our criminal law system and other institutions grounded in punitive structures. With new tools in hand, the opportunities for healing and finding a mutually beneficial path forward become more accessible.

I especially find hope in the means to achieve genuine criminal law change reflected in Unitive Justice criminology theory and practice described in Chapter Eleven. But first, in Chapter Six we consider how to build a bridge from here to there.

* * *

Invitation to Journal. Consider these questions:

    a. Describe your experience with punitive justice.
    b. Does the retributive justice system feel fair to you?
    c. What do you recall about the "war on crime" and the multiple slogans that politicians used in their campaign ads during the punishing decades? Did these slogans influence how you voted?
    d. What are your aspirations for the Unitive States in the decades to come?

CHAPTER SIX
TWO BRIDGES FROM PUNITIVE TO UNITIVE JUSTICE

Thus far, I have described a pretty dismal state of affairs. Before we move beyond the punitive world to consider the new unitive model of justice, it is important to understand that they are not a difference in degree, they are a difference in kind. As Albert Einstein famously said, "No problem can be solved from the same consciousness that created it." Changing our state of consciousness is the key to system change.

The broken state of affairs we now experience is evidence of duality consciousness being shared by many, perhaps most people. Many band-aids are applied in our attempt to fix the punitive system, but the brokenness continues because one fix followed by another does not get at the root of the problem. If we apply big band-aids, perhaps the formerly prosecuted can become the prosecutors, but even this is not system change. System change requires more, not a mere rearrangement of the hierarchy, but a new level of consciousness.

This passage in the U.S. Declaration of Independence is as true today as it was in the 18th century: "[A]ll experience hath shewn, that mankind are more disposed to suffer, while evils are sufferable, than to right themselves by abolishing the forms to which they are accustomed."

The good news tucked in that quote is *while evils are sufferable*—we may be approaching a time when it is no longer tolerable to endure the forms that arise out of duality consciousness, no matter how accustomed we are to them. Perhaps the depth of the brokenness delivers our existential moment—the moment when we muster the will to let go of what we now have and actually do what it takes to move to a new level.

TWO FUNDAMENTAL SHIFTS IN CONSCIOUSNESS

On my journey from punitive justice to Unitive Justice, it became clear that punitive justice depends on dualistic thinking and consciousness that is heavily invested in the *past*. Understanding history is important for it holds lessons that inform our actions in the present and future, but seeing the past through a lens that does not chain us to the past is key. You don't have to let go of the past; it is already gone. It is our mind's attachment to the past that imprisons us. It is the stories we tell ourselves about the past that keep the past in control. To be present to the joy and peace of this moment, we must create our release from the prison of our past.

Our traditional legal system is so focused on past wrongs and seeking retribution and revenge for what happened in the past, it is as if the past is the only aspect of time that is important. Determining how much must be paid *in the future* for what happened *in the past* is what transpires in our courtrooms every day. The result is that the past shapes the future in its own image, with little regard for what is real in the present.

The present, the now, is what is most important. Only in the *present* does healing occur and it is healing that ensures a brighter, better future. What is the cost of the legal system's perpetual misuse of time? One lost opportunity after another to create peace, generate mutual wellbeing and experience the freedom of forgiveness.

In order to commence our journey to Unitive Justice, there are some important preliminary steps we must take. Two that are fundamental to system change are, 1. we see the past differently and 2. we achieve unified goals. I first encountered these two lessons in *A Course in Miracles*, but it was when I learned about what Taylor Paul and Prince Bunn did to transform their prison culture that I saw how seeing the past differently leads to achieving unified goals. I now understand how they are both essential when implementing system change.

I call upon Taylor and Prince to be our teachers. They created a path to Unitive Consciousness and Justice as Love, even while confined in one of the most severe manifestations of punitive justice—prison. Determined to earn their release from life-plus-many-year sentences in prison, they transcended the punitive system, as we must do to experience Unitive Justice.

Taylor and Prince were physical captives in the punitive system; they could not walk away. But they realized that hanging on to their old ways and focusing on a desire for retribution and revenge for what happened in the past was their death sentence. Giving up that old attachment allowed them to ultimately *transcend* the prison system and the duality it reflected, but their transformation took time.

When Taylor and Prince were convicted and sentenced, their egos told them that going to prison was the worst thing that could happen to them. Their long sentences meant they would die in prison, which, for them, was an insufferable possibility. To change that outcome required a total transformation. They eventually saw that it was their long prison sentences that gave them the time they needed to transform so they could earn parole. When they came to see the benefit to them of their long sentences, they realized that being in prison at this time in their lives was in their best interests. They now acknowledge that their long sentences saved their lives.

Fortunately, when they were sentenced the get-tough-on-crime policy of abolishing parole had not yet become law in Virginia. They still had the possibility of being released—if a miracle happened. This was their existential choice: die in prison or create the miracle that would get them out. They chose the miracle. Their example may, in fact, show us that the magnitude of the breakdown we are now experiencing is just what we need to propel us toward true system change.

The earlier versions of Taylor and Prince could be aggressively defensive, their hearts shielded by thick walls to protect them from pain. Where did their transformation begin? When they saw the past differently. This enabled them to disarm their egos and give up their defensive barriers so they could genuinely connect. Their first step in this direction was to seek to understand other inmates before expecting to be understood. This led them to develop compassion for their prison peers, regardless of what they had done in the past.

In a very intentional way, they began interacting with the men in the pod by being fully present and loving toward them, especially gang members—men who lived by a code of violence. Taylor describes the way they engaged these men in conversation as being so present to them that he and Prince could feel the connection. He explains this as *showing them that we saw their humanity so they themselves could see their humanity*. Taylor coined the term "radical tenderness" to describe this interaction, one that produced results that no punitive measure can ever achieve.

Taylor and Prince were humanizing the prison environment. To build connection, they knew the labels that designated separation had to stop, labels like "gangster," "thug," "hoodlum," or the use of gang names. So, Taylor and Prince began speaking of the inmates as family members—as fathers, sons, brothers, uncles, and nephews. Bringing attention to their roles as family members had an important impact on the inmates—it helped them more clearly see their humanity and how it served them. Taylor and Prince modeled the courage required to do what many would consider impossible, especially for them—they transformed their prison pod with lovingkindness and radical tenderness. Instead of being the problem, Taylor and Prince were becoming the solution.

This is a lesson in understanding that everything that happened in the past was in our best interest. Just as Taylor and Prince came to see that their long prison sentences were a blessing, similarly, we begin to see that, as bad as it was, the past *was* in our best interest. At a minimum, the past shows us what we do not want in the future. The new possibilities that can then emerge enable us to go forward together in a mutually beneficial way—this allows us to achieve unified goals.

It is in perpetually seeking conflicting goals that brings conflict and trauma to our endeavors. Instead, unified goals eliminate the hurdles of opposition and adversarial contests that characterize duality. Unified goals unite the power of everyone in a synergistic process, an upward spiral, as they work in concert to achieve mutually beneficial action.

Taylor and Prince provide a clear example of what "unified goals" means. They came to see that being in prison and achieving the transformation needed to earn parole were *unified goals*—one supported the other. Their freedom from the desire for retribution and revenge permitted them to go from conflicting goals to the unified goals of, 1. structuring their time in prison so it was consistent with their release from prison and 2. achieving that release. Having unified goals opened the door to experiencing Justice as Love through the services imbued with lovingkindness that they provided to other inmates during their incarceration, some of which are described later in the book. Coming to that outcome depended on both seeing the past differently and achieving unified goals.

Achieving Justice as Love depends on being free of a desire for retribution and revenge; Love and revenge are mutually exclusive. A desire for retribution and revenge for anything that happened in the past is a personal prison. Dwelling on past wrongs may trigger hyperarousal, increased vigilance, resistance or outright defiance, and then aggression. Stewing in retribution and revenge is both unhealthy for us and the cause of much of the suffering in the world.

As long as we seek revenge, we live with blinders on and cannot see reality. We cannot be present to this moment, yet in the moment is where miracles occur. But how do we release the chains of the past? We must release our past conditioning so we can see the past differently. This frees us from the misuse of time—chaining the future to the past while disregarding the present. As we open a portal to total forgiveness, this shift in perception is our contribution to all time—to eternity.

VARIOUS TECHNIQUES FOR SEEING THE PAST DIFFERENTLY

You don't have to let go of the past; it is already gone. Focusing on the past is just another form of perception and both are distorted by misunderstanding, prejudice and projection. If you believe that your right to seek revenge for past injustices, pain, disappointments and other deprivations that you hold on to is valuable, the prospect of seeing the past differently might give rise to fear of loss—fear of losing your right to revenge. This must be weighed against the value of having peace, mutual wellbeing and the freedom of forgiveness today and in the future. How will you use your time?

There are several ways to release attachment to the past. In this moment, you may choose to see what happened in the past as in your best interest. With this shift, nothing needs to be forgiven. This eliminates the complexity and innuendo; this opens the door to freedom. You may intentionally extend gratitude from your heart to the gifts contained in the events in your past—even for the gifts you have not yet recognized.

Or you may reinforce your intent to release the past by writing what it is that keeps your mind attached to the past, then burn the paper (in a safe way) as you envision releasing what you are hanging on to. Some let the past go using breathing techniques, as this can help you experience the "now." Meditation can also help free you from attachment to the past. Peace comes with giving up attachment to the past because this permits you to be in the *now*. In the "now" is where the creative process unfolds—it happens nowhere else.

My experience of being stuck in the past often played out like this. In my mind I repeatedly played the movie of what happened in the past while I continuously rehearsed how I would argue my theory of the case when the confrontation with the person who angered me arrived. While I was doing this, the toxins this mental prison released were flooding my system and adding layers to the already existing energy blocks in my body. As these energy blocks become tightly bound, they become aches and pains and ultimately manifest as illness and dysfunction.

Fortunately, I learned a technique to reverse this process when, about 20 years ago, I discovered Vipassana meditation as taught by S. N. Goenka.[1] It teaches how to selfgovern the mind using a process that reverses the energy blocks, a slow and sometimes painful process, especially early on as the bound up energy unwinds. This is achieved by mentally scanning the body and just observing what you encounter, without reacting. At first, focusing my mind for more than a second or two was impossible. It was in recognizing how undisciplined my mind was when I began this practice that I made the choice to no longer live my life like that. As I practiced the technique over the years, I slowly unwound many of the energy blocks—a process that continues. It is hard, though no longer painful, and I expect to continue working on it all of my life. It is a choice I made that becomes easier with practice.

You can also control your thoughts and not let every stressful event or situation that comes to mind take over. By creating a sense of safety through consistency, routine and familiarity, these conditions create a "therapeutic web" that is one way to deal with any traumatic events.[2]

Seeing that the past was as *it needed to be* to teach you the lessons you had to learn frees you for the journey forward. You may not recognize the truth in this immediately. It may even take years, but at some point, the fact that you cannot create a new system while remaining in the consciousness of the old system becomes real for you. Creating a new system requires transcending the past.

Your intention to create change will fail if it is lukewarm. Change cannot be made in the present if it is still tethered to the past. Commitment to change must have a cause that will endure and surmount the barriers you encounter, or it will not last. System change requires that you go deep.

When peace and wellbeing become more important than revenge for what happened in the past, you begin to experience freedom. It is true that duality thinking leads to harmful acts—see these acts as the wrongdoer's cry for Love. Forgive them, for they know not what they do.[3] When we are functioning in the lower parts of the brain, as a practical matter, we do not know what we do.

We are fortunate to have an example of this lesson on a much larger scale and in the realm of foreign policy. When the Marshall Plan was implemented at the end of WWII, the U.S. extended aid, not only to allies, but also to former enemy nations, aid to rebuild their nations. The primary goal of those who wrote the Marshall Plan was to achieve the unified goal shared by both former allies and foes who fought in this bloody war: peace and the rebuilding of the war-torn countries. Seeking retribution would have made achieving this goal impossible. That was a lesson learned at the end of WWI when the victorious nations sought heavy reparations against Germany, laying the foundation for WWII. As predicted, lasting peace with our former foes, Germany and Japan, continues to this day.

To do otherwise is to pass on to our children the moral predicament of living in duality. So long as we continue down this path, we cannot teach future generations how to live life guided by lovingkindness. Escape from dualistic thinking is difficult while we are in it, even as the world confronts us with the disorder and destruction that the belief in duality brings us. We must choose—is projecting the past into the future what we want for our children and grandchildren, or do we declare that it ends with us?

WHAT ABOUT ACCOUNTABILITY?

As the contours of system change begin to emerge, there may be some who are wondering, if we choose to see the past differently, what about accountability on the part of those who caused harm? Management consultant, Margaret Wheatley, provides insight into what this question reflects:

> Those of us educated in Western culture learned to think and manage a world that was anything but systemic or intercon-
> nected. It was a world of separations and clear boundaries: boxes described jobs, lines charted relationships and accountabilities, roles and policies described the limits of what each individual did

and who we wanted them to be. Western culture became very skilled at describing the world with these strange, unnatural separations.[4]

When we begin to see through the eyes of Unitive Consciousness, the structures that give rise to the need to control others and be sure they are punished begin to diminish. Conflict still occurs, but accountability is handled differently in a unitive system. Accountability is one's recognition and acceptance of *self-responsibility*. Of course, this requires a new set of structures that create the conditions in which this is likely to occur, structures that support selfgovernance as the means of correcting one's harmful behavior. With this understanding of accountability comes dignity, self-esteem and freedom from control by an outside authority; it may even lead to benevolence. These outcomes are the opposite of what control and punishment produce. It reflects genuine system change.

Unitive Justice does not immediately stop widespread crime or authoritarian oppression and abuse. Unitive Justice Circles will not provide a quick stop to injustice at home or abroad. As we plant the seeds of Unitive Justice and nurture them with loving care, we will have parallel systems. The punitive system will continue—it does maintain a level of order that is better than chaos—but it will slowly diminish in importance as people learn of the unitive option. When positioned adjacent to Unitive Justice, punitive justice cannot endure.

We begin to create small communities where Justice as Love becomes the norm—these are the seeds of system change. We can fairly quickly transform a school culture or a neighborhood. A prison culture can be transformed when the necessary tools are provided. Churches, temples and mosques can accelerate this culture shift by leading with their teachings about peace, Love and forgiveness. As the people in these communities take Justice as Love to the larger community, they shine a light on the injustices of the punitive system, ridding us of the dark corners where punitive justice hides from the truth.

The first step toward escaping duality is to realize we have a choice, that we can choose Unity. Because our mind is the most powerful device that we have to effect change, by changing our mind in one instant, we can change our world in the next. As more people choose Unitive Justice to address conflicts and guide behavior, our need for the punitive system wanes like a candle with a short wick. If we are persistent, our grandchildren and great-grandchildren will reap the benefit of our efforts to create small Unitive Justice enclaves that eventually spread far and wide.

We need not seek Unity—it is our inherent nature. Our task is to seek and find all of the barriers we have made against it, the false beliefs and illusions we project on our world to maintain the illusion of separation. When we recognize that the world is not dualistic, we wake up in the worldview of Unity.

Unity requires a re-design at every level: our identity, our understanding of individuality, our understanding of "other," the core beliefs that make up our ideological infrastructure, as well as our social/institutional structures—including justice. Traditional institutional structures that have as their foundation the belief that separation is reality are obsolete.

"Out beyond ideas of wrongdoing and rightdoing, there is a field. I'll meet you here."

Rumi, The Book of Love: Poems of Ecstasy

* * *

Invitation to Journal. Consider these questions:

> a. Does it seem plausible to you that seeing the past differently permits you to release any desire for retribution and revenge and this permits you to achieve personal freedom? Does it cause you fear or discomfort? Why or why not?
> b. Describe an example of a conflicting goal in your life and how that impacts your ability to move to resolution.
> c. If you see the past differently and give up your desire for retribution and revenge, how might that help resolve the conflicting goal that you described? Would it help achieve unified goals?
> d. What are the advantages of viewing the world without judgment or a desire for revenge?

Suggested Viewing: Two videos about giving up retribution and revenge, and how powerful that choice is.

Amish schoolhouse tragedy: Pennsylvania's Charles Carl Roberts case, available at https://www.youtube.com/watch?v=661vq-3yqXY (10 min.).

Nickel Mines & Amish Forgiveness. 15 Years Later, available at https://www.youtube.com/watch?v=n3leZB719ws (7 min.).

CHAPTER SEVEN
NEW CHOICES

Old institutions are tenacious, and they have long tentacles rooted in history and many choices our ancestors made. Diverse influences—law, history, religion, science, politics, culture—all keep us entrenched in old structures. We become like fish swimming in murky water, not realizing a different world is possible while we slowly suffocate. We accept the status quo, often thinking that policies that serve the interest of only a few will still serve the common good. Or perhaps we think that change is not possible. It is.

When Martin Luther King, Jr. addressed the nation from Riverside Church in New York City on April 4, 1967, about the interlocking injustices of racism, poverty, and militarism, he asserted, "...the whole structure of American life must be changed."[1] That is a big ask, but King was right. The flaws are so deep and so wide that we must create a way to start anew.

Unitive Justice is a theory designed to help us do this. The theory reveals a deeper understanding of what is possible. This may even give rise to a new story about Lady Justice. Her blindfold signifies she does not need to see the material world—she functions in a realm beyond the physical—the realm of Unity.

The evolution to a new understanding of justice may begin as a slow process. As one thought follows another, we question, discuss and struggle. More insight brings more awareness. Our experiences help us discern the path more clearly. Sometimes we will fall back into dualistic thinking, but we continue on. We may slip and fall then struggle to get up, but the journey to our destination has begun. The arc of justice is a force in itself. It propels us toward Love—if we are willing.

Unitive Justice theory helps identify the underlying forces, actions, beliefs, and institutional designs at the root of the injustice in our traditional system. It also helps us imagine how to create a workable model of justice that can honestly be called Justice as Love. Justice as Love addresses crime and wrongdoing, but not by answering harm with more harm—it seeks to heal and unify. You will discover that these structures are also a guide for living. As this new insight informs your life and activities, perhaps you will notice that you begin to show up differently, make different choices and act differently toward others as you move forward.

How did Unitive Justice theory emerge? John Stuart Mill advised, *"We advance knowledge only by subjecting our most treasured beliefs to careful scrutiny."*[2] (Emphasis added.) A treasured belief for many of us is that our punitive justice system is just, a belief I realized must be scrutinized.

As I began to identify various structures that hold our traditional system of justice together, an important and recurring question arose: what structure would serve the same system function (such as the system's guiding moral principle, its goal, how it ensures security and order, etc.) but do so *without being punitive*? I began knowing that the traditional justice system is hierarchical, judgmental, and punitive, so the new system must be non-hierarchical, non-judgmental, and non-punitive.

But the new system could not be defined by what it is not—I had to discover what Justice as Love *is*. I made it a two-step process: first, identify a structure that is essential to a punitive system and determine what function it serves, and second, ask what could replace it that transcends punitive thinking? Eventually, what emerged was a comparison of fourteen fundamental structures that characterize a punitive system with fourteen structures[3] of Unitive Justice, aka "Justice as Love."

HOW UNITIVE JUSTICE THEORY IS ORGANIZED IN THIS BOOK

In this book, the structures of the punitive and unitive systems are set out as 14 Arcs from punitive justice to Unitive Justice. What begins to appear is a path from a punitive system to a unitive system. These 14 Arcs are set out in the chart below and on the inside front cover.

14 ARCS FROM PUNITIVE JUSTICE TO UNITIVE JUSTICE

INDIVIDUAL TRANSFORMATION – BE THE CHANGE

	Structure	Punitive	Unitive
Arc 1	SECURITY/ORDER	FROM RULES	TO VALUES
Arc 2	GOVERNANCE	FROM CONTROL	TO SELFGOVERNANCE
Arc 3	COMMUNICATION	FROM DECEPTION	TO HONESTY
Arc 4	ASSESSMENT	FROM JUDGMENT	TO INSIGHT
Arc 5	INTERPERSONAL	FROM DISTRUST	TO TRUST
Arc 6	INNER STANCE	FROM SELF-DOUBT	TO COURAGE
Arc 7	GUIDING MORAL PRINCIPLE	FROM PROPORTIONAL REVENGE/HARM ANSWERS HARM	TO LOVINGKINDNESS/ HEAL/DO NO HARM

COMMUNITY TRANSFORMATION – DISCOVERING OUR SHARED HUMANITY

	Structure	Punitive	Unitive
Arc 8	BENEFIT	FROM SELF-INTEREST	TO COMMUNITY
Arc 9	SOCIAL FRAMEWORK	FROM HIERARCHY/ TOP DOWN	TO EQUALITY/INCLUSION
Arc 10	SAFETY	FROM PUNISHMENT	TO CONNECTION
Arc 11	GOAL	FROM COMPLIANCE	TO MUTUALLY BENEFICIAL ACTION/WHOLENESS
Arc 12	FOCUS	FROM EVENT	TO CONTEXT
Arc 13	ANIMATION	FROM OPPOSITION/ CONFRONTATION	TO SYNERGY
Arc 14	ENERGY/SPIRIT	FROM FEAR	TO LOVE

© 2021 Sylvia Clute

Because the structures of each system are set out in side-by-side columns, one might assume that the two systems are opposites, but this is not the case. Unitive Justice is a unified world with no separation, but Unitive Justice theory requires the use of language to describe it and language is, by its very nature, linear. Quantum physicist David Bohm describes the problem of language being linear and inadequate when describing abstract concepts—like Unitive Justice and the theories it contains. Bohm writes:

> So, whether we like it or not, the distinctions that are inevitably present in every theory, even an 'holistic' one, will be falsely treated as divisions, implying separate existence of the terms that are distinguished (so that, correspondingly, what is not distinguished in this way will be falsely treated as absolutely identical). We have thus to be alert to give careful attention and serious

consideration to the fact that our theories are not 'descriptions of reality as it is' but, rather, ever changing forms of insight, which can point to or indicate a reality that is implicit and not describable or specifiable in its totality.[4]

Unitive Justice is not the opposite of punitive justice. Unity/Love is all-encompassing—it holds duality within it, as duality is merely blindness to Unity/Love. Unitive Justice is universal. We need only lift the veil of duality consciousness to be present to Unity. Unitive Justice removes the blinders that sustain the punitive system.

The 14 Arcs are organized into two categories of seven Arcs each: personal transformation and community transformation. This is another distinction used merely for clarity. These categorizations help frame the pedagogy for teaching the theory and thinking about its implementation; they do not indicate fragmentation or separation.

The "personal transformation" category is considered from the perspective of what individuals can put into place, beginning with change within themselves. The "community transformation" category is considered from the perspective of how we engage with others in creating system change using Unitive Justice theory, as these seven Arcs are more relational. Two Arcs, the guiding moral principle (from proportional revenge to lovingkindness) and the energy of the system (from fear to Love) are foundational throughout the entire system. Still, to make it easier, we consider one of them in the personal transformation category and one in the community transformation category.

This individual process unfolds as one moves forward, but the experience will not be the same for any two people. Once you experience Unitive Consciousness, you may not stay there. For most of us who are crossing the bridge from duality consciousness to Unitive Consciousness at this time in human history, one moment we are in Unitive Consciousness but in the next, we lapse into our old beliefs and behaviors.

When we eventually realize that our duality consciousness manifests the punitive world we experience—we are the cause, and our punitive world is the effect—we are present to the root problem. When we operate in the realm of duality, we use the concept of good and evil to explain perceiving ourselves as separate from others. When we transcend duality, we see that what we thought was evil actually reflects a broken link to

Oneness. When we look deeply enough, we find that harmful acts are a cry to be reconnected; they are a cry for Love.

In the moments we experience Unitive Consciousness, we discover that this new level of consciousness becomes the cause and lovingkindness is its effect. With this comes the end of our system blindness.

I intend for this book to provide a series of windows through which you, the reader, look at one aspect of Unitive Justice and then another. To do this, I describe processes and practices through which many of us have *experienced* Unitive Justice; it is through experiential learning that Unitive Justice begins to emerge as an attainable reality. You then see that separation is not real and that fear of the "other" is a dualistic construct. Once you experience Unitive Justice, you can no longer believe that punitive justice is the best we can do. Only in dualistic consciousness can retribution and revenge be understood as justice.

The chart on the next page and on the inside back cover is a version of the Arcs that includes only the unitive structures.

THE DIFFERENCE A THEORY MAKES

In our practice of Unitive Justice, we find that having a defined theory makes a significant difference. Comparing 14 punitive and 14 unitive structures, as Unitive Justice theory does, provides a clear path from where we are now to where we can go to create real change in the justice system and beyond.

When we understand the balance, harmony and simplicity of a unitive system, it is difficult to apply the term "justice" to what happens in our criminal law system. Unitive Justice theory makes it clear how punishment undermines connection—the absence of connection is what leaves a community with punishment as its only means of imposing control. (This is an example of how a punitive system causes a number of the problems it is supposed to address.) Unitive Justice theory also clarifies how strengthening connection is the key to implementing a system with no punitive elements. As connection is strengthened, the need for punishment is diminished because people who are bound by a strong connection tend not to harm one another.

Unitive Justice theory transcends the punitive system. It asks different questions because it reflects a different level of consciousness. It redefines the container that holds the justice system in place. The forms of exchange are different, and relationships are different because the paradigm has shifted.

UNITIVE JUSTICE AND RESTORATIVE JUSTICE

In reading this book, you may be wondering how Unitive Justice differs from Restorative Justice. Perhaps the most significant difference is the fact that Unitive Justice has a defined theory. The field of Restorative Justice (RJ) is well known for its circle processes, but some note that RJ's lack of a theory to define what it is and how to practice it is a limitation. In the last chapter of his book, *Crime, Punishment and Restorative Justice: From the Margins to the Mainstream*, Ross London wrote: "[W]hile it has achieved outstanding results in thousands of programs, [RJ] has remained a marginal development because it has failed to articulate a theory and set of practice applicable to serious crimes and adult offenders."[5]

Dominic Barter, the creator of the Restorative Circle process that we use in our Unitive Justice training and practice, and Mikhail Lyubanski concur, "[T]he modern restorative justice movement has no single origin, no unifying theory, and no dominant approach."[6] Not only is a cogent RJ theory lacking, but other authors also note that "a universally accepted and concise definition of the term has yet to be established."[7]

Even John Braithwaite, a prominent advocate of Restorative Justice, concedes, "There is no consensus within the social movement for restorative justice on what should count as unjust outcomes."[8] No consensus on what is unjust?

Does this mean that in Virginia the term "restorative" can be used to whitewash torture? A Washington Post opinion piece indicates this may be is the case:

The commonwealth's criminal code and the Virginia Department of Corrections refer to solitary confinement as "restorative housing." That's an Orwellian euphemism that obscures what it is: isolating human beings in a maximum security setting, often for long periods of time. Inmates call it "the hole" or "the jail within the jail." We are not alone in considering it cruel and unusual punishment — a sanitized term for torture.[9]

We hope that Unitive Justice theory will provide the clarity needed to avoid the contorted terminology sometimes found in the larger Restorative Justice movement. Despite this limitation, Restorative Justice has made a significant difference in the field of conflict resolution and justice. Many schools have been especially well served by Restorative Justice as an alternative to zero tolerance discipline and it provides a beneficial diversion for juvenile courts that is less harsh than the traditional system.

* * *

Invitation to Journal. Consider these questions:

a. Is this your first introduction to Unitive Justice?
b. Have you experienced anything that is similar to Unitive Justice? If so, what was it and what are the similarities?
c. Is the shift from punitive justice to Unitive Justice something you are interested it? If so, why? If not, why not?

CHAPTER EIGHT
THE 7 ARCS OF INDIVIDUAL TRANSFORMATION

The first seven Arcs of Unitive Justice theory provide a framework for individuals to achieve personal transformation, regardless of their environment. Achieving individual transformation then provides a foundation for subsequent community and systemic change.

INDIVIDUAL TRANSFORMATION – BE THE CHANGE				
	Structure	Punitive	Unitive
Arc 1	SECURITY/ORDER	FROM RULES	TO VALUES
Arc 2	GOVERNANCE	FROM CONTROL	TO SELFGOVERNANCE
Arc 3	COMMUNICATION	FROM DECEPTION	TO HONESTY
Arc 4	ASSESSMENT	FROM JUDGMENT	TO INSIGHT
Arc 5	INTERPERSONAL	FROM DISTRUST	TO TRUST
Arc 6	INNER STANCE	FROM SELF-DOUBT	TO COURAGE
Arc 7	GUIDING MORAL PRINCIPLE	FROM PROPORTIONAL REVENGE/HARM ANSWERS HARM	TO LOVINGKINDNESS/ HEAL/DO NO HARM

BRIEF OVERVIEW OF ARCS 1-7

With Arc 1, the unitive structure of values begins our journey into the inner workings of the unitive system. We begin with values because living out of values strengthens connection. As values are established, we go next to Arc 2 and the unitive structure of selfgovernance–living out of one's values requires selfgovernance. Values and selfgovernance lead to Arc 3, honesty, a keystone value that naturally emerges alongside selfgovernance. Honesty leads to Arc 4, the unitive structure of insight, and insight leads to Arc 5, the structure of trust. As the system takes shape, Arc 6, the structure of courage, is necessarily present—this system change will require a good measure of courage. Arc 7, the unitive structure of Lovingkindness is a cornerstone of all the other unitive Arcs.

Note: In the process of creating a vocabulary that describes Unitive Justice, we need terms that convey clear and concise concepts. For example, we need to address the confusion reflected in statements like "kids learn positive values here and negative values there." In the lexicon of Unitive Justice, there is no such thing as a "negative value;" values are positive. Instead, we might describe what is being called "negative values" in this statement as beliefs, learned behavior or perhaps conditioning. This makes for less confusion when we use the term "going from rules to values."

To clarify what I am referring to when I describe the structures referenced in the 14 Arcs, I will begin the description of each Arc by defining the key terms being used.

ARC 1: SECURITY/ORDER
FROM RULES TO VALUES

rules: laws, requirements or guidelines intended to govern conduct within a particular activity or jurisdiction. Rules are generally written and enforced by those who control that activity or jurisdiction. The role that rules play may also be found in widespread beliefs or norms. Other terms for rules: statutes, tenets, regulations, entrenched beliefs.

values: internal moral guidance adhered to through selfgovernance and reflected in shared positive community norms that are modeled by and maintained within the community. Other terms for values: principles, ethics, morals, standards.

When I use the term "values," it means core human values that are found in all cultures, on all continents and among all people. The law of Love is universal. I sometimes hear people say, "Your values are different from mine." They are not talking about core values. Core values are not meaningful to some and not others—they embody our shared, inherent impulse for goodness. The core values I refer to include honesty, integrity, generosity, kindness, trust, courage, lovingkindness, and other human values that are found in communities worldwide. Whether you are in a big city or a remote village, these aspects of human nature are understood.

I believe Buckminster Fuller was referring to core values when he said: "On personal integrity hangs humanity's fate."[1] Our values, not our rules, may spare our species from self-destruction.

There is an interesting interplay between rules and values. For example, honesty is a value, and rules against lying are designed to achieve a similar outcome. But telling the truth because you are honest is not the same as telling the truth because you fear the consequences you will suffer if you do not. One is the result of an internal moral compass and selfgovernance, while the other is compliance with what others dictate. While values may be breached, they do not depend on what others do—values provide a moral compass that lies within each of us. This permits us to create community-based processes guided by values for addressing harm and conflicts.

When those who write the rules are people of integrity, the difference between rules and values is diminished. When lawmakers are guided by self-interest, the difference between rules and values can be significant.

OVERALL WEAKNESSES OF A RULES-BASED SYSTEM

Each structure found in a punitive system has particular weaknesses associated with it, but the problems associated with rules are especially numerous. In a rules-based system, such as our traditional legal system, recurring themes highlight its shortcomings. First, rules generally tell us what NOT to do, and the list only grows longer; eventually, the scope and reach of the rules become oppressive and difficult to administer.

Second, when the state deals with rule violations, i.e., crime, the state is pitted against the individual. The imbalance that results is addressed using a lot of due process band aids to level the playing field, but this makes the system so complex that the unfairness may be compounded. Third, rules are enforced with punishment and punishment further undermines connection. Fourth, rules can be used to legalize anything, whether it is moral or not.

Fifth, the Rule of Law can be a source of protection for citizens, but it can also be form and no substance—dictators and autocrats exploit this weakness. Sixth, rules are easily abused, and lastly, rules depend on compliance and they don't work without it.

THE FIRST WEAKNESS: RULES TELL US WHAT NOT TO DO

Rules generally tell us what we are NOT to do—do not go over the speed limit, do not commit robbery, do not commit murder, do not lie under oath. A major problem with rules telling us what not to do is that each time a new harm is invented, the official list of rules must be expanded to prohibit it before violators may be charged or convicted. One example is when a student brought a Taser to school for the first time, so the school disciplinary code was expanded to prohibit bringing a Taser to school. The school disciplinary code was already many pages of small print because new violations had been continually added over the years. The following image is *just one of seven pages* in a disciplinary rule book detailing the acts prohibited in a Virginia school district and the level of punishment for each prohibited act.

Pre-K - 5th Grade Discipline — Levels

Offense/Violation		1	2	3	4	5	Police Documentation Required	Safety and Security Consult
Fighting, Assault & Battery, Bullying, Hazing (Cont'd)								
FA1	Fighting: Mutual Contact between Students – Serious Injuries Requiring Medical Attention			●	●	●	🚓	
FA2	Fighting: Mutual Contact between Students – No Weapon/Minor Injuries That Do Not Require Medical Attention		●	●				
F1T	Minor Physical Altercation	●	●					
HR1	Harassment (shoving, throwing objects at someone)		●	●	●	●		
H1Z	Hazing		●	●	●	●		
H01	Homicide - Firearm Against Staff				●		🚓	
H02	Homicide - Firearm Against Student				●		🚓	
H03	Homicide - Other Weapon Against Staff				●		🚓	
H04	Homicide - Other Weapon Against Student				●		🚓	
KI1	Kidnapping/Abduction				●			
ST1	Stalking				●		🚓	
TI1	Threatening Staff Member (physical or verbal threat or intimidation)				●		🚓	
TI2	Threatening Student (physical or verbal threat or intimidation)	●	●	●	●	●		L5
Gambling								
G1B	Gambling	●	●	●				
Gang Activity								
GA 1	Gang Activity	●	●	●	●	●		L1-L5
Improper Use of the Internet/Internet Safety								
T1C	Unauthorized Use of Technology and/or Information	●	●	●	●	●		L5
T2C	Causing/Attempting to Cause Damage to Computer Hardware, Software or Files	●	●	●	●	●		
T3C	Violations of Acceptable Usage Policy	●	●	●	●	●		
T4C	Violations of Internet Policy	●	●	●	●	●		
Other Conduct								
S3V	Other Code of Conduct Violation	●	●	●	●	●		
Possession, Use or Possession with Intent to Sell or Distribute Alcohol								
AC1	Alcohol Use			●	●	●	🚓	
AC2	Alcohol Possession			●	●	●	🚓	
AC3	Alcohol Sales/Distribution				●	●	🚓	
Possession/Use of Communication Devices								
C1M	Beepers	●	●	●				
C2M	Cellular Phones: Student possession of cell phones at Richmond Alternative (alternative program) is prohibited.	●	●	●				
C3M	Electronic Devices (laptops, iPods, MP3 Players, etc.)	●	●	●				

THE SECOND WEAKNESS: AN IMBALANCED SYSTEM

During the criminal process, the might of the state is pitted against the individual, resulting in an imbalance in administering justice. When this system was instituted in the U.S., the colonists recognized this was a problem. Rather than address the root cause, our founders sought to level the playing field by instituting due process limitations on the might of the state. For example, due process requires that citizens know what particular acts are prohibited before they are charged with violating them or subjected to punishment. This protection means if an act is not yet made illegal, a person may not be charged with breaking the law. This is especially problematic in the age of the Internet.

When the Internet and social media make interconnected, instantaneous and worldwide communication possible, new harms can spring up faster than the cumbersome punitive justice system can respond with new laws to make them illegal. The number of potential violations in this chaotic and technically complex environment has grown exponentially; the system is unable to respond in a timely manner.

The 2016 Presidential election in the U.S. is a good example. Officials had not foreseen the need for specific laws regulating social media and enforcement mechanisms to prohibit other nations from using the Internet to interfere in our democratic election. When officials realized our system was under a cyber attack, they had to rely on existing laws designed for an earlier era to address the situation as best they could.

Cyberbullying is another example of how rules are not up to today's challenges. What remedies, if any, exist to address the frequent hurtful or threatening comments made on social media? The legal remedy may depend on whether such statements are determined to be speech or conduct. Does the First Amendment protect hurtful commentary as free speech? Or is it an act of libel or defamation, which may give rise to either a civil action or a criminal charge? David Hudson, Jr. writes in an American Bar Association article: "There are certain things that people shouldn't be able to say online. There definitely is a line somewhere, but the courts haven't really defined where that line is."[2] Nor have our legislatures.

In theory, we are to be informed of what acts are prohibited, but the notice we receive may be superficial or merely implied. The school rule book described above is one example. Public schools are a state agency, so due process requires that parents receive a copy of the disciplinary rule book that lists pages of violations and punishments that apply to their children. Parents sign a statement saying they received the booklet and understand its contents, but some, perhaps most, don't even look at them.

Outside the school setting, citizens are simply presumed to know the rules regarding what is legal and what is not, although many would not know where to find a code book. This imputed knowledge is used to justify punishing those who violate the rules—they supposedly knew what they did was wrong. Perhaps not; sometimes even the courts disagree on the interpretation of a given law.

In addition, due process is supposed to ensure punishment is fairly administered, but the rules are now so complicated that it can require a high-priced attorney to figure them out. You may not get your share of due process if you don't have a good lawyer.

THE THIRD WEAKNESS: RULES UNDERMINE CONNECTION

Rules often reinforce separation and give rise to distrust. Rules can undermine our connection to each other, but connection is the glue that holds relationships together. Typically, we don't harm those whom we feel connected to. Because connections are weak in a punitive system, compliance must be compelled and punishment is the primary means of enforcement. Punishment further undermines connections, as do other punitive structures—control, deception, judgment, distrust, hierarchy, and so on.

THE FOURTH WEAKNESS: RULES AREN'T NECESSARILY MORAL

Rules can legalize anything, whether it is moral or not, if those responsible for writing the rules so choose. Colonization was legal. Slavery was legal. Apartheid was legal. A clear example of an immoral law that impacts many of us today is the legalization of usury, i.e., lending money at very high rates. Legalized usury is why interest on credit card debt can now be so high.

Usury was deemed immoral for centuries by all major religions, and for good reason. When the wealthy lend to those who are impoverished at rates of interest that are so high that the borrowers are hard-pressed to ever repay the loan, it fosters a deep divide in the community. It further concentrates wealth in the hands of those who are already rich and makes climbing out of poverty even more difficult for those with so little.

Despite the long-standing moral condemnation of usury, in the late 20th century, many state legislatures in the U.S. legalized usury by passing laws that abolish limits or raise the legal interest rate to as high as 36%

per annum. This is the rate allowed in the Virginia statute governing payday lending set out below. This encourages lenders to set up business in poor neighborhoods where the circumstances of some residents are so dire that uninformed borrowers or those with no other option will agree to pay this usurious rate of interest. Even when made legal, usury remains immoral.

> § 6.2-1817. Authorized fees and charges.
> A. A licensee may charge, collect, and receive only the following fees and charges in connection with a short-term loan, provided such fees and charges are set forth in the written loan contract described in § 6.2-1816.1:
>
> 1. Interest at a simple annual rate **not to exceed 36 percent**; [emphasis added]
>
> 2. Subject to § 6.2-1817.1, a monthly maintenance fee that does not exceed the lesser of eight percent of the originally contracted loan amount or $25, provided the fee is not added to the loan balance on which interest is charged;
>
> 3. Any deposit item return fee incurred by the licensee, not to exceed $25, if a borrower's check or electronic draft is returned because the account on which it was drawn was closed by the borrower or contained insufficient funds, or the borrower stopped payment of the check or electronic draft, provided that the terms and conditions upon which such fee will be charged to the borrower are set forth in the written loan contract described in § 6.2-1816.1; and
>
> 4. Damages and costs to which the licensee may become entitled to by law in connection with any civil action to collect a loan after default, except that the total amount of damages and costs shall not exceed the originally contracted loan amount.
>
> B. A licensee may impose a late charge according to the provisions of § 6.2-400 provided, however, that the late charge shall not exceed $20.
>
> 2002, c. 897, § 6.1-460; 2008, cc. 849, 876; 2010, c. 794; 2020, cc. 1215, 1258.

Rules are only as good as the values that stand behind them. Whether or not our laws are moral is—or should be—an essential element of our civic dialog, debate, and ultimately, agreement. It serves us well to measure each law by the moral standards that we, the community members, want our laws to embody.

THE FIFTH WEAKNESS: RULES CAN BE FORM WITH LITTLE SUBSTANCE

Another weakness that is rarely acknowledged is that the term "the rule of law" has two distinct meanings; one way of defining it protects citizens, and the other serves those in control. When used to protect citizens, the term "the rule of law" means "a moral principle of how government power is to be used. It specifies that government power may be invoked:

- only when authorized by law,
- pursuant to legal procedures which give the people subject to government authority the ability to demand a justification for official action,
- and on the basis of laws that reflect a public purpose that treats people as equals."[3]

The above definition of the term "the rule of law" ties rules to values.

A second use of the term means those in control may pass any law they desire, moral or immoral—they just pass the law before they enforce it. It is more accurate to call this the "rule of men," not the rule of law. We saw this use of the rule of law being applied when Putin claimed the annexation of a large swath of Ukraine following a sham election in 2022, then declared he would defend it as a part of Russia.

The Nazis—any totalitarian regime for that matter—are among the most notorious examples of how the law is used to legalize injustice and immorality. The Nazis plundered, murdered, and executed the Holocaust only after passing laws or issuing orders that made their acts "legal." Form trumped substance. The fact that Nazis adopted laws pursuant to some established procedure was all it took to legalize their immoral actions. Their rule of law made a mockery of justice.

An MSU College of Law article on Auschwitz provided this insight: "Legally, the Nazis had a fixation on records and legality. Committed to the bureaucracy of death, they were scrupulous in making sure that their actions were backed by the force of law."[4] The article states, "The capacity for human cruelty and evil is practically unlimited. But, this individual level question often misses the role that political, social, and legal inputs played in creating the system." Many forces are at play in sustaining an unjust regime, and the rule of law argument is often one of them.

Because there is no one to control those in control, leaders who lack integrity can get away with whatever they want, rules or not. Joseph Stalin's mass systematic killings went unpunished. Mao's Great Leap Forward killed 45 million people in four years[5] without legal consequences.

THE SIXTH WEAKNESS: RULES ARE EASILY ABUSED

The above examples also demonstrate a sixth weakness: rules are easily abused. Rules are not inherently bad; they can be effective in maintaining order and protecting safety. Good rules can guide how we conduct ourselves and help protect us from being violated by others. Sometimes our safety depends on obeying the rules.

The rules that govern traffic on roads and highways are an example of good rules; they apply to everyone, and everyone benefits from them. I want everyone who drives on the roads I drive on to comply with the traffic rules. But even traffic laws may be abused to benefit those in control. One example is using traffic fines to extract additional funds from the poorest residents.[6]

Examples of lawmakers using rules to serve their own interests are common, and often destructive.

THE FINAL WEAKNESS: COMPLIANCE IS TEMPORARY

Lastly, even with punishment as a lever, rules often achieve control on a superficial level, and compliance is temporary. Those subject to the rules may opt not to comply with them and instead engage in civil disobedience. When punishment is not a deterrent, rules alone do not work. For some, beating the rules is their end game. Rules can fail us when we most need them.

Rules are an important part of our everyday experience, and I am not suggesting that we abolish rules. But I do suggest that we pay more attention to whether or not our rules align with our values.

Courts and legislators tell us where to draw the line between legal acts and illegal acts. Due process, in theory, requires that the line be the same for all of us, for diverse communities and circumstances. But even if this was how it actually worked, is that the best way for decisions to be made? Often, the circumstances are unique to the particular individuals involved and "one-size-fits-all" can do more harm than good. In addition, as times change, some rules become outdated and need to be rescinded, but that may be difficult for legislators to do.[7]

As a trial attorney, I quickly realized that rules often do not produce fair results. There are many dedicated, honest people who work within the justice system, but they are working within a flawed structure. Despite the best of intentions, the cumbersome court process used to enforce rules can produce unfairness. How can we achieve justice when an assessment of one's conduct and its consequences depend on a convoluted legal analysis, who has the best lawyer or whether the judge leans politically to the right or the left? It is not unreasonable to think, "I don't want to know what the law is; I want to know who the judge is," as Roy Cohn famously said.

Often, we accept rules without asking, a. are they moral? b. do they serve the community? or c. how do they impact our institutions and us? Our system blindness may keep us from seeing any alternative.

Is there another alternative? In other words, do the rules have to be imposed by our legislators and others in control? Or might the guidelines for how we conduct ourselves be shared values instead of rules, norms that are generally accepted and maintained by those who live in a community?

VALUES IN THE UNITIVE SYSTEM

How does a Unitive Justice system replace the weaknesses of the punitive system with strength and consistency? We go from rules to values as our primary source of guidance. In fact, the fear of punishment is only one of the reasons why people comply with laws and rules. Many of us comply with most rules because of the values that we hold, such as honesty, integrity, respect and concern for others. The new system builds on this inherent goodness.

In a unitive system, values are not used to legalize things that are immoral because, by definition, values are moral and the rules that apply are grounded in values. Values provide no cover for dictators and autocrats to pretend like they are doing what's right, nor are values subject to abuse. When people live out of their values, compliance is not an issue and need not be enforced. Values are a powerful means of diminishing the role traditional justice plays and in bringing peace and security to a community.

Values do not require voluminous code books. Unlike rules, values guide us in what we ARE to do, not in specific instances, but generally—be honest, generous, kind and trustworthy. Whatever the circumstances we find ourselves in, values provide an internal moral compass that keeps us on track as caring, honest people.

Rules are written in regulations and code books, but values must be lived through selfgovernance and taught by example. Values are maintained by mutual consent, by being an integral part of a way of life. Values are invisible, but we know they are present and practiced when we see the results. Our values demonstrate our level of humanity. When we see what values do, it is clear that they transcend rules.

Going from rules to values is system change at a deep level. I learned a lot from Taylor and Prince about how to do this, even while in a punitive system. In their determination to earn parole despite life-plus sentences, they made the rules less important in their pod by elevating values. For example, when an inmate loaned items to others, but in return, extracted a high price from the borrower (a form of usury), a fight might erupt if the high price was not paid. To circumvent this practice, Taylor and Prince created a "charity box" where they kept extra toothpaste, toothbrushes, soap, sodas, etc. When a man needed something, he could get it from the charity box and did not have to borrow it from another man in the pod. No one was punished for not replenishing what they took from the charity box. This modeled values like generosity and lovingkindness; it extinguished the inmate-imposed rule and simultaneously circumvented a source of conflict.

A values-based system is not a new idea. The African system of Ubuntu is an ancient community-based system founded on shared values that are central to the traditional African understanding of humanness and ethics.[8] Native cultures, such as Aboriginals, Maori, and First Nation Americans are values-based systems grounded in the Oneness of all things.

The imposition of Western justice on civilizations around the world was perhaps expected to replace their ancient practices of community justice, but the roots of those indigenous practices survive. A type of Renaissance of ancient practices is taking place, as community-based justice is now making inroads into our Western understanding of justice. These ancient teachings help us understand our interconnectedness and how values build and support connection.

In cultures and systems that already embrace the essence of Justice as Love, there is no need to apply UJ theory or practice to what has long existed. This includes many aboriginal and indigenous cultures, and some religious traditions that have embraced lovingkindness as their guiding light for centuries. Some of the oldest cultures have understood this aspect of our humanity since the beginning of recorded history. Perhaps they will find the comparison of the punitive and the unitive structures of interest, but I don't expect it to change what they do. Perhaps we will find ways for indigenous and aboriginal traditions and Unitive Justice to be mutually-supportive, as we seek to advance our unified goal of creating a gentler, kinder world.

We are in a precarious world where dualistic beliefs prevail. The reality of Unitive Justice is a long-term project, yet perhaps more urgent now than ever before. Values, not rules, may be what saves humanity from itself.

* * *

Invitation to Journal. Consider these questions:

a. What values did you learn as a child, and who taught you those values?
b. What values have you chosen later in life that are different from those you were taught as a child?
c. How do these values continue to guide you, especially when you need to make quick decisions and you cannot wait for rules to be applied?
d. What first step might you, as an individual, take to strengthen the values of your family, workplace or community?

Suggested Viewing: A simple classroom experiment with third graders demonstrates the impact rules that are based on our differences have on our relationships and how quickly such rules can destroy our interconnectedness. It also demonstrates the importance of being guided by values and the inclusiveness that results. A short video about the experiment is called *Jane Elliott's Blue Eyes Brown Eyes Experiment*, available at https://www.youtube.com/watch?v=X97JTH7UCq4 (4 min.; if you cannot access it with this link, please search on YouTube for that title).

ARC 2: GOVERNANCE
FROM CONTROL TO SELFGOVERNANCE

control: the process of dominating others and restricting their freedom through physical, mental, or emotional coercion; wielding influence using fear tactics, be they blatant or covert. Control is territorial and requires perpetual enforcement. Other terms for control: oversight, dominion, domination, regulation, guidance, management, supervision.

selfgovernance: internal self-control and self-mastery; being one's own master; the ability to exercise the function of regulation upon oneself, making the intervention of an external authority unnecessary. Other terms for values: principles, ethics, morals, standards.

CREATING LANGUAGE FOR THIS DISCUSSION

Before we consider the second Arc, from Control to Selfgovernance, I would like to create a distinction between the words "control" and "power." This will give us more precise language when we speak about the two models of justice.

In the English language, we hear Hitler and Gandhi both described as "powerful" men. It seems curious that we can use one term to describe two men who stand at the opposite extremes of violence and non-violence.[1] This glosses over the brutality of Hitler's control and diminishes the emphasis on Love as power reflected in Gandhi's work. We can clarify our language by using the words "control" and "power" to designate this important distinction.

The compelling and dynamic term "power" comports well with the quality possessed by those who draw others to join them without coercion or control. In this framework, power is internal, a reflection of the guiding values, the ethos within the individual that guides their actions. Power is earned through integrity, honesty, and courage, by extending forgiveness, kindness, generosity, expressing remorse, and doing unto others as one would want to be done to oneself. Others are inspired to follow and emulate those who are powerful. Power is built on trust.

Mahatma Gandhi was a man who possessed power, as did Martin Luther King, Jr. and Nelson Mandela. One with power may often experience peace, as did Buddha, Christ, Bahā'Allāh and many of their followers. Power and peace are mutually supportive. Power is economical, requiring the expenditure of minimal energy to accomplish much. No armies are required to maintain power. Mandela exercised power from a prison cell for decades. I will use the term "power" to describe leaders who attract people to their cause through their integrity and consistency.

In contrast, Hitler, Stalin, and Mao imposed control. Each required massive armies and multiple layers of security forces to maintain control. The term "control" works well when describing the process of dominating others, and restricting their freedom using some form of coercion. Control is achieved through attack, might, strength, force, manipulation, violence, pressure, or fear. The attraction that our egoistic mind can have to those in control is another force that supports control—perhaps seeing them as the model our ego wants to emulate. The means used to secure and maintain one's control preclude peace, but it can achieve periods of enforced compliance. I will use the term "control" when referring to those in the hierarchy who use force and coercion to impose their will on others.

PUNITIVE JUSTICE SEEKS TO IMPOSE AND MAINTAIN CONTROL

In Chapter Two, we considered the history of the punitive law system. Despite its failure to meet our expectation of justice, the strength of the punitive system lies in the fact that its structures do one thing well—they provide a means for those in control to impose and maintain control, but there are shortcomings to this approach.

Control is territorial, temporary, fleeting, and unpredictable. Maintaining it requires constant vigilance and being ready to punish those who refuse to comply. As rebellion is a constant threat, the one exercising control cannot rest for fear control will be lost when one's back is turned. Enslavers, dictators, and occupiers know this all too well. And control can also be lost when it is taken away by those who possess greater might, as in the case of the slave states that lost the American Civil War to the Union forces,[2] and Hitler, who lost World War II to the Allied Nations.

Control and fear are interlinked. Control is achieved in the punitive system by instilling fear of the consequences of disobedience—fear of physical pain, fear that something tangible or cherished will be taken away, or even fear of the punishment to be suffered in the hereafter. Paradoxically, fear fuels the desire for greater control—fear of scarcity, loss, defeat, and fear of the unknown give rise to the imposition of more layers of control.

The punitive system's dependence on control is one of its glaring weaknesses. Because control depends on compliance and collapses without it, people who overcome the fear of the punishment that may be inflicted are able to simply not comply. When resistors engage in peaceful civil disobedience, the compliance and submission that control depends on are lost. Those seeking to impose control are disarmed.

Refusing to comply using peaceful civil disobedience forces a difficult choice on those seeking to impose control. Because they only have punishment to enforce their will, it must be escalated each time a little punishment does not work. Escalating the punishment of nonviolent resistors quickly becomes demonstrably disproportionate and, therefore, violates the system's moral justification for answering harm with harm— i.e., *the harm done is no longer proportional*. Abusive rulers are left with two difficult choices: disproportionately punishing the nonviolent resistors and being condemned for acting immorally or just giving up.

When the British faced this dilemma in India, they eventually gave up, and Gandhi's nonviolent movement prevailed. Gandhi's non-violent movement was largely responsible for Martin Luther King, Jr.'s embrace of nonviolent action. After traveling to India to investigate this revolutionary movement, King wrote:

> It was a marvelous thing to see the amazing results of a nonviolent struggle. India won its independence, but without violence on the part of Indians. The aftermath of hatred and bitterness that usually follows a violent campaign is found nowhere in India. Today a mutual friendship based on complete equality exists between the Indian and British people within the commonwealth.[3]

It is true that a violent revolution was avoided, but the system change was limited. After the British accepted defeat, citizens of India took over the system the British had instituted. Although it may be a big improvement, replacing the British hierarchy with an Indian hierarchy is not system change. When the British were no longer the common enemy, Gandhi's work was undermined by the partition of India and Pakistan and the continuing conflicts between Hindus and Muslims. The punitive system continues, but with a new group in control.

Sometimes political leaders argue for nonviolence as a tactic, but not as a principle they are willing to adhere to themselves. When riots erupted in Baltimore in 2015, President Obama's call for an end to the violence was met with skepticism. One critic, Natasha Lennard, observed that "[c]alls for an end to the riots are not calls for peace, but a return to violent order."[4]

Another critic, Bruce A. Dixon, pointed out the inconsistency of President Obama's call for the poor people of Baltimore to remain peaceful, nonviolent and respectful of the law when he himself relied on violence. Dixon wrote:

> This is a notion that should either make us laugh out loud, or cry, it's hard to decide which. President Obama, you see, also claims the law entitles him to drone-bomb hundreds, perhaps thousands of civilians across Asia and Africa whose names he doesn't even know based upon their "profiles" or their proximity to supposed "terrorists," also frequently unknown by name. The president, along with his outgoing and incoming attorneys general assure us this is all perfectly legal.[5] We have to take their word for it, because they've made the precise legal language of the rule they say permits this classified – a secret.[6]

Once again, inconsistency and hypocrisy are characteristics often present in the punitive system.

Our judicial system depends on the use of force to maintain control. This fact is reflected in the sheer amount of incarceration in the U.S. The American criminal legal system holds almost 2.3 million people in 1,833 state prisons, 110 federal prisons, 1,772 juvenile correctional facilities, 3,134 local jails, 218 immigration detention facilities, and 80 Indian Country jails, as well as in military prisons, civil commitment centers, state psychiatric hospitals, and prisons in the U.S. territories.[7]

Over time, efforts at benevolent reform of the punitive justice system have made little difference in the exercise of control. Efforts to reform the system are swallowed up, adapted, and even adopted as a reason to expand the punitive system.[8]

SELFGOVERNANCE LEADS TO FREEDOM

Instead of seeking control, can we create a system in which the need for control imposed by others is reduced by one's own selfgovernance? In other contexts, "selfgovernance" is often used to mean autonomy for an organization or governmental entity, such as local government self-rule. Here, I am using the term to refer to an individual's selfgovernance as a means of living in accordance with core values by choice. The Greek philosopher Plato taught that without selfgovernance, there is no freedom. Unless individuals govern their pleasures and desires, they are enslaved to them.

Selfgovernance is integral to Unitive Justice. The transition from control to selfgovernance is a shift from fear and toward Love. It demonstrates an important principle to those who believe they must rely on force and physical might to maintain control—those being controlled can instead choose freedom—freedom from control. Selfgovernance provides the freedom to take ownership of your life and to make your own decisions.

I learned the importance of selfgovernance being one of the first steps in creating unitive system change from Taylor and Prince. Early in their efforts to create prison culture change, they introduced the concept of selfgovernance to the men in their pod, a diverse group of about eighty-five men of different ages, races, religions, and gang affiliations. Some might assume that teaching selfgovernance to this particular group of men in a prison setting was impossible, but they are wrong. Taylor understood how to become the solution to the problems he previously caused. He knew that many of his peers in prison could also be the agents of the change they wanted to see happen. The way Taylor and Prince achieved this was ingenious.

Some correctional officers (COs) took pleasure in using the prison rules to regulate even minor aspects of the incarcerated men's lives. Taylor describes this as "keeping their foot on the necks of the inmates." When the men reacted with anger and noncompliance to harsh punishment for minor infractions, it could result in a longer prison sentence. Taylor devised a way to turn this situation upside down.

Taylor asked Prince to post some signs on the walls where everyone could see them that simply said, "SELFGOVERNANCE." He expected this to spark the curiosity of the men and that would lead to an opening to help them see their conflict with the COs in a new light. When Taylor and Prince were questioned about the signs, they suggested that if their pod mates used selfgovernance to follow the rules in the prison rule book, not as an act of compliance, but because they *choose* to, the COs would not need to say anything to them.

Taylor instructed them, "If the rule book says your shirt must be tucked in, tuck it in. If it says your name tag is to be on your left lapel, wear it on your left lapel." Complying with the rules would deprive the COs of their justification for using force to maintain control; they could no longer justify punishment in the name of public safety. It worked. Taylor and Prince modeled strictly following the rules as an act of defiance, and others began to follow.

Unexpectedly, following the official rules turned out to be a "violation" of the unofficial rule that let the COs be abusive and get away with it—they were just controlling unruly inmates. The inmates' compliance with the official rules turned out to be a form of civil disobedience towards the COs!

Surprisingly, following the official rules had the same impact as an act of nonviolent civil disobedience. As Martin Luther King, Jr. explained, the nonviolent approach does not immediately change the oppressor's heart—it first does something to the hearts and souls of those committed to it. King said, "It gives them new self-respect; it calls up resources of strength and courage that they did not know they had."

Finally, just as MLK said, it reaches the opponent and so stirs his conscience that reconciliation becomes a reality."[9] This is precisely the impact that following the prison rules *as an act of selfgovernance* had on the peers of Taylor and Prince, and eventually on many of the prison staff and administrators.

As complying with the prison rule book became the norm in their pod, other changes began to occur. The inherent dignity of the incarcerated men began to be reflected in their conduct. Living according to values seemed to emerge naturally. Soon, the men began to follow their own internal moral compass, and simultaneously, violence in their pod decreased and subsequently became rare. It is important to note that threats and force were not used to achieve this end.

The men in the pod achieved freedom through selfgovernance, but it also had the effect of revealing their shared humanity, and this provided a significant step toward achieving a positive self-image. Selfgovernance had the collateral effect of benefitting the COs as well as the men in the pod. The COs were safer, they didn't have to spend hours of overtime writing incident reports to justify the punishment. And they got to go home on time; this meant they could spend more time with their families. The hierarchy between staff and the inmates diminished.

You might ask, "What is the difference between compliance and self-governance? Didn't the men simply comply with the rules to avoid punishment?" No, they demonstrated their dignity and self-worth by showing they didn't need outside control. This is an important distinction. Selfgovernance is empowering; compliance is disempowering. Selfgovernance requires no coercion; enforcing compliance requires a proverbial whip.

Taylor says that selfgovernance happens when "a person comes into their own," when they realize that "being on the side of right is not so bad after all." It felt good when he began to do good, and he decided he wanted more of that. It was consistent with whom he was becoming, or perhaps this was his authentic self that was always there, waiting to be discovered.

Selfgovernance is achieved by the individual, but when two or more who have self-mastery join together, this creates an emerging force that enhances the potential to manifest Justice as Love. The community can support its members in this transformation. It is helpful to have a guide or code of conduct for the individuals aspiring to selfgovernance, such as the 14 Arcs to Unitive Justice. The 14 Arcs help clarify the behavior the group is seeking to achieve, it provides a measure of the community's level of success, and brings light to where more attention is needed. Before a community system is established, individuals on this path may use the Arcs and Unitive Justice Circles (described at the end of this chapter) on a smaller scale, laying the foundation for greater change to come.

* * *

Invitation to Journal.

a. Do you consider selfgovernance a realistic alternative to control by an outside authority?

b. When you read that Taylor and Prince implemented self-rule in their prison pod, what were your thoughts about that? Did it challenge any preconceived ideas that you had about people in prison?

c. Do you see the possibility of men in a prison pod experiencing joy as they assume control by exercising selfgovernance? Can you imagine something comparable to this happening in your life? If so, what might that look like?

d. Do you recognize selfgovernance in your own life? If so, how does it show up?

Suggested Viewing: Will Smith uses the term "self-discipline" in this video, but the message also applies to selfgovernance. *Self-Discipline - Best Motivational Speech Video* (Featuring Will Smith) https://www.youtube.com/watch?v=ft_DXwgUXB0 (10.17 min.).

ARC 3: COMMUNICATION
FROM DECEPTION TO HONESTY

deception: the act of causing someone to accept as true or valid what is false or invalid;[1] giving a misleading or untruthful account of conduct, intentions or events. Other terms for deception: half-truth, exaggeration, tall tale, little white lie, lying.

honesty: the act of giving a fair and truthful account of conduct, intentions, or events. Other terms for honesty: candor, frankness, veracity.

THE PUNITIVE SYSTEM OFTEN DISTORTS THE TRUTH

After twenty-eight years of trying various types of civil cases and having a ringside seat in some criminal actions, I do not apologize for using the term "deception" to describe what often happens in the punitive system. Deception is not an occasional problem in the legal system; it is inherent in its flawed design.

Why is deception so common? One reason is because in a punitive system it is often unsafe to be honest. It is a win-lose, winner-take-all system where the cost of losing can be enormous. In a criminal trial, honesty can speed up your conviction and punishment and perhaps even cost you your life. In a civil case, you can lose your business, home, custody of your children and also your reputation. Some conclude that it is safer to lie than tell the truth.

In a court of law, each witness takes an oath to tell the truth, leading us to believe telling the truth is of paramount importance. But sometimes lying is simply ignored. Perjury, the law that makes lying in court a crime, is so narrowly defined that a lot of untruthfulness must be ignored. To be prosecuted, the perjury must occur while a person who is under oath swears falsely about a *material matter or thing*, i.e., something related to a central issue in the case. If it is about something deemed to be of less importance it will not be prosecuted. The system would bog down if perjury were more broadly defined and routinely prosecuted.

But sometimes telling a lie is legally sanctioned because telling the truth is secondary to other considerations. In a criminal trial, the accused is confronted with the might of the state. In an attempt to correct this significant imbalance, the 5th Amendment provides that the accused cannot be forced to admit guilt. This is accomplished by giving defendants, even those who are guilty, the right to plead "not guilty." A system that must sanction an untruth that goes to the most important issue in the case, as happens in criminal cases, is inherently flawed.

Some rules that are supposed to help get at the truth have collateral consequences that can discourage honesty. The right to cross-examine witnesses in a criminal case is intended to help the judge or jury ferret out truth from lies. But because victims of crime are needed at trial to prove the state's law was broken, in this role, these witnesses are deemed to be agents of the state. As state witnesses, crime victims can be ruthlessly challenged on cross-examination by defense attorneys. After having been the victim of a violent crime, this can be a re-traumatizing experience. This is just one of several attributes of the punitive system that deter rape victims from pursuing charges,[2] and one reason why the truth remains untold.

The procedural rules regarding when the truth is supposed to be told and when a party is *legally* permitted to avoid telling the truth are complicated. Some statements, when made to a spouse or one's attorney, are considered privileged and therefore are not admissible as evidence—this truth can remain hidden. However, if a statement might provide evidence of guilt (i.e., it is an "admission against interest") made to someone not within the scope of privileged communication, the statement is admissible. The theory is that people are more likely to be telling the truth when they admit to wrongdoing that can get them punished, so this type of statement is presumed to be reliable. This is the rule that gives us "jailhouse snitches." Being able to catch the defendant or the adverse party making admissions against interest that are admissible in court is a useful skill for prosecutors and defense attorneys to possess.

Sometimes our policies promote lying in unexpected ways. Here is an example of how difficult it is to get out of this trap.

When I began practicing law, Virginia was a common law state, which meant that, upon a divorce, the property of the marriage went to the spouse who held title to the property. The husband could manipulate this provision by bringing a number of papers to his wife and directing her to sign them without making it clear that she was signing the title to their joint property over to him. Or, he might have arranged things so she never had legal title to the property in the first place.

When there was an opportunity to adopt equitable distribution in Virginia (i.e., the property is divided based on equitable principles, not mere title) I worked for that change. While the new law was an improvement, the problem of dishonesty remained. The current version of the Virginia code now provides that the property of the marriage will be divided based on the relative contributions of each party to the wellbeing of the family and what each put into the acquisition and care of the property acquired during the marriage.[3]

These factors set in motion a contest over who was the best and worst partner in the marriage. The attorney's role is to show that their client was a dutiful, diligent, committed spouse while the other spouse was a louse. The distortions that occur in this struggle, the outcome of which can determine the future trajectory of a spouse's life and fortune, can be brutal. Few litigants in these cases have an interest in a non-partial telling of their story.

The battle over custody of the children can be even more brutal and damaging. Sometimes, a child is used as a witness against the other parent, which can have life-altering consequences. After many years in this gladiator pit, I concluded that it is immoral to pit one spouse or parent against the other in an adversarial process where the truth too often takes a back seat to winning. It is not a good way to find the truth or promote honesty, and it further undermines relationships.

Divorce cases were not the only cases where I saw dishonesty used to win cases. In this win-lose system, pressure for the "evidence" to be told in a way most likely to convince a judge or a jury is an incentive to distort the truth in any type of case, because it is the judge or jury who decides which litigant wins. The punitive justice model requires trial attorneys to be good storytellers, even when the facts make it an uphill battle. They must shape the facts into a winning story and then seek to minimize or exclude evidence that contradicts their clients' claims.

In this adversarial punitive system, honesty may help your opponent win, hasten your defeat, or increase your punishment. As a result, attorneys readily admonish their clients never to say things like "I'm sorry" or "I made a mistake"—to anyone. To avoid costly blunders, attorneys often control the narrative by speaking on behalf of their clients.

The complex rules regarding when it is legal to avoid telling the truth and when it is worth taking the risk to lie can make a trial an elaborate game of skill and obfuscation. Having an attorney with the necessary legal expertise to win in court—innocent or not—is often the determining factor. The overall result is that truth is elusive at best and absent at worst. We celebrate when truth prevails, but what about all the other times?

How is this complex system experienced by laypeople who get caught up in it? This is how Taylor Paul and Prince Bunn describe their experience of the problem of honesty/distortion in the criminal legal system.[4]

TAYLOR:

They say that justice is blind, and I tried to figure it out for so many years. Prince and I, we talk about it all the time and just trying to get a grasp, an understanding of it. It's like you're talking about two concepts of truth when you go inside that courtroom, and it's sort of like a good versus evil or a prosecutor versus defense, and between the two, somebody is telling the truth, and somebody is not. So it appears, because justice is blind, so it appears.

The job of the prosecutor is to find the defendant guilty, and in some cases, regardless if that person is guilty or not. The job of your defense attorney, if you had that money, if you were getting a lot of money or something, or you had a family that was wealthy or had some money, then they probably got you a lawyer, and that lawyer's job, because you paid him, is to get you off whether you are guilty or not. So where's the truth between the two?

PRINCE:

And then the lawyer that you're talking about, he comes in, and he says to you, "Well, we're trying to find a loophole," that's what they call it. A loophole at the expense of somebody else's life, and then I heard a thing the other day that said "it's better to be rich and guilty than poor and innocent in this country."

TAYLOR:

Wow.

PRINCE:

Yeah, that's what I heard, man, and I thought about it. All right, you get in the courtroom, and then, all of a sudden, numbers are being thrown at you, plea bargains are thrown at you, and you are wrestling with yourself in the back, in the holding pen, or in the cell, as you're pacing back and forth. Whenever you go outside for rec, trying to find a loophole, but the loophole is basically, in my opinion, an avenue for dishonesty to come forth, you know what I'm saying?

Real talk, because if you know that you are guilty, and I'm saying I had a situation with a couple of my offenses where I actually committed malicious wounding, I shot this guy, and I wound up beating this case, but then I got convicted on a robbery that I didn't even do—in the same system. I go into the proceedings for the thing that I did do and get found not guilty. . .

TAYLOR:
Then you get found guilty for something you didn't do.

PRINCE:
. . . So, I sat back, and I said, well, now this is where the thing about your honesty comes into play because now I'm like, I could've easily went in there and said that I had shot this guy, but now, mind you, I'm already facing other charges as well. I already had the murder charge, and this was just some more charges that had been added to me. So, my thought was, yeah, I'm looking for loopholes. I'm looking for loopholes, and the loopholes were just opportunities to further lie and escape accountability for my actions, bro. And I think that until a man finds some personal integrity within himself, there is no hope, okay, because we were talking about restoring life, so that was then, this is now. . .

Lying is heavy, man. It burdens you because you have to constantly be mindful of what it is that you said, whoever you lied to, because that person that you lied to, they remember these things because it deeply impacted them, so they're going to be like detectives. They're going to be tearing things apart, trying to get to the truth that you're supposed to be dealing with. You've got to get away from the lying because it ain't no future in it.

TAYLOR:
. . . I remember reading Just Mercy *by Brian Stevenson, and there was a part that he was talking to one of his comrades when he first gets down to Alabama, and he's trying to do some things in this justice system that was totally corrupt, and his partner told him, and they were talking about the people that were on death row and capital punishment, and he told him that if you have no capital that you shall be punished. . .*

And this court-appointed lawyer who's probably chummy with the prosecutor that comes in and tells you, "Hey, man, you better take this, or they're going to do this, or they're going to do that," and then for you, . . . you found out that that whole thing that they were trying to give you was a lie. You wouldn't get as much time as he said you were going to get if you went to trial. Still, this particular defense attorney that they appointed to you, who only gets no more than $100 or $200 to defend you and most of the crimes, he comes to you and just tells you a lie *just to get you to write it off, and he can go on about his day because he's not getting paid a whole lot of money. Is that a reason for him to lie and not be truthful and dishonest?*

So how do you not be in that circumstance? Probably by being what we call an L7, and if you don't know what an L7 is, then you go to the board, and you draw an L, and then you put a seven over top of it, and you will see a square, meaning that you just take care of yourself and be truthful in your own life, and you do not have to go inside of courtrooms. You do not have to be in front of a prosecutor. You do not have to get a court-appointed lawyer, and you do not have to spend your hard-earned money or your mother or family's hard-earned money, trying to hire an attorney, all because you're being truthful in your own life.

A deeper problem remains. The punitive law system is designed to narrowly focus on offender guilt in a criminal case and on defendant liability in a civil case. What about the underlying systemic conditions that fuel crime, harm and misunderstandings? The court process is not designed to look at a continuous, coherent picture that leads to long-term solutions.

"Is it safe to be honest?" is a question that we learn to ask at an early age, especially if misjudging the answer comes with severe consequences. In school, students might learn that the principal's office is not a safe place to be honest—it hastens their punishment. Some children are told by their parents that disclosing the truth will result in punishment. Teachers who attend my training programs are sometimes hypervigilant about discussing what actually happens at school; they have learned that can cost them their job. Fortunately, the traditional punitive system is not our only choice.

UNITIVE JUSTICE INSPIRES HONESTY

Unitive Justice requires honesty and does not work without it. When I began to experience the Unitive Justice Circle, I realized the huge difference it makes when people are not afraid to tell the truth, because they see that it actually serves their own interest to do so. Going from distortion to honesty is system change at its best!

For people to be honest, it must be safe to be honest. Unitive Justice provides spaces where you can be honest, without risking your reputation, property, or life, and this removes the pressure to deceive. "The truth will set you free" is an old adage, but for the truth to set us free we must walk toward the truth, even when it is painful.

Honesty is a pillar of Unitive Justice. These are things that I learned about honesty *after* leaving the courtroom.

- When it is safe to be honest, people tend to be honest; this convinced me that people are inherently honest.
- Every conflict has a distinct context, a set of circumstances that gives rise to a specific conflict at a particular time. Being truthful permits us to discover the information contained within our conflict—information that often reveals the underlying brokenness out of which the conflict arose. Only when we discover this underlying brokenness can we begin to address it.
- When we tell the truth, we take responsibility for our feelings and actions. Honesty reflects integrity—we are who we say we are regardless of where we are or who we are with.
- Honesty builds connection. Truthfulness is essential for us to connect at the level of our shared humanity; this is where transformation happens. When we connect on this level, we naturally wish no harm to the person who, at that moment, we see as fragile and precious. This may sometimes occur even when the person has done egregious harm, if the circumstances have been created in which transformative change may arise.
- We must be honest if we are to connect at the level of our shared humanity. When we connect at this level, we discover that our differences do not disappear, but they are no longer a reason for judgment or separation. This opens a world of new possibilities. We discover that our differences actually enable us to achieve much more together than we can ever do alone. It begins with being honest.

An example of justice that rewarded truth-telling is found in the Truth and Reconciliation trials in South Africa. After years of civil strife during Apartheid between 1960 to 1994, this racially divided nation took a new approach. Rather than launching a multitude of criminal trials to address years of human rights violations (abductions, killings, torture), the nation offered amnesty to those who honestly admitted they committed these crimes. Building on the values inherent in the African system of Ubuntu, these trials showed how an open heart more readily leads to the truth. Instead of punishment, those who took responsibility for their crimes were extended amnesty and acceptance in the community.

Sometimes, getting to the truth in these trials inspired forgiveness. Instead of asking that their tormentors be punished as retribution and revenge would have it, some victims of terrible atrocities connected to something greater than themselves. Some spontaneously embraced those who had caused harm.

The Truth and Reconciliation process rewarded truth-telling with amnesty, but it was not designed to get at the root causes—the step of using the harmful acts to uncover the underlying conflict dynamic out of which the years of violence arose. Perhaps future truth and reconciliation processes will be designed specifically to facilitate this deeper level of healing.

Honesty is not just about telling the truth to others; it is also about being truthful with yourself about who you are. Prince Bunn often talks about his long walk to the mirror when he had to be fully honest with himself and admit who he had become and all the people he had harmed or disappointed. Being truthful with himself was essential to Prince's transformation.

Honesty is telling the truth, as you know it, about factual events. However, being honest doesn't mean being rude, unkind, or aggressive. A statement like, "Your hair is ugly but not as ugly as your face—I'm just being honest," does not get a pass. Honesty and being considerate must go hand in hand.

Creating a safe environment for truth-telling does not depend on just one structural element. Unitive justice is a system that works because the structural elements are mutually supportive—they create an upward spiral. Shared values support equality and inclusion. Values and equality support insight and selfgovernance, strengthening connection, community, and trust. Trust leads to honesty, and honesty opens the door to new possibilities. New possibilities give rise to mutually beneficial action and this strengthens the community.

Instead of punishment, the reward for being honest can be mutually beneficial action where the interests of all are served, and no one has to lose. This can lead to unified goals. The power of unified goals is unknown in the punitive law system. Once the transformative nature of being honest is experienced, it is difficult to find any benefit in dishonesty. It is in honesty that our authentic power lies.

* * *

Invitation to Journal. Consider these questions:

a. Do you believe the complex way we go about providing due process in the courtroom to help achieve fairness actually achieves fairness?
b. If our legal system is accommodating dishonesty, might this impact our culture as a whole? If so, how does this impact manifest?
c. What, if any, obstacles to being honest do you experience in your life?
d. Have you had the experience of working or living in an environment where genuine honesty was the norm? If so, how did this impact the culture? If not, how did the lack of honesty impact you?

Suggested Viewing: A short YouTube clip from the trial scene in the movie, *To Kill a Mockingbird*, shows the defense attorney, Atticus Finch, cross-examining Mayella, the state's key witness in proving a trumped-up case of assault and rape against a Black man. This scene reminds us of many reasons why a witness may not feel safe telling the truth in the adversarial setting of a trial. This particular case had a context that included domestic abuse and racial violence, neither of which was addressed by the criminal trial. The video, "To Kill a Mockingbird (4/10) Movie CLIP - Atticus Cross-Examines Mayella," is at https://www.youtube.com/watch?v=44TG_H_oY2E (4 min.). Doing a search for video clips from *To Kill a Mockingbird* will find other examples from the movie.

ARC 4: ASSESSMENT
JUDGMENT TO INSIGHT

judgment: considered decisions intended to result in sensible conclusions, but preconceived perceptions believed to be real often taint the decisions. Other terms for judgment: expectations, evaluation, assessment, perception, differentiation, condemnation.

insight: discovery of new information about the inner nature of an act or events; an act of discerning deeply that reveals information and possibilities that were not previously seen. Other terms for insight: vision, wisdom, intuition, acumen, understanding.

PUNITIVE JUSTICE AND JUDGMENT

A punitive system relies on judgment—discerning the divide between who is guilty or innocent, who is good or bad, who is with us and who is against us. We judge who is unimportant, who is evil or ugly. The problem is that judgment is based on preconceived notions that we hold about other people and things, along with the belief that our perception is real. In fact, we project our judgment on them and there may be no truth in it. Our perception is informed and shaped by our beliefs, be they true or not.

We often judge another without realizing our perception is like looking in the rear-view mirror—it is a view through the lens of the past. As we focus on the speck in another's eye, we are blind to the log in our own.[1] As judgment proliferates, separation from one another deepens, and human relations deteriorate.

The punitive justice system cannot exist without multiple levels of judgment. That's why we call those at the pinnacle of the system "judges." They first judge the accused. Then, if found guilty, they judge what measure of punishment they deem to be proportional to the crime. Judges judge each issue raised on appeal. Parole boards judge when it is time for a prisoner's release, and probation officers judge if a violation has occurred post-release. Often, the public continues to judge those who bear the label "criminal" long after their debt to society has been legally paid.

We rely on judgment, even knowing it is a flawed tool for getting at the truth, including for those who judge as a profession. How many wrong decisions do our judges and juries make daily in courtrooms around the nation?

More than 180 death sentences have been commuted since 1973 because evidence later proved these people were innocent—innocent people sentenced to die! An average of nearly four wrongly convicted death-row prisoners have been exonerated (*i.e.*, cleared of blame) each year since 1973. There was an average of five exonerations per year from 2000-2011. "In 96% of states where there have been reviews of race and the death penalty, there was a pattern of race-of-victim, race-of-defendant discrimination, or both."[2] And how many have been wrongfully convicted and put to death? This alone is a reason to think twice about how flawed judgment often is.

Modern brain science provides evidence that judgment is not as reliable as we once thought it was, a finding with significant implications for the justice system. A finding that goes to the heart of the legal process is that using an adversarial process to address conflict can damage mental and cognitive resources. It can trigger a fight, flight, freeze or appease response in those engaged in the process—not a good environment for making life-changing decisions. This science is beginning to impact how some lawyers practice law, especially in the field of Collaborative Law.[3]

Judgment is like a prison that chains us to the past. Judging always comes with a price—it is as though our judgment is the setting of the price and the price we set we have to pay. When we focus on achieving retribution for what happened in the past, we are not thinking about the present or creating for the future—imagine the price of that. We often send our youth to pay the price for our judgment, even when it is terribly mistaken—yet another price we pay. Judgment is guided by unconscious programming that lies in the recesses of the mind, like an invisible hand guiding our judgment and influencing our decisions. This gives rise to the illusion that we are being completely rational, even when our decisions are misguided, mistaken and irrational. Judges and juries are subject to this same mental conditioning.

We must ask: is a judge or jury, hearing bits and pieces of evidence molded by attorneys whose aim is to win by making the other side lose, the best way to judge guilt and innocence? Is this a reasonable way to make decisions about life and death?

This unconscious programming may also help sustain the double moral standard that permits us to see our harming others as moral, perhaps even redemptive. Thinking we are the "good people," we are quick to judge the harm done by those whom we judge to be "bad people" as immoral and destructive, even when we are doing essentially the same thing. This double moral standard is the guiding moral principle of punitive justice, described in Arc 7, from proportional revenge to lovingkindness.

We cannot be free so long as we imprison anyone in our judgment and condemnation—the jailer cannot leave his port. Until we experience it, we may not be able to appreciate the release and peace that comes from meeting ourselves and our brothers and sisters without judgment. When we recognize one another at the level of our shared humanity, we begin to see that judging them has no more meaning than them judging us.

UNITIVE JUSTICE AND INSIGHT

The human mind is complex and intriguing; it is not linear. It is as though the mind is a house with many rooms—some that we easily enter and exit, and some that seem to trap the thinker, making escape difficult. Some rooms can only be entered when we are in a connected state of mind. These special rooms are where we encounter insight.

Insight is a mental portal that opens to inner sight and access to knowledge and understanding that was previously inaccessible. Insight paves the way for more refined thinking and actions. It permits us to be forward-looking, not focused on the past, as judgment requires.

This leads to understanding people, issues and contexts free of the projection of one's own judgment. Insight leads to understanding the cause of one's own pain and the pain of others, letting it be acknowledged and perhaps seen in a new way.

The Unitive Justice Circle described at the end of this chapter is especially well-equipped to help us access insight. With insight, participants might see how they meet their needs in ways that perpetuate the conflict dynamics and systemic brokenness. It brings participants to recognize their shared power and connection, seeing a future in which they can go forward *together*. This paves the way to take the goal from merely seeking compliance to achieving mutually beneficial action, as will be described in Arc 11.

Here is an example of the difference addressing a student fight in a circle and achieving insight can make. Two high school boys, John and Ramon (not their real names), got into a fight in the school gym. Interest in the conflict by other students spiked because Ramon was Black and John was white. However, in the safety of a circle, they quickly got to the root of their conflict, and it was not simply an issue having to do with race. They were both school athletes. As they engaged in reflective listening, they figured out that Ramon was intent on hanging out with John who was a star athlete, but John rejected his overtures of friendship. Ramon reacted to this hurt by being rude to John. This escalated John's rejection of Ramon, increasing Ramon's embarrassment and anger. They realized that, as one hurt compounded another, the deepening wedge between them led to the fight.

As they sorted out the underlying dynamics, each student owned up to how he had unwittingly contributed to the escalation. They agreed to make a point of being helpful to one another in ways that fit their particular situation. John would ask Ramon to play on his team in gym class, and Ramon, the better student, would help John with some of his homework assignments. This circle took about thirty minutes. It was a minor conflict, yet the resolution represented a step toward system change—until we discovered a systemic hurdle in its implementation.

With the students' consent, their signed agreement was shared with the gym teachers. They were asked to *support* the students in living into the terms of their agreement, not with threats of punishment, but with encouraging words and actions. The circle facilitator was unaware of a "Conduct Contract" used in the traditional disciplinary process that students were required to sign after a fight and staff members were expected to enforce. Later the facilitator discovered that the gym teachers assumed the agreement entered in the Unitive Circle Process was just another "Conduct Contract." It was not. We hoped to replace judgment and punishment with kindness and understanding, perhaps even enthusiastic support. This incident provided an important lesson in how unforeseen hurdles may arise when seeking to create system change.

Insight into a gym fight may not seem like much, but the principles are much the same when seeking peace at the international level. Robert McNamara served as Secretary of War during the Vietnam War. Years later, McNamara met with the Vietnamese military leaders who led their fight against the Americans.

In the documentary *The Fog of War*, McNamara describes this meeting and how it became clear that both sides marched into that war blinded by their own projections, judgments, and mistaken beliefs about the other. It was the clash of our illusion with their illusion that propelled us into war. McNamara realized that, if the Americans had better understood the history of the Vietnamese and their determination to secure their independence from all other nations, including China, he would have approached the conflict differently. If the Americans and Vietnamese had sought insight instead of relying on judgment, it could have changed the course of history and saved millions of lives. When insight replaces judgment, we discover that values, wholeness and connection can be achieved.

* * *

Invitation to Journal. First, in your journal, draw the pieces of a puzzle that represent major events in your life up to this point in time. Then, write

> a. Which experiences most stand out among the pieces of your life's puzzle?
> b. Describe how each piece of your puzzle influenced where you are today.
> c. Can you imagine re-ordering some of the pieces, reclaiming others, and even creating new pieces to produce more harmony and stronger relationships as you go forward?
> d. Record any insights that arise.

Suggested Viewing: The documentary *The Fog of War* may be viewed at https://www.youtube.com/watch?v=nU1bzm-BW0o (1 hr., 23 min.).

ARC 5: INTERPERSONAL
FROM DISTRUST TO TRUST

distrust: suspicion or doubt of the honesty or reliability of another. Other terms for distrust: mistrust, suspicion, cynicism, skepticism, disbelief, lack of confidence.

trust: relational interdependence that strengthens relationships and makes human interactions more functional because it is built on shared values. Trust begins on the individual level, then becomes a community value. Other terms for trust: confidence, faith, conviction.

NOTES ON THE NATURE OF TRUST

Trust is a unique value. It is difficult to define and even more challenging to measure, yet we know what trust is. Trust is relational and it is personal. We build trust one interaction at a time, one day at a time. Being trusted by someone is a huge responsibility. The trust we place in those whom we love to not harm us is as precious as any gift we can give. When someone extends trust to us and we honor that trust, we affirm their dignity, their personhood and our connection to them.

Trust has an internal reward—the greater the trust among individuals, the more harmonious their relationships are likely to be. Trust is like a shortcut, a bridge that strengthens relationships and makes human interactions more functional. Trust fosters openness and flow.

Trust and faith are closely related and are sometimes used to mean much the same thing. For example, "I have faith in the president," might be expressed as "I trust the president." Perhaps the difference can be described as trust is what we extend to other living beings (e.g., people and dogs), but faith we extend to things beyond this realm. In Hebrews 11:1–6 it says, "Now faith is the assurance of things hoped for, the conviction of things not seen."

Trust is different from confidence. You might have confidence in a person's intellectual or physical ability and then be disappointed in their performance but still trust them.

We extend trust knowing it comes with the risk of being betrayed, yet trusting it won't be. When we innocently extend trust, as a child does, its betrayal can be devastating and life-long. Trust is built and held in place by shared values. It can be lost in a moment when those values are violated. When trust is absent, suspicion emerges to undermine our interactions.

A violation of our safe space or our body is life-changing. The violation of this particular trust is like the tearing of a precious fabric that can never be repaired. A woman who is raped, a child who is molested, an inmate who is raped and has no escape. Will they ever again know what it is like to be genuinely trusting?

When I was growing up in a small rural community in Colorado, between the late 1940s and early 1960s, we never locked our doors, day or night. I don't recall seeing a key to our home when I was a child. We trusted our neighbors and those who lived in our community to honor the security and serenity of our home. After my father passed away, my mother lived alone in a small home without air conditioning. Even when I was a young adult, I recall her leaving the kitchen door open on hot summer nights to get the benefit of the night breeze that came in through the screen door. She never lost sleep worrying about someone breaking into her home.

When our children were small and we lived in rural Virginia, I recall the first time I came home and discovered that our home had been broken into. Little was taken, but it was not about the things, it was the intense sense of personal violation and loss, the destruction of trust in those in my community. The violation of my sense of safety, even in my own home, was traumatic. The second time our home was burglarized we installed a security system that sounds an alarm when a window or a door is impacted when the system is on. Just being present to the loss of trust in my community that this reflects is depressing. And I realize, especially in the South, there are those whose homes have never been safe places for them or their children. I believe at the time in which we now live, this feeling of distrust is prevalent among nearly all of us who live in the U.S.

Now, I live in a metropolitan city in the South, and I definitely do not experience that level of trust, at home or elsewhere. Even when I leave my home for a short time, I lock the door. When I am home alone during the day, I sometimes lock the door and if someone rings the doorbell, I don't open the door unless I know who is there. I no longer live in a community where I trust others as we did when I was a child. Obviously, I have a lot of work to do to restore trust in my community.

How did distrust become so prevalent? Is the objectification of "the others" so widespread in our culture that it is like water is to fish? Is our separation now so deep and wide that we are drowning in it? Perhaps the answer lies in our duality consciousness.

DISTRUST IN THE PUNITIVE SYSTEM

A punitive system is a hostile environment for trusting relationships. The dualistic worldview of "us versus them" and "good versus evil," to which the punitive system is tied, reinforces and sustains distrust of others. What's more, all of the structural elements of the punitive system promote distrust—deception, proportional revenge, self-interest and every other punitive structure. The punitive system depends on judgment, but it is based on projections and perceptions that are often wrong; this fuels distrust. The adversarial nature of the punitive system undermines trust because adversaries must guard their self-interests.

The problem is compounded by the hierarchy found in every punitive system. It promotes separation, undermines connection and promotes distrust. Checks on those at the top of a hierarchy are often difficult to impose, and where such checks exist, they tend to be weak. As a result, abuse of authority and control can arise in every hierarchical group, profession or institution. A punitive system is not a trusting environment.

TRUST IN THE UNITIVE SYSTEM

A quick review of the structural elements of the unitive system makes it clear that each one builds trust. Each structure, from values to Love, replaces the punitive system's structures that undermine trust. Trust becomes natural and easy in the new system.

The Unitive Justice Circle that you will read about later is an important process for building trust within a community. It provides experiential learning in how to build trust following a conflict or breakdown. As mutual understanding grows in stage one of the circle, trust begins to build. In stage two, when participants begin recognizing their interconnectedness and shared humanity, this results in a high level of trust.

When the circle process ends in a mutually beneficial outcome, it heightens our trust in others and even in our own ability to do what is honorable and right. When root causes are addressed and no longer fester, trust among community members is strong. When everyone wins and goals become united, trust wins.

Trust is tied to other values. Trusting a person depends on their honesty, integrity, fairness and courage. Values such as these instill trust. Trust nurtures trust. The more trust you extend to others, the more others are likely to trust you. Trust is essential for healthy relationships and strong communities. Structures that build trust are essential for the betterment and welfare of humanity.

A system of Unitive Justice sustains trust within our relationships, neighborhoods and communities. As trust grows, so do honesty, fairness and kindness. As trust spreads from one block to another, the neighborhood changes. This type of wellbeing at the local level fosters the wellbeing of the state and nation.

System change requires a lot of trust. If you step into the role of modeling for others how system change is to be achieved using Unitive Justice theory and practices, others will extend their trust to you because you offer what they deeply desire. Your commitment to honor their trust is crucial. The gift they give to you and you give to them when this interaction occurs is the giving and receiving that will bring peace.

* * *

Invitation to Journal. Consider these questions:

a. Think of a person whom you trust. Describe the characteristics of that person that cause you to trust them.
b. Think of a person whom you distrust. Describe the characteristics of the person that cause you to distrust them.
c. Of the two sets of characteristics, which most accurately describes how you see yourself when you meet a person for the first time?
d. Which set most accurately describes how you interact with someone who is central to your life—your spouse, a parent, a sibling, or your immediate supervisor?

e. Is there anything you might choose to change? If so, describe the change you want to make and why.

Suggested Viewing: The video called *Why Trust is Worth It* is an artistic portrayal of trust. It is available at https://www.youtube.com/watch?v=cWypWe9UAhQ (3 min.).

An additional video suggestion: a podcast of Brene Brown on Oprah's show talking about *The Anatomy of Trust.* It is available at https://www.youtube.com/watch?v=HX7pxiwzSzQ (27.17 min.).

ARC 6: STRENGTH
FROM SELF-DOUBT TO COURAGE

self-doubt: a feeling of insecurity regarding one's worth, value, ability or power. It leads to conformity, accepting a low bar for one's purpose in life, depression and other negative outcomes. Other terms for self-doubt: insecurity, meekness, timidity, temerity, low self-esteem, uncertainty, indecision.

courage: the *moral bravery* to do the right thing even in the face of disapproval, opposition or rejection; the *emotional bravery* to be vulnerable, present to one's own pain or to be present to the pain of others or to practice radical tenderness even in the face of entrenched callousness; the *intellectual bravery* to question one's thinking or to risk discovering new ideas, or to discern and tell the truth; the *spiritual bravery* to discern one's purpose or the meaning of life; the *civic bravery* to responsibly exercise one's role as a citizen and to be a player in writing a new version of history where all are deserving of dignity and respect; and the *physical courage* to act in the face of fear or risk of physical harm. Courage allows us to do the extraordinary, even while we think we are ordinary. Other terms for courage: daring, fearlessness, grit, heroism.

In a punitive world, we are constantly judged, and judgment leads to self-doubt. Continually getting messages that you are inferior, inadequate, unworthy or "the other" takes a toll. Self-doubt is destructive and debilitating.

Growing up, I continually got the message that I was inferior because I was a girl. When I entered law school, there were still quotas for women and minorities, a judgment that we were not worthy of the profession, but they would make an exception for a few of us.

To be sure, men are subject to judgment that leads to self-doubt, as well. We judge some men for not being the right type of man for a multitude of reasons, or not being relational enough or too soft. Racism is another form of judgment, learned from an early age, a message to people who aren't white that they are less worthy. The resolution of separation is always found in connection.

There is a desire on the part of some whom I have encountered to dismantle white superiority using the same old tactics. Racial healing is not achieved in reorganizing the punitive system's hierarchy by driving white people out. Racial healing will come with the inclusion of Black people and other minorities in any and all roles because we recognize our shared humanity, the value of our diversity, and this achieves our unified goals. The election of Barak Obama as President demonstrated that we can do this. This is in our mutual best interest. It's true, we now have to overcome the backlash to Obama's election, but it is a reaction of some, not the leading force. The prevailing trend, albeit too slow, is toward Unity.

You may be surprised to learn that many lawyers find themselves subject to self-doubt, and the problem begins early in law school. The structures of punitive justice undermine connection, leaving us feeling isolated, unsupported and alone—conditions that fuel self-doubt. Trial lawyers often deal with depressing cases that reflect the deep brokenness in our society. This may help explain why lawyers are 3.6 times more likely to suffer from depression than non-lawyers.[1] The American Psychological Association identifies depression as the most likely trigger for suicide.[2] According to CDC data, lawyers are "ranked fourth when the proportion of suicides in that profession is compared to suicides in all other occupations in the study population (adjusted for age). They come right behind dentists, pharmacists and physicians."[3]

Self-doubt is unavoidable when you believe that you or what you are doing is not worthy, of little value, or that you sometimes contribute to the ugliness in the world. Self-doubt makes the system look so big and ingrained that you think there is nothing you can do about it.

When I think about the moments of self-doubt that I experienced as a trial attorney, what comes to mind are instances when I was forced to choose between the lesser of two evils, one injustice or another. Repeatedly being in a situation where you are not proud of what you are required to do contributes to self-doubt.

One instance that comes to mind is when I would confront the ethical duty to report a client who told me they intended to commit a crime. When I practiced law, adultery was a crime in Virginia, and I handled many divorces. One brave legislator tried to abolish this law, one that we all knew a good number of attorneys and judges violated with impunity. His attempts to abolish adultery as a crime were met with charges that the legislator wanted to condone sin and immorality, so that law remained in effect as long as I practiced law.

Of course, attorneys have a duty of confidentiality regarding client-attorney communication, but there are exceptions, and the intent to commit a crime is one of them. What did I do when I thought perhaps a client was going to tell me about their intent to commit adultery? I would tell them there are some things that it's best not to share with me, and I changed the subject. This was not something I liked to do, but complying with a rule that I knew would cause my client harm when it should not be on the books due to the hypocrisy it reflected was not something I was willing to do either. I was faced with a choice between a legal injustice and a rule violation. Moments like this gave rise to self-doubt.

I faced another conflict early in my career when I took court-appointed cases involving juveniles charged with a crime. In my last case like this, I represented two Black grade-school children who were charged with shoplifting shoes at a local store. They admitted they took the shoes and I felt the best lesson for them would be to honestly accept responsibility. When their trial began, and the shoes were set before them, I asked them if they had taken those shoes from the store. They said they did and I advised them to plead guilty. The judge could not have been kinder to the children. He said he hoped they had learned their lesson and that this would not happen again. He suspended judgment for a period of time, after which he would dismiss the charges if they got into no further trouble.

Shortly after that, I attended an ethics course for attorneys representing juvenile clients. The course instructor stated that what I did was unethical—a criminal defense attorney was duty-bound to instruct their clients to plead not guilty, even when they were, to force the state to prove its case. I felt that saying they were not guilty when they were guilty was a poor lesson for these children to learn, especially if they got away with it. I never represented another juvenile charged with a crime. I had three young children of my own at the time, and that was not a lesson I wanted them to learn. I was not going to play a role in making it a lesson that other children learned.

In the next few years, my teenage daughter and son each faced a traffic charge in juvenile court. In each case, I asked them if the charge, as read, sounded accurate. When they said it did, I advised them to plead guilty. I am confident that the lesson in honesty and accountability this provided them was more important than forcing the state to prove its case against them.

As I learned more about Justice as Love, it became progressively harder for me to continue to practice law. In the 1990s, I settled on what I thought was a way I could make lemonade out of the lemons I was dealing with—I would specialize in representing victims of childhood sexual abuse. I thought this was a good use of my legal skills because childhood sexual abuse is especially disempowering, but I could help empower my clients by giving them a fairly safe venue in which to confront their perpetrator. I could force the perpetrator to appear for depositions, answer interrogatories and even take the stand at trial. I knew they might choose to plead the 5th Amendment, but they could not ignore their victim. I worked with my clients' therapists to carefully prepare them for trial so it would not be a traumatic encounter that caused further harm.

One of these cases brought up an inherent conflict of interest that was actually a turning point in my legal career. These were cases that required a lot of preparation time. As most of my sexual abuse clients had limited resources, I had to take them on a contingent retainer—I was paid only if we won the case and collected the judgment. I would then receive one-third of what was collected.

In one case I represented a teenager who had been sexually violated by her father. We were a few days before the trial and I was preparing her to testify when she turned to me and said, "I don't want this. I just want my dad without the bad stuff going on." My first thought was my contingent fee. If we didn't win the case and get a judgment that could be collected, I would not be paid for the many hours I had invested in the case.

It was gut-wrenching to realize that a conflict between my interest in being compensated and my young client's interest in reconciling with her father was what first came to mind. It was made more difficult by the fact I had tried to settle the case to spare this young girl from testifying against her father in court. The father's attorney must have believed we wouldn't go to trial; he would not negotiate in good faith. I explained this to my client and her mother. I know it was a difficult decision for them, but we tried the case and "won," in that the jury ruled in favor of my client. A juror called me after the trial to say that jurors should be afforded counseling after hearing such evidence. The win did not give my client what she wanted—her father without the bad stuff going on. This experience cemented my determination to leave this profession.

Facing a conflict of interest involving a fee was unusual for me, but public defenders frequently find themselves in this position. Often, they are assigned to represent indigent criminal defendants facing an array of charges, some minor and some major, all for a set fee. In Virginia they are paid a flat fee of $120 for a case in district court and $1,235 for a circuit court case (i.e., a court of record) that involves a possible sentence of 20 years in prison.[4] The pressure to get a quick resolution and move on to the next case so the attorney can make enough to pay overhead can be significant. As Taylor and Prince described earlier, a common solution is to encourage the client to take a plea bargain and not go to trial.

When you are in a profession that fuels self-doubt, you get accustomed to it. You might not even realize that you are trapped in a persistent state of self-doubt. When you can exist within the walls you build to protect yourself from the judgment and attacks of others, you can ignore your self-doubt—much of the time. It becomes easier to go along to get along or to keep earning the paycheck than to do what your inner moral compass tells you to do. You might even try to disguise your self-doubt with macho behavior, bravado, and even breaking the law, thinking this shows you are strong.

Self-doubt undermines your ability to face disapproval, opposition or rejection and still remain grounded in your inherent dignity and worth. Self-doubt inhibits your ability to live life fully or discern the meaning of life. It makes you feel small, unwilling to risk extending radical tenderness or lovingkindness, or to discover new opportunities, often because you fear being judged or rejected. Being fully present to another person is inhibited by self-doubt—it takes courage.

For me, one of the most painful aspects of self-doubt is that it often begins early in life, when we are children. Imagine the self-doubt that all of the children who have been sexually abused live with throughout their lives. Imagine the self-doubt experienced by children who are called demeaning names or told they are worthless by their parents, other adults, and other children. A punitive culture is an especially cruel environment for children.

It can seem that the easiest choice is to stay in your comfort zone—as dark and debilitating as it is—unwilling or unable to step out. But how do we overcome self-doubt?

ANSWERING SELF-DOUBT WITH COURAGE IN THE LEGAL PROFESSION

I now believe that many attorneys find an antidote to the self-doubt fed by the nature of their work by finding opportunities to be courageous by challenging the status quo. There are many opportunities for attorneys to do this because they hold the keys to this punitive world. The attorneys who enjoy the profession tell me they are proud to help clients experience at least some justice in a system where the hurdles to justice abound. Eking out a win here and a win there for individuals or groups who are treated unjustly in the punitive system justifies the work they do. It is like a perpetual David and Goliath battle that goes on in the punitive system, work that, in one way, may help sustain the system—small victories help distract our attention from the system's flaws.

As one of the few women practicing law in Richmond, Va., when I started in the 1970s, I had many opportunities to lunge into this David and Goliath struggle, mustering the courage to fight for a little justice here or there. When I began practicing law, I was immediately confronted with the centuries of judgment and injustices that reflected the inferior status of women. Virginia's law provides that English common law is still operative in Virginia, so long as it is not explicitly rejected by the Virginia code or its Constitution.[5] Many of the old laws relating to women and children had not yet been rejected.

As a result, at that time, Virginia still had the "family doctrine," a rule from English common law that said the husband was the master of his household and the hand of the state would not reach into his domain. As long as women were voiceless, there was no way to change how things were and had been for centuries.

In the 1970s, women could be left with no property in a divorce or when their husband died. The criminal code included no crime of marital rape; sex with his wife was a husband's right, regardless of the circumstances. The traditional common law doctrine of *feme covert* that said a woman's legal identity merged with the husband's at marriage meant that she had no legal rights independent of her husband, leaving wives with no legal redress. Yale Law School professor, Reva Segal, observed, "No nineteenth century court . . . granted a battered woman the right to sue her husband for damages for assault. Instead, state courts effectively closed the door to such suits by transforming the common law fiction of coverture [i.e., one legal identity for both spouses] into a substantive common law rule of interspousal tort immunity."[6] Tort immunity means no *civil* legal redress exists for a wrongful act (other than under contract). When women had no legal redress, needless to say, children did not either.

I mentioned earlier that I eventually chose to specialize in representing survivors of childhood sexual abuse in an attempt to do something that I felt was valuable with my legal skills. I immediately encountered legal barriers. Tort immunity is a convenient legal theory that bars a civil suit for a harm done. When I began practicing law, the common law doctrine of intra-family tort immunity was still in effect—a doctrine that said one family member could not bring a civil suit for damages against another family member. This barred any civil suit against a family member for child sexual abuse.

Consistent with intra-family tort immunity, courts viewed the family as the husband's domain, so what happened at home, even child sexual abuse, was best left to the "family government," and that, of course, was controlled by the husband/father. Reva Siegel summarized the results: "In creating a new protective sphere around the privacy of domestic relations, courts, while speaking in formal, neutral terms, acted to shield middle- and upper-class men from risking the evils of publicity merely for their inevitable 'frailties of nature' and 'the mysteries of passion.'"[7]

The issue of childhood sexual abuse was further complicated by a non-legal theory that said such allegations were never true. Beginning with Freud, many in the therapeutic community argued that an allegation of childhood sexual abuse arose because of mental illness on the part of the victim and her fantasy about having sex with her father. This effectively barred criminal charges for child sexual abuse, as well as civil redress, because the experts would testify that the abuse never happened. Paul Lombardo explains, "Equally troublesome for those bold enough to unmask their assailants is a legal system unprepared to address allegations of harms long past, accustomed instead to a counsel of indifference toward claims so difficult to substantiate."[8] It was not until the 1970s and later that some therapists rejected the "mental illness" theory and believed the children.

As long as there was no civil or criminal redress for incest, childhood sexual abuse was a "perfect crime."[9] It was not until the 1980s that the doctrine of civil intra-family tort immunity began to wane in Virginia,[10] and therapists were available to serve as expert witnesses regarding the harm caused by childhood sexual abuse. As a result, when I began trying civil sexual abuse cases in the 1990s, they were among the first in Virginia.

But we had not yet addressed all the hurdles in civil cases for childhood sexual abuse. We still had to overcome the two-year statute of limitations on bringing a case that began to run when a minor turned 18. A victim had to file suit by age 20 or forever be barred from filing a civil suit. Most survivors have not healed to the point of being able to confront their perpetrator that early in life. It may take being out of the reach of the perpetrator for a number of years, plus years of therapy before the idea of going to court against a perpetrator can be entertained. This short statute of limitations continued to protect the perpetrators who sexually abused children.

This civil statute of limitations had to be extended to make the playing field more even—a small piece in this maze of injustice that seemed doable. By this time, I was working with a number of adult survivors who were willing to step into the role of David in their fight against Goliath, and to do so for as long as it took. Dulaney Collins was a leader among them, as was Debbie Sneller and others who demonstrated enormous courage. We got to work. We found a patron and several co-patrons for a bill that extended the statute of limitations in these cases. Adult survivors shared their experiences of childhood sexual abuse with the relevant legislative committees and in many public arenas. The bill that extended the childhood sexual abuse statute of limitations was signed into law in Virginia in March of 1991.

I filed one of the first suits under the new law, Starnes v. Cayouette, 419 S.E.2d 669 (1992). The Circuit Court held that the statute could not be applied retroactively because that violated the Virginia Constitution's provision that protected vested property rights. I appealed that case to the Virginia Supreme Court, and on June 5, 1992, the day the Virginia

Supreme Court decision was handed down, Dulaney and I met at the courthouse to get a copy. The Virginia Supreme Court upheld the lower court ruling with only one dissenting vote. I told Dulaney that we had lost and she was devastated. She asked if there was anything we could do. I told her we could amend the Constitution of Virginia.

Those who had worked to pass this statute planned to meet the following day to either celebrate or commiserate the Virginia Supreme Court decision. After seeing the devastation on Dulaney's face when I told her we had lost, I was not going to that party to tell the survivors who had worked tirelessly to pass the statute that we lost and it was over. Dulaney and I went to my office and prepared a handout for the party the next day that described a plan for amending the Virginia Constitution.

A later article about amending Virginia's statute of limitations in these cases reported that "Despite this additional lengthy delay [caused by losing in the Virginia Supreme Court], advocates for a new law appear unfazed by their court setback."[11] Nothing could be farther from the truth. We were heartbroken, but we were fighting for the dignity of those who had been violated for centuries in this dark corner of the punitive law system and we weren't giving up.

In July, 1992, we held a press conference to announce our intent to amend Virginia's Constitution, followed by a multi-year effort that involved many adult survivors building the groundswell of voter support to pass the amendment. A multitude of speeches were given and signatures were gathered across the state to demonstrate citizen support. The proposed amendment had to be approved twice by the Virginia Legislature and then approved by the voters. We followed each step of the plan and in November of 1994 over 65% of the voters of Virginia approved this amendment, a high margin for a constitutional amendment in Virginia.

The new law went into effect on January 1, 1995.[12] Adopting this constitutional amendment can be seen as a monumental victory, but for me, it is another small victory in an ocean of injustice. It was yet another band-aid on a flawed justice system that protected perpetrators of child sexual abuse and violence toward women for centuries. The problems with the punitive system evolve, but they don't go away.

When I practiced law, I accepted the unpleasantness of the profession as inevitable—it's just how things are, be a big girl and trudge on. The David versus Goliath moments kept me going longer than would have otherwise been the case, but they are not the answer we need.

I recognize that accepting the unpleasantness of one's profession that comes with working in a punitive culture is not limited to those in the legal profession. Several people in the business world tell me they are in the same situation, and many in the teaching profession share the same sense of resignation.

FROM SELF-DOUBT TO COURAGE: PHYSICAL, MORAL, EMOTIONAL, INTELLECTUAL, SPIRITUAL AND CIVIC COURAGE

We often think of courage being limited to the bravery displayed in the face of physical danger. In the definition of courage on page 118, we add moral courage, emotional courage, intellectual courage, spiritual courage and civic courage. Embracing Unitive Justice will require all of these types of courage at one time or another. However, the structures of Unitive Justice support each aspect of courage, making them less daunting in the new system.

When self-doubt becomes a way of life, reaching inside for that spark of courage—all types of courage—is the remedy. Self-doubt and courage are both states of mind, so finding the courage to cure self-doubt does not depend on anyone else—it is solely up to you.

The Arcs to Unitive Justice provide a place to start. You can conquer self-doubt by daring to follow your internal moral compass and achieve selfgovernance, rendering submission to rules unnecessary. The mental shift from self-doubt to courage is reflected in giving up judgment to gain insight. When we have the courage to be honest, we leave behind the self-doubt that prompts us to deceive others. We replace the self-doubt that keeps us narrowly focused on our own self-interest with the courage that enables us to focus on the community's wellbeing as a better way to meet everyone's needs, including our own. A community that is non-judgmental and non-punitive, one that offers a means to address conflict in ways that achieve mutually beneficial outcomes—that is a community that supports the journey from self-doubt to courage.

Where does one find the courage to overcome self-doubt? Perhaps the turning point comes when you realize that self-doubt robs you of your dignity and that you are better than how you show up now. Instead of mustering the courage to merely fight the punitive system with band-aids, addressing symptoms but not root causes, and achieving just a little justice here or there, we find the courage to transcend the punitive system to experience a new reality in which justice is Love—that is real system change.

COURAGE IN THE UNITIVE SYSTEM: TRANSCENDING THE PUNITIVE SYSTEM

As I continued to develop Unitive Justice theory, it became clear that Justice as Love will never be found in a punitive system; they are mutually exclusive. We only find Justice as Love when we muster the moral, intellectual, and spiritual courage courage to transcend the punitive system. There we find the truth that we, on some level, have always known exists.

To think about this new application of courage, let's begin by imagining two armies at war in the punitive system. Each side fears the other. Each side sees themselves as the "good" people and the other as "evil." The evil people are seen as deserving of the harm done to them, the retribution and revenge that is intended to teach them a lesson. Each side sees their interests as being in competition—for one side to win, the other must lose. And they are willing to invest enormous resources in defeating the other, directing resources to the task of destruction, including sacrificing the lives of many bright and gifted youth.

In this world, they understand courage as what arises in the face of the physical harm that war inevitably fosters. Such courage is rewarded, and it inspires others to continue the fight.

Now imagine those two warring groups finding a way to overcome their desire for retribution and revenge. They recognize their shared humanity. Finally, they see that everything in the past serves their self-interest, so they no longer seek revenge for past actions. This permits them to transcend the punitive mindset and beliefs that justify war. They no longer fear the other but instead see that they are interconnected. They are One. Their apparent differences don't disappear, but they are not a cause of judgment and separation. Instead, they see their differences as a gift, a resource that enables them to expand what they can accomplish together far beyond what they can do alone.

As I write this, I am listening to news reports of atrocities committed by Russian soldiers in Ukraine. I am fully aware of how farfetched what I am saying may seem, but to believe there is no possibility of transcending the past leaves us doomed to continue as we are. I think of how many times the Lord's Prayer is recited around the world, "forgive us our trespasses as we forgive those who trespass against us." Are those words meaningless? Do we say them only to ignore them? In duality consciousness the answer is yes, they are meaningless. But duality consciousness is a choice. We can choose differently.

When the blinders of retribution and revenge are removed, a whole new set of possibilities emerge that cannot even be imagined when we fear the "other" and are committed to their defeat. These new possibilities are outside the old norms. When the cost of retribution and revenge no longer consumes our resources, they are available for other purposes. And additional resources are available because of the expanded capacity that overcoming our differences and joining forces manifests. This does not require sacrifice, as no one has to lose. At this level, what we give is given to ourselves. Our goals are unified.

Imagine this type of engagement, collaboration and mutual respect happening between Jews and Palestinians, Ukrainians and Russians, North Koreans and South Koreans. Imagine this being how the Americans and Chinese proceed into the future. Imagine what having the courage to transcend the punitive system in these circumstances could produce.

Courage is required to manifest this new reality, to lift the veil of duality and experience Unitive Consciousness. One example of courage inspires another, and goodness grows. As all thought creates form on some level, as we shift from dualistic thoughts to unitive thoughts, we begin to create what we ask for in the Lord's Prayer: ". . . Thy Kingdom come, Thy will be done, *on Earth as it is in Heaven.*" With the courage to transcend duality consciousness, something approaching Heaven on Earth is possible.

Perhaps most of us do not yet understand how unique this moment is in human history. Visionary philosopher, Jean Gebser, describes this era as a time when human consciousness is evolving to a new level,[13] as do the writings of Sri Aurobindo, Pierre Teilhard de Chardin and *A Course in Miracles*. In the mid-19th century Baha'u'llah, founder of the Baha'i faith, declared the unification of the entire human race into an all-embracing, spiritually mature world civilization based upon divine principles of justice and Love, and Unity in diversity is now possible.[14] While achieving Unitive Justice may not have been possible in the past, this emerging new consciousness may indicate that the time for its manifestation has come.

I can only imagine such a reality on an international scale, but on a much smaller scale I have experienced it. If it is a possibility at the micro level, when it is repeated over and over, it becomes a possibility at the macro level. It can even become the norm.

* * *

Invitation to Journal. Consider these questions:

> a. What thoughts about your circumstances come up as you consider the structure of self-doubt and the structure of courage?
> b. Are there occasions when you use courage to make the punitive system more bearable and to do what you can to make it a little more just? If so, what are those circumstances?
> c. Are there occasions when you experience the leap from the punitive mindset to the unitive mindset? If so, how do you describe that experience?
> d. What is the most courageous thing that you have ever done?

Suggested Viewing: *Woman Has Removed Over 300 Hooks From Sharks' Mouths | The Dodo Wild Hearts*, available on YouTube at https://www.youtube.com/watch?v=G8LmxwOgBhA&t=10s. (4 min.) This is an extraordinary demonstration of courage, despite all the conditioning we have to distrust sharks.

If you are up for a longer video, I recommend *Bringing Down a Dictator* by A Force More Powerful, http://www.aforcemorepowerful.org/films/bdd/ (55 min.). This is an inspiring documentary about an uprising that used humor and nonviolence to bring down Slobodan Milošević, the former dictator of Yugoslavia.

ARC 7: GUIDING MORAL PRINCIPLE
FROM PROPORTIONAL REVENGE/HARM ANSWERS HARM
TO: LOVINGKINDNESS/HEAL, DO NO HARM

proportional revenge: the level of punishment is relative to the severity of the crime or harm for which punishment is being inflicted. Other terms for proportional revenge: an eye for an eye, tit for tat, getting even, just desserts, payback, measure for measure, retribution, retaliation.

lovingkindness: the extension of kindness and compassion toward all living beings based on one's moral duty as a human to do so. This moral standard applies equally to everyone, harm to another is not condoned as moral. We respond to harm as a call for Love. Other terms for lovingkindness: goodness, gentleness, tenderness, humanity, radical tenderness.

The moral arc of the universe is long, but it bends toward justice. Or does it? It depends on how high or low we set the bar for what constitutes justice.

"Justice" is a powerful, compelling word that, for many, may be associated with concepts like mercy and healing. That is not necessarily what justice means in our retributive system of justice. Answering harm with harm is deemed just so long as the harm done to achieve revenge is equal in measure to the harm to which one is reacting—it is proportional. Who decides what is proportional? Often the one inflicting revenge.

The set of scales is an appropriate symbol for this retributive justice model, a system in which harm answers harm in equal measure. In the United States, we use common phrases, like "the punishment fits the crime," "I want to get even," or "it's tit for tat," often without realizing that these terms are describing the moral principle that underpins the punitive model of justice, i.e., proportional revenge.

The "justice" in proportional revenge lies in balancing one harm against another, as in "an eye for an eye, a tooth for a tooth." It used to be literal, but now it is usually figurative, e.g., the crime being balanced with the years in prison, or a child stealing a candy bar and then getting a whipping. Any dispute about what measure of revenge is required to achieve justice is usually decided by the decision-maker, such as legislators writing the criminal code, judges meting out sentences, the parent, or the one with more might who is seeking revenge.

There are several unspoken, largely unexamined premises in the moral theory of proportional revenge. The way it is often presented can camouflage the fact that measuring the morality of our retribution by the measure of harm chosen by our attackers means that, in this model of justice, morality has no objective measure—it is always relative to what our enemies do. In effect, our enemies define the measure of our morality.

Another unspoken premise: for the moral principle of proportional revenge to work requires two standards by which we measure whether the test of morality is met—one for "us" and one for "them." This double moral standard—unacknowledged by those in the system—permits us to claim that, for example, the killing done by us, the "good" people, is moral because we are killing the "bad" people. At the same time, we condemn those who want to kill us, labeling them as "evil" or "enemies" because they are killing us, the "good" people.

When both sides view the other as evil and themselves as good, as is often the case, they both use this double moral standard in their defense. Each justifies their attacks and counterattacks as self-defense while claiming self-righteous innocence for what they do. It is as though each side declares, "Our killing is moral; yours is not," imagining themselves to be morally innocent as they rationalize that those whom they harm bring the harm they experience upon themselves—"they made us do it." When each side sees the harm done through the lens that favors them, even when both are doing the same thing, it is illogical and hypocritical. This flawed moral compass guarantees morally flawed results.

This dysfunction is sustained by a widely-shared belief that justice *requires* proportional revenge. As a result, we keep doing what we have always done, even when the outcome causes more harm rather than reducing it, and there is no end in sight. The deeper, underlying forces that could be examined to create healing and end harm are neither acknowledged nor addressed in this game of retributive ping pong.

The killing becomes endless, while each death on one side affirms that side's negative judgment of the side that caused it. At the same time, those doing the killing often see each death of an adversary as a "victory," an occasion for celebration. Each side sees a different reality because of their projection of guilt on the other.

Proportional revenge can apply to any harm answered with harm at any level. The proportional revenge system of justice implemented in our courts is replicated by smaller punitive systems farther down the line. The anti-snitching phenomenon is an example—if you hurt someone by snitching on them, *i.e.*, reporting their crime, they see retribution as your "just rewards." They are merely answering one harm—someone snitching on them—with another—their retaliation for the snitching. When a church excommunicates a member for disobeying church rules, this is also proportional revenge.

In our system blindness, we fail to recognize that retributive justice fuels cycles of violence and perpetuates trauma. The survivor/victim cycle flows into the enemy/aggressor cycle, and back again. Victims become aggressors and aggressors become victims, as shown in the cycles of violence depicted in the model on the next page.

Cycles of Violence

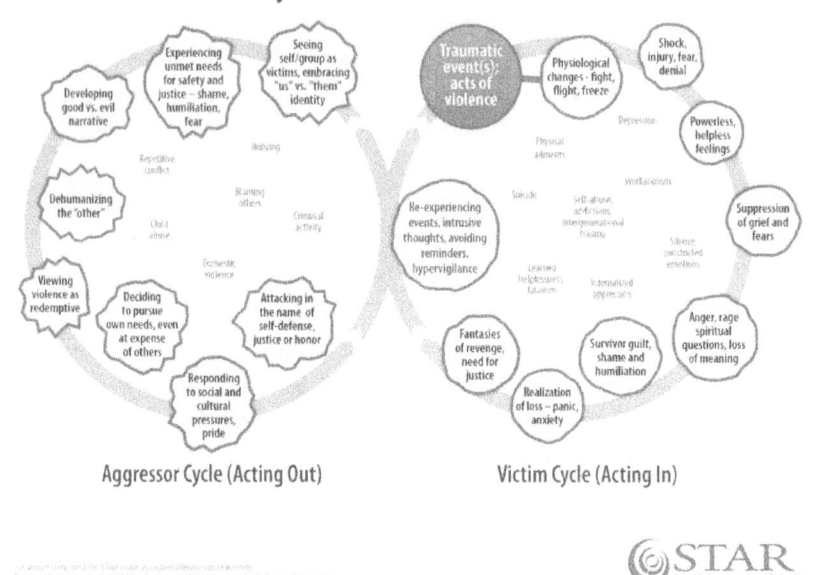

Reprinted with the permission of Eastern Mennonite University.

Questions such as how trauma arises, how it impacts social and individual wellbeing, how trauma plays into victimization and into offending behavior,[1] and *how proportional revenge fuels the cycles of violence* are important policy issues. Answers to these policy issues are found by delving into the context of what happened and discovering why and how the harm arose. The fact the punitive legal system is not designed to consider the context is a serious structural flaw.

HOW DO WE TEACH OUR CHILDREN PROPORTIONAL REVENGE?

How do our children learn proportional revenge? One way is by a parent spanking their child. The child violates some rule or otherwise upsets the parent, and the parent's reaction is to spank the child to teach the child a lesson—classic proportional revenge. While we don't often make this connection, it is clear that spanking, slapping, taking their toys away, and even a "time out" is how, by example, we teach our children about revenge.

The parent may feel it is justified or necessary, but it is proportional revenge. "Certainly you can get a child's attention [by spanking], but it's not an effective strategy to teach right from wrong," said Dr. Robert D. Sege, a pediatrician at Tufts Medical Center and the Floating Hospital for Children in Boston. He was one of the authors of the strongly worded 2018 policy statement of the American Academy of Pediatrics that recommends that parents not spank their children.[2]

Not all agree. Consider the argument in favor of spanking made by Fitzhugh Dodson, a clinical psychologist and best-selling author of books on parenting. He argues that many discipline problems can be solved using his "pow wow approach."

> It's my pow, followed by his wow, he explained, demonstrating how he would swat a child's bottom. A poor mother is left with nowhere to go. She's mad at the kid, has had it up to the eyebrows with him, and longs to give him a big smack on the behind, but she's been told she shouldn't. She should, and it's good for her, because it releases her tension. And the child definitely prefers it to long parental harangues.[3]

Proportional revenge may feel good in the moment, but it does not provide a lasting solution. Recent studies have shown that corporal punishment is associated with increased aggression and makes it more likely that children will be defiant in the future—in time, they will engage in their own proportional revenge. According to the Academy of Pediatrics spanking is associated with outcomes similar to those of children who experience physical abuse.[4]

There was considerable consternation when, in 2000, the Academy of Pediatrics recommended that corporal punishment in schools be abolished in all states. According to Dr. Elizabeth T. Gershoff, a professor at the University of Texas at Austin who has studied corporal punishment in public schools, children "need to know that you have their best interests at heart. . . If the kid doesn't trust the parent, then they're never going to want to do what they say."[5] Without connection, there is no social capital or bond to hold us together, to create harmony, one with another. Without connection, some form of punishment to coerce compliance becomes the only tool in the toolbox from one generation to the next.

Whatever the context, when proportional revenge serves as the moral compass for our measure of justice, we are relying on a seriously flawed tool. There is a compelling argument to be made that the flawed moral principle of proportional revenge is a destructive force in the world. Here are two examples.

THE STANFORD PRISON EXPERIMENT: SIX LESSONS ABOUT RETRIBUTION

Where a punitive system is in operation, its well-known patterns are easily identified. The Stanford Prison Experiment was not real life, but it nonetheless demonstrates the internal workings of punitive justice in a penal institution, even in a shortened span of time. (*See* Suggested Viewing below.) The study was conducted by a group of social scientists in the early 1970s to understand the development of norms and the effects of roles, labels and social expectations in a punitive system, such as a prison environment. In the study, they examined the psychology of imprisonment as a means to better understand why prisons are such negative, abusive places.[6]

Two theories were that prisons attract bad people, inmates and staff alike; another theory was that the environment causes good people to behave in abusive, harmful ways.[7] The experiment was designed to differentiate between what people bring into a prison environment from what the prison environment brings out in the people who are there. Perhaps unwittingly, the structures of a typical punitive system were systematically built into the Stanford Experiment design, such as proportional revenge, hierarchy, judgment, confrontation and punishment.

Under the supervision of psychologist Phillip Zimbardo, a mock prison was set up in the basement of the university's psychology building, complete with a closet that served as a solitary confinement cell. Twenty-one male students, identified as the most normal and healthy among those who applied, were selected to participate. Half of the group was randomly designated to serve as guards. These young men were given uniforms and dark glasses and were charged with keeping order in the mock prison. The others were given the role of prisoners. They were soon to be stripped of their individual identities.

To heighten the reality of the experiment, Zimbardo arranged for members of the Palo Alto Police Department to simulate arrests of the "accused" and bring them to the station house. They were then charged with a fictitious crime, fingerprinted, and blindfolded by the police before being taken to the mock prison. Upon arrival, they were stripped by those designated to be guards and given prison uniforms that had a number on the front and back. The number would serve as their official identification.

The students designated as guards, some of whom had previously considered themselves pacifists, quickly exerted abusive control and imposed severe discipline on the prisoners. For instance, on the first night, the prisoners were awakened at two in the morning and made to do push-ups and other arbitrary tasks.

On the morning of the second day, the prisoners rebelled, ripping off the numbers on their uniforms and barricading themselves in their cells. The reaction of the guards was to exert greater control. They stripped the prisoners, sprayed them with fire extinguishers, and threw the rebellion's leader into solitary confinement in the dark, locked closet. The guards' behavior became more abusive and sadistic as the experiment progressed. In a few short days, the guards had withheld the prisoners' food, denied them bathroom privileges, forced some prisoners to sleep on the bare floor, and most were punished with nudity and sexual humiliation.

Correctional institutions are unique in that the isolation of their closed environment can heighten the conforming effect of violence and retribution. This was poignantly demonstrated in how rapidly the Stanford Prison Experiment participants, all mentally healthy male college students, conformed to its anti-social environment.

After 36 hours, one prisoner became hysterical and was released from the project. Four more were released due to extreme depression, crying, rage, and anxiety. Slated to last two weeks, the experiment was terminated after six days.

Zimbardo reported that those who designed the project did not expect either the intensity of the change in conduct or the speed with which it happened. In this environment of repression, those whose role gave them unrestricted control over the others quickly fell into less-than-humane conduct. Those subject to control were soon reduced to survival mode.

This experiment illustrates the following five lessons about a punitive system. First, one of the primary justifications for the punitive system is that it is necessary to maintain control for us to be safe, but its adversarial nature may actually make it *difficult* to maintain control. The guards saw their interest served by using their superiority to impose control over the prisoners. The prisoners saw their interest served by resisting the guards and even rebelling. The system remained broken until it failed completely.

The second lesson relates to how easily hierarchy slides into abuse. The traditional justice system is hierarchical. Hierarchy often comes with the means to impose control, bolstered with a sense of superiority, entitlement, and less-than-full accountability. Hierarchy opens the door for abuse, as quickly happened in the Stanford Experiment. By the end of the first day, the guards exhibited their superiority by being abusive towards the prisoners.

The third lesson is that the punishment often has to be escalated to be effective. When a little punishment doesn't achieve compliance, what happens? More force must be applied by those seeking to impose control, but more force further erodes social capital. As connection was further destroyed, the guards in the Stanford experiment had to continually escalate their punishment to maintain control. This inevitably leads to the punishment no longer being proportional. Thus, it violates the moral standard that is supposed to justify its use.

Fourth, the Stanford Prison Experiment demonstrates the hypocrisy of the double moral standard the punitive system requires. Harm answers harm, but for this to seem rational, one harm must be deemed moral and the other immoral. Thus, the guards in the experiment felt justified in escalating their punishment of the prisoners because the "bad" noncompliant prisoners needed more punishment to force them to comply. At the same time, the guards saw the prisoners' resistance as unreasonable and not to be tolerated, without considering the merit of the prisoners' resistance. Of course, the prisoners reversed the good versus evil labels. The system's hypocrisy becomes apparent when the whole is considered.

The fifth lesson is that the punitive system is structurally weak. The parties on the opposite sides must not engage in meaningful dialogue—if they do, they soon discover the system's inconsistencies. Instead of encouraging people to work together, the structure divides people and makes them adversaries, even enemies. Structurally, the punitive justice system is dualistic and that undermines cooperation, connection and resolution. This experiment quickly unveiled a sadistic tendency that can emerge, a dark bent of human nature that a punitive system feeds.[8] Sustaining this weak system depends on being trapped in a bubble of blind self-righteousness and the belief separation is reality.

9/11: RETRIBUTION AND REVENGE ON AN INTERNATIONAL SCALE

Based on news reports and security analysis available online, the events before, during and after the attack on the World Trade Centers in New York City on September 11, 2001, commonly called "9/11," provide another example of how retributive justice is deeply flawed. When we turn to revenge in reaction to violence and conflict, it demonstrates the truth in the old adage, "live by the sword, die by the sword."

The U.S. was clearly attacked on 9/11, and many innocent people were killed and injured. Why? What motivated that attack? If we consider proportional revenge as a motive for that attack, it may help explain this event, what preceded it and what followed.

Decades of U.S. action in the Middle East that fueled animosity toward the U.S. preceded 9/11. Any number of prior events could have led the 9/11 attackers to justify their acts as retribution for prior injustices —their desire for "an-eye-for-an-eye" justice. One injustice that continues to cause resentment in the Arab world was the CIA's direct involvement in an Iranian coup in 1953. The ruling Prime Minister, Mohammad Mosaddegh, wanted to nationalize the Iranian oil fields that were controlled by the British. The CIA was actively involved in removing the Prime Minister from office and replacing him with the Shah, Mohammad Reza Pahlavi, a man who more readily accommodated the interests of the western nations.[9] When U.S. leaders preach democracy, but then the U.S. government actively helps destroy the democratic system of another nation, we can reasonably expect revenge at some point.

There are other acts that may have motivated the attack on 9/11. The fact that fifteen of the nineteen hijackers who carried out the 9/11 attacks were from Saudi Arabia,[10] a U.S. ally nation, is a reason to especially consider what was happening in Saudi Arabia at that time. The hijackers were educated, intelligent men willing to die for their cause. Perhaps they were motivated by religious beliefs, and the cause for which they were willing to die was to force the U.S. to remove its large and strategic Prince Sultan Air Base from Saudi soil.

By 2001, Prince Sultan Air Base had become an important intelligence center involving satellite communications, imagery analysis, radio and other systems related to U.S. theater command and control in the Middle East.[11] A report in Military News in 2019 acknowledged: "The presence of U.S. troops in Saudi Arabia, home to Mecca and Medina, Islam's holiest sites, has always spurred opposition in the kingdom."[12] Perhaps devout Muslims found the airbase intolerable because its presence violated the sanctity of their two most holy sites.

If the goal of the 9/11 attacks included a commitment to get that U.S. air base moved away from Mecca and Medina and out of Saudi Arabia, the attacks were successful. Nineteen months after 9/11, the U.S. air base was dismantled and moved to Qatar. Whatever the hijacker's motive may have been, the 9/11 attack has all the markings of revenge for what they perceived to be earlier U.S. transgressions.

Immediately after 9/11, the hearts of people worldwide opened to the United States. A few weeks before President George W. Bush left office he nostalgically recalled the outpouring of love and support for the United States in the first dark days after the attacks:

[J]ust a few weeks after September the 11th, 2001—I said that America would always remember the signs of support from our friends... I remember the American flag flying from every fire truck in Montreal, Canada. I remember children kneeling in silent prayer outside our embassy in Seoul. I remember baseball players in Japan observing moments of silence. I remember a sign handwritten in English at a candlelight vigil in Beijing that read, "Freedom and justice will not be stopped."

That was a short moment when President Bush could have embraced this worldwide unity and used it to promote worldwide peace. Instead, the compassion extended to the U.S. was quickly extinguished by his call for revenge.

On September 17, 2001, President Bush announced that the U.S. would take the path of retribution and revenge to answer the harm done on 9/11. He said:

I want justice. And there's an old poster out West, as I recall, that said, 'Wanted: Dead or Alive.' . . . All I want, and America wants [Osama bin Laden] brought to justice. That's what we want.

When the U.S. first attacked Afghanistan in October 2001, few seemed to notice that the possibility of a nonviolent response to the attack had been tossed aside. Preparations for war ensued and many joined in the calls for vengeance. Few protested the escalating violence.

The war that began in Afghanistan spread to a war against Iraq in 2003. Many Americans thought the attack on Iraq was retribution for 9/11, so they saw it as justified. President Bush offered the proportional revenge theory that Iraq possessed weapons of mass destruction, but it did not. President Bush may have used this moment in time, when Americans were primed to attack in the Middle East, as an opportunity to attack Iraq for reasons other than its (nonexistent) weapons of mass destruction—it's not clear what the policy objectives were.

Not only did the widespread compassion for the U.S. immediately after 9/11 evaporate when President Bush called for revenge, but thereafter, the U.S. was hard-pressed to find nations willing to join our "coalition of the willing" to help fight our war in Iraq. When we say we desire peace, but our actions defeat peace, we cannot expect peace. Conflicting goals never lead to harmony. When we seek peace through retribution, the silent reply is, "seek but you will never find."

As of 2018, nearly 7,000 United States soldiers had died fighting the wars in Iraq and Afghanistan[13] and an unusually high percentage of young veterans have died since returning home, many from drug overdoses, vehicle crashes, or suicide. According to a Brown University report, approximately 500,000 civilians have been killed as a result of the fighting and it caused over 8 million war refugees and displaced persons.[14] The U.S. federal price tag for the post-9/11 wars is over 5 trillion dollars,[15] but the final bill has not yet been paid. War, of course, did not produce the peace and security we were promised.

When he called for revenge, President Bush ignored the lessons taught by earlier leaders like Buddha, Genghis Khan, Jesus, Hitler, Mahatma Gandhi, Stalin, Martin Luther King Jr., Saddam Hussein, Nelson Mandela and now, Vladimir Putin. History repeatedly teaches us that escalating violence does not make a leader revered in the annals of history—as Genghis Khan, Hitler, Stalin, Saddam Hussein, Putin, and many others like them demonstrate. Those on the list who extended Love, both in good times and bad—Buddha, Jesus, Mahatma Gandhi, Martin Luther King, Jr., Nelson Mandela and others like them—are the revered leaders in history. Revenge is not a winning strategy. It is in Justice as Love that power lies.

Through the ages, the consistent moral standard reflected in lovingkindness has been rejected by those who control through fear and violence, but now this punitive approach poses an even greater threat than in the past. As some rulers now possess weapons of war capable of total annihilation, answering harm with more harm has the potential to destroy life as we know it.

At this dangerous moment in history, adopting lovingkindness as our guiding moral standard and Unitive Justice as our practice is our means to escape self-destruction. Unitive Justice permits us to see the whole and its many parts, allowing us to access the information needed to understand root causes and find solutions to diverse problems. In seeing the whole, shared interests emerge, leading to unified goals. As any one problem is solved, a path to resolving others opens up.

For my readers who feel anxious or uncomfortable at the very idea of lovingkindness being our moral norm, rest assured that it will not manifest immediately. However, we can begin to create the bridge from here to there—"there" being a place where lovingkindness seems rational and not threatening. We can begin to build a culture in which Unitive Justice is the norm by beginning locally, in the places where we have influence and possess power.

Some might question, "How do we extend lovingkindness to those who are a threat, such as a child molester or rapist?" Confusion or doubt about how lovingkindness might apply in the face of conflict, even violence, is understandable. While we are immersed in the present system and are being taught that retribution and punishment constitute justice, Justice as Love may seem implausible.

Violence begets violence. As we begin to create Unitive Justice systems that address conflict early on and as we address the root causes, we are changing the societal conditions out of which acts, be they good or bad, arise. Lovingkindness begets lovingkindness. As we create societal conditions that support mutual understanding, acts of kindness will increase and the frequency of harmful acts will decrease.

Some people object that the positive results of Unitive Justice take too long to produce. They prefer the quick compliance that punishment and revenge aim to achieve. After conflict erupts, the punishment-and-revenge approach may result in enforced compliance, but this is not peace. Perpetually enforcing compliance consumes valuable resources and it takes time to repair the further wounding and conflict that result from a retributive response. The time and money we invest in creating Unitive Justice is well spent.

THE GUIDING MORAL PRINCIPLE OF UNITIVE JUSTICE: LOVINGKINDNESS

Unitive justice is based on the moral principle of lovingkindness, a mandate to do no harm, to extend kindness and compassion to others, even those who have wronged you. Wrongdoing is addressed, but not in ways that compound the harm. Moreover, the moral standard of lovingkindness applies equally to everyone, without exception.

Lovingkindness implies nonviolence, even nonresistance. We offer our adversaries what we want for ourselves—lovingkindness. The power of Unitive Justice lies in this internal moral consistency—no double moral standard is required or allowed. In Unitive Justice, we seek to achieve unified goals through peaceful means.

The independence movement led by Mahatma Gandhi in India after World War II is an example of lovingkindness and the moral authority it embodies. The British Empire in India seemed impervious to attack until Mahatma Gandhi and his devotees used nonviolent civil disobedience against the Empire. Embodying the power of Love that Gandhi recognized in the teachings of Jesus and other spiritual teachings, he called upon his followers to follow the path of nonviolence instead of answering harm with harm. Nonviolence applies the moral principle of lovingkindness and one moral standard for all. Using the power of lovingkindness, Gandhi's people drove the British out of India without firing a single shot.

One might argue that perhaps the British Empire was already on the verge of collapse when Gandhi emerged, but there are other compelling examples of the power of lovingkindness being triumphant over vengeance and violence. Maria Stephan and Erica Chenoweth, experts in nonviolent resistance,[16] report the following:

> From 2000 to 2006 organized civilian populations successfully employed nonviolent methods, boycotts, strikes, protests, and organized noncooperation to challenge entrenched power and exact political concessions.
> Successful uprisings took place in Serbia (2000), Madagascar (2002), Georgia (2003) and Ukraine (2004–05), Lebanon (2005), and Nepal (2006)." Their findings "show that major nonviolent campaigns have achieved success 53 percent of the time, compared with 26 percent for violent resistance campaigns.[17]

Stephan and Chenoweth contend that there are two reasons for the success of nonviolence. First, a commitment to nonviolence enhances the domestic and international legitimacy of the group and this encourages broad-based participation in the resistance. As recognition of the grievances being redressed increases, internal and external support for the protesting group and alienation of the target regime grow. This, in turn, undermines the regime's political, economic, and military control.[18]

The second reason Stephan and Chenoweth give for the success of nonviolent action is that it deprives the regime of its justification for violent counter attacks against the insurgents.[19] This approach highlights the immorality of attacks that violate proportionality, causing regime violence against nonviolent movements to backfire against the regime. When those who are attacked act more morally than those in control who are attacking them, the claimed moral superiority of those in control disappears.

I suggest that there is a third reason that nonviolent action is successful—the moral consistency of their action. Those being attacked are willing to sacrifice to bring about change that benefits not only themselves, but everyone, including those who are attacking them. They are fighting to make what they want for themselves available to others—they have one unified goal. The moral consistency of the protesters stands in direct contrast to the moral inconsistency of those seeking to impose control using violence.

OTHER EXAMPLES THAT DEMONSTRATE THE MORAL PRINCIPLE OF LOVINGKINDNESS

My belief that we can shift away from punitive justice is reinforced by the fact that there are people, albeit few in number now, who model how to live according to the unitive principles described herein, even though they may have never heard of Unitive Justice. Their faith tradition, family norms or perhaps their internal moral compass guides how they show up, despite what is happening in the world around them. Those who live by unitive principles often do so out of the limelight and unknown to many of us—until a tragedy occurs and their response is clearly outside the norm.

LANCASTER COUNTY, PA.

On October 2, 2006, in a small Amish enclave in Lancaster County, Pennsylvania, a man murdered five young school girls, wounded others, and killed himself in a planned attack. The gunman was a milk tanker driver who served some of the Amish farms in this area. He was married and had three children. His co-workers reported that they noticed a disturbing "change" in him over a couple of months before the attack. However, the week before the shooting, he appeared to return to normal, and he was even upbeat and jovial during this time. It is speculated that this change came when he decided to carry out the attack.[20]

Before he shot the girls, some adults and boys in the classroom escaped or were told to leave. It was the girls whom he singled out in this attack. The entire community was terrorized and devastated by the event. Remarkably, the people of this quiet community sought no revenge.

Instead, after the attack, some of the elders visited the killer's widow to offer forgiveness. The families of the slain girls invited the widow to their children's funerals. The Amish requested that contributions sent to them be shared with the widow and her children. And over thirty members of the Amish community attended the funeral of the man who killed and maimed their children.[21]

After this violent attack, the attacker's mother sometimes cared for a teenage girl who survived the attack but was confined to a wheelchair and had to be fed through a tube. She bathed her, sang to and read stories to the girl who could not talk.[22]

Following the example of the Amish, the mother of the man who killed the girls also forgave her son. She said that the world needs more stories about the power of forgiveness and the importance of seeking joy through adversity, so she shared her story with many audiences. "I realized if I didn't forgive him, I would have the same hole in my heart that he had. And a root of bitterness never brings peace to anyone. . . We are called to forgive."[23] She is an example of how those touched by lovingkindness can sometimes embrace and extend it to others.

CHARLESTON, SOUTH CAROLINA

On the evening of June 17, 2015, a twenty-one-year-old man with an automatic weapon murdered nine people during a Bible study session at the historic Emanuel Church in Charleston, South Carolina. The young man grew up in the midst of racial hatred fueled among white nationalists by their aversion to having a Black man as President. White supremacy was on the rise.

An investigation revealed that the murders were probably motivated by fear of losing white privilege and a desire to seek revenge for what the young white man perceived as unfairness to white people. After the church massacre, Gov. Nikki R. Haley immediately called for the death penalty for the young offender.

The family members of those who were murdered did not speak of revenge. One said, "You took something very precious away from me. I will never talk to her ever again. I will never be able to hold her again. But I forgive you. And have mercy on your soul." And another said, "I acknowledge that I am very angry, but she taught me that we are the family that love built. We have no room for hating, so we have to forgive."[24] They responded based on their values and with Love in their hearts.

One report noted that it was "as if the Bible study had never ended as one after another, victims' family members offered lessons in forgiveness, testaments to a faith that is not compromised by violence or grief."[25] The state and nation were moved.

At the time of the murders, a Confederate flag flew on the South Carolina capitol grounds, placed there in 1961 as a symbol of the "states-rights rebuff to racial desegregation."[26] Before the murders, it was unimaginable that the African American community had the power to remove the Confederate flag from the capitol grounds without igniting another war. Their response to the murders showed, however, that they did have that power, but not in the way we would normally expect. The forgiving response of the survivors of the murder victims, in stark contrast to the state's symbol of hate, was an exercise of their power.

When contrasted with the loving response of the families, many members of the South Carolina legislature were embarrassed by the racialized symbol flying on their capitol grounds. A movement began among legislators to take it down. After a long and sometimes passionate debate, they voted to remove the Confederate flag from the South Carolina capitol grounds. This is an example of how the power of Love wins over fear.

These two tragedies demonstrate how lovingkindness has an internal moral consistency, the consistency of wanting for others what you want for yourself. The Amish in Pennsylvania and the members of Emanuel Church asked nothing for themselves that they were not willing to give to others, including those who harmed them. They showed us the moral strength of lovingkindness and their commitment to do no harm, regardless of the circumstances. When seen next to the power of lovingkindness, the moral inconsistency and moral weakness of proportional revenge, an eye for an eye, is evident.

Compared to the scale of our punitive justice system, these examples are small and involve few people. However, there are larger examples. Martin Luther King, Jr. and his followers ended legalized segregation in the U.S. using non-violence and lovingkindness rather than revenge.

UNITIVE JUSTICE STRUCTURES EVIDENT IN THESE TRAGEDIES

In addition to Arc 7, from proportional revenge to lovingkindness/do no harm, that was modeled by the Amish in Pennsylvania and the members of Emanuel Church, Arc 1, from rules to values stands out. There were no rules that required either community to respond with lovingkindness. They were directed by something else, perhaps their internal moral compass, their religious values and the strength of their selfgovernance.

Values are taught by modeling them; they are learned by example. While it's true that violence begets violence, it is also true that generosity begets generosity, and lovingkindness begets lovingkindness. A community grounded in values needs few rules. Moved by the forgiveness of Emmanuel Church members, the South Carolina governor and legislature demonstrated courage and generosity of spirit that previously had been beyond their reach—they removed the flag that represented a symbol of hate to so many.

We might assume that values must be slowly cultivated over time, learned from generation to generation. But there are times when circumstances are such that a sudden shift toward Love and values occurs. Removing the Confederate flag from the South Carolina capitol showed us how this can happen.

We may think defeating our enemies using physical might is the path to victory, but it was the gentle, yet mighty, defenselessness of the Amish and the Emanuel Church members that fiercely moved the hearts of those of us who watched. Guided by shared values such as forgiveness, generosity, trust, integrity and kindness, they brought honor to their communities as no sword of retribution could ever do. They inspired others to live more lovingly. Perhaps "be defenseless" is what Jesus instructed us to do when he said, "turn the other cheek."[27]

* * *

Invitation to Journal. A shift in beliefs can mean giving up what was once important, perhaps even endangering what connects you to others with whom you associate—friends, perhaps even family. Consider these questions:

a. How much has the moral principle of proportional revenge been a keystone of your life and relationships?

b. How would giving up proportional revenge as a guiding moral principle and embracing lovingkindness (the idea that harm to another is never moral) impact your life and your relationships?

c. How do you assess the pros and cons of doing so? What fears does this give rise to?

d. How are you already using lovingkindness as a response to harm in your life? When you do, how does that impact your relationships?

Suggested Viewing: What can happen when those in control are unrestrained is poignantly demonstrated in a short documentary on the *Stanford Prison Experiment*, available at https://www.youtube.com/watch?v=760lwYmpXbc (29 min.). It is a compelling example of why we must have system change.

A second Suggested Viewing is a short TEDx presentation by Erica Chenoweth (mentioned above) called *The Success of Nonviolent Civil Resistance*. She describes how she came to understand the power of nonviolent civil resistance. It is available at https://www.youtube.com/watch?v=YJSehRlU34w (13 min.).

CHAPTER NINE
THE 7 ARCS TO COMMUNITY TRANSFORMATION

The next seven Arcs in Unitive Justice theory provide a framework for community transformation. This is where the individual transformation considered in Arcs 1 – 7 provides the foundation for taking the process to a deeper and broader level with Arcs 8 - 14. Without individual transformation, there will be no community transformation.

COMMUNITY TRANSFORMATION – DISCOVERING OUR SHARED HUMANITY			
	Structure	Punitive	Unitive
Arc 8	BENEFIT	SELF-INTEREST	TO COMMUNITY
Arc 9	SOCIAL FRAMEWORK	FROM HIERARCHY/ TOP DOWN	TO EQUALITY/INCLUSION
Arc 10	SAFETY	FROM PUNISHMENT	TO CONNECTION
Arc 11	GOAL	FROM COMPLIANCE	TO MUTUALLY BENEFICIAL ACTION/WHOLENESS
Arc 12	FOCUS	FROM EVENT	TO CONTEXT
Arc 13	ANIMATION	FROM OPPOSITION/ CONFRONTATION	TO SYNERGY
Arc 14	ENERGY/SPIRIT	FROM FEAR	TO LOVE

BRIEF OVERVIEW OF ARCS 8 – 14

Arc 8, from self-interest to community, begins to weave our individual role into the whole. A healthy community is what you help to create when you live out of your values and selfgovern, you are honest with yourself and others, when your insight replaces judgment, trust begins to blossom and courage overcomes self-doubt. These individual traits are the foundation of a strong community that enables individuals to be the best they can be.

Without manifesting these principles in our lives, the Golden Rule and many other moral teachings are mere words, window dressing, aspirations that change nothing—leaving us to struggle in the darkness of duality for millennia.

With Arcs 8-14, we see our self-interest is served by living in a strong community where we feel included and connected. This reduces any desire for retribution, opening the way to mutually beneficial action. We naturally consider the whole, the context. The synergy that manifests is an expression of the Love that abounds when we are free of duality thinking, lifting us in an upward spiral. As we implement the seven Arcs that transform our community we discover our *shared* humanity.

ARC 8: BENEFIT
FROM SELF-INTEREST TO COMMUNITY

self-interest: a concern for one's own interest or advantage, without regard for the impact on others. Self-interest depends on a belief in separation and having a dualistic worldview. Other terms for self-interest: self-absorption, self-centeredness, self-involvement, egoism, egotism, narcissism, disconnection, disunion.

community: in association or kinship; humans sharing one humanity expressed as unique individuals living collectively out of shared values. What we can do together far surpasses what we can do alone. Other terms for community: family, neighborhood, social bond, shared sense of connection.

A NOTE ABOUT SEPARATION, CONNECTION, AND REALITY

Self-interest and community depend on two distinct underlying beliefs: separation and connection. Self-interest depends on the belief that we are all separate, while community depends on the insight that we are all connected. These beliefs are mutually exclusive. They are also different in that self-interest is plagued with inconsistencies and contradictions, while community embodies consistency.

U.S. culture is known for its attachment to individualism—an elevated status for the individual that implicitly denies our interconnectedness. Ironically, the functional value of this belief in separateness requires that it be a *shared belief*, a belief grounded in our connection! Indeed, the belief that separation is real supports the dualistic system only so long as it is one of our most widely shared beliefs. This internal contradiction is resolved by acknowledging that it is *connection* that is real, not separation.

A challenge in recognizing connection is that separation appears to be confirmed by our everyday physical existence. Our sense of touch seems to confirm that we are separate. With our eyes, we see others as different—how can we be connected to "those people"? Our sense of smell and taste also seems to tell us that each of us is a separate physical entity.

For centuries, the belief in separation also had an ally in science. The belief in separation was reinforced by the teachings of traditional Newtonian physics, the prevalent scientific theory throughout much of the 19th and 20th centuries. Newtonian physics was based largely on the premise that the atom is the fundamental building block of our existence and that the atom is composed of bits of matter separated by empty space. Seeing the world through this prism led Newtonian physicists to conclude that matter is our fundamental reality. The belief in the reality of materialism became widely shared.

From this material understanding of the world, we constructed our perceived reality based on how matter functions. We deduced that all events are local and unconnected to the larger world. We concluded that we can separate ourselves from what we do to others, even to the point of harming others and thinking it is done without harm to ourselves, not seeing the patterns that our choices contribute to, or their impact on our loved ones and us.

In the early 20th century, the new science of quantum physics began to emerge and now, early in the 21st century, this new science is redefining our fundamental reality. Just as Newtonian physics confirmed separation in past centuries, the new science of quantum physics indicates that, while the laws of matter apply at the gross physical level, a more fundamental reality exists beyond matter—an all-encompassing field of energy in which separation does not exist.[1] Quantum physics teaches us that connection is our true reality and there are no exceptions.

We appear to be separate individuals at the physical level, but our uniqueness is held at the quantum level in diverse patterns and flows of energy that exist in unending wholeness. We are born in time and space, but also exist beyond time and space.

Now the belief in connection as reality is growing. We are discovering what is and always was true—connection is inherent in who we are and it is lived in community. As the Dalai Lama affirms, "Without the human community, one single human being cannot survive."[2]

PUNITIVE JUSTICE AND SELF-INTEREST

The punitive justice system is riddled with problems, yet it persists. How the criminal law system serves self-interest provides an important insight into the system's longevity. In Chapter One, I referred to the work of criminologist Nils Christie and his famous treatise, "Conflicts as Property." His work is especially relevant to this arc, from self-interest to community. Christie argued that the criminal law system is an institution designed to serve the self-interest of those who control it—not the interests of those involved in or impacted by crime.[3]

The French philosopher and social theorist, Michel Foucault, expounds on self-interest in the punitive justice system in his book, *Discipline and Punish*. Foucault argues, in essence, that the punitive justice system is not merely flawed, it is inherently corrupt because of the extent to which the self-interest of those who control the punitive system is the guiding principle. His thesis is that the criminal law system is a clever design in which corruption is so integral to the system that it is not seen by those who believe the myth that the law is universal in its application.[4] Our deference to the status quo is so ingrained that self-interest can be dismissed as "it's just how it is," suggesting a habit and an apathy that are difficult to escape.

This is compounded by the criminal court process that asks narrow questions—what law was broken, who broke it and what will be their punishment? This narrow focus keeps the larger context from being considered. We are thus distracted from considering whose self-interest the punitive system benefits, and how the benefits are achieved. Nor do we consider the human needs, met and unmet, and the societal/institutional conditions that are perpetuated because our attention is directed to the event, while our system blindness is a veil that keeps the context out of sight.

Actions such as these defy and deny our interconnectedness and result in harm to ourselves and to others. They lead to conflict and violence. We might think such actions serve our interests, but this requires ignoring the fact that the apparent benefit is short-term and limited to the material level. Our undivided connection may be invisible to the eye, but it is real.

UNITIVE JUSTICE IS THE EMBODIMENT OF COMMUNITY

The punitive system sees a breach of state or federal law as a crime to be punished, something for the state to handle outside the community. This provides no opportunity to address the underlying causes.

In contrast, Unitive Justice sees a harmful event as a breach of community values and a wound to our interconnectedness. The harmful event is addressed by bringing community members together to consider the event and draw upon their wisdom about the context—the people involved and the conflict dynamic from which the event arose are both relevant. Determining what must be done to achieve a sustained resolution is found only in community.

The punitive system looks at a harmful event at close range and sees only a few actors. If we expand the lens, we eventually see patterns that involve all of us—our choices, even our disinterest and neglect, are aspects of the whole. Of course, our care and concern are also parts of the whole. What happens at the local level defines the community and, cumulatively, communities define the whole. Only when we see the connection between our choices as individuals and larger societal conditions do we recognize our power to shape our lives and create systemic change.

Unitive Justice nurtures the individual internal factors and the core values that promote individual and community wellbeing—honesty, trust, generosity, integrity, lovingkindness, and mutually beneficial action. We can choose anew and be guided by our sense of community and connection.

From self-interest to community applies to the notion of community in every realm. For example, good public education is an investment in community wellbeing to benefit everyone. By all of us investing in the education of everyone's children, some of the resulting benefits are a well-trained workforce, active and engaged citizens, abundant creativity, heightened gross national product (GNP) and a lower rate of crime. Security is likewise a community issue. My security, and that of my family and group, is enhanced by ensuring the security of others. Community wellbeing is achieved by recognizing that every life matters. What we give is given to ourselves.

When community becomes our focus, lawmakers will see the benefit of laws governing our market economy that are designed to promote the wellbeing of all. We can write regulations to reward those who keep the environment clean, create sustainable production processes and pay fair wages. This will surely produce clean air and water, healthy citizens, and life-protecting processes more effectively than the self-interest that now keeps these benefits from being universal. Let's experiment to see if a moral market economy leads to moral vitality in commerce and trade. As the end is always an embodiment of the means, this may produce the widespread prosperity that now seems beyond our grasp.

Despite our belief in separation, our need to be connected in community is a basic human need. Only in community do we discover our full potential. Individual wellbeing depends on connection, and connection requires community—that is where an individual achieves the sense of wholeness that is the highest dimension of oneself.

A 2015 study of several thousand lawyers in four states to determine how those in the legal profession measure happiness supports this conclusion. The study was conducted by law professor Lawrence S. Krieger and social scientist Ken Sheldon.

The research showed that it is not the extrinsic measures—prestige, status, money or even becoming a partner in the firm—that bring the most happiness.[5] It is a heightened experience of intrinsic values and internal work motivations[6]–having the opportunity for self-improvement (with guidance from others), intimacy, and altruism—that predict happiness.[7] Each identified measure of happiness confirmed by this research depends on being in a community.

The study found that public service attorneys (e.g., public defenders) are happier than attorneys in large, prestigious firms, despite the latter's elevated status and higher earnings.[8] This is because the greatest sense of wellbeing comes from internal factors, like connection and integrity, not external ones, such as income or a corner office.[9]

In prestigious law firms, while each increase in billable hours produces moderately more income, the increased hours also produce slightly less happiness.[10] Even a sixty-two percent increase in the income earned by junior partners over senior associates (an increase of about $69,000 per year) brought the partners no greater happiness than the associates.[11]

The shift from self-interest to community is an important step to our future wellbeing—perhaps it is a key to our survival. We do not control our own fate independent of the fate of others, nor can we create systemic change as individuals. This is done in community. We may build walls to separate us, but connection within what cannot be divided is our innate nature. The gift of connection awaits where separation ends. Only truth is true.

* * *

Invitation to Journal. Consider these questions:

a. How does self-interest show up in your life?
b. How does self-interest impact your relationships with others?
c. Are there some with whom you experience the type of community that is described in this Arc? If so, what are the characteristics that define that community? How is self-interest set aside?
d. What examples are you presently aware of where people are seeking to replace self-interest with the value of community? Are you aware of any corporations that are seeking to do this, and if so, how?

Suggested Viewing: Oprah Winfrey's interview of Buddhist monk, Thich Nhat Hanh examines peace, suffering and nonviolence. Hanh shares advice on how we may move toward connection and community. *Oprah Winfrey talks with Thich Nhat Hanh Excerpt – Powerful* available at https://www.youtube.com/watch?v=NJ9UtuWfs3U&t=918s (22 min.).

If you are up for a longer video, *The Feminist in Cellblock Y* considers how individual beliefs about manhood become toxic patriarchal norms, at what cost and how to create change. Available at https://www.youtube.com/watch?v=JYxTzsabkH8 (1 hr. 15 min.).

ARC 9: SOCIAL FRAMEWORK
FROM HIERARCHY/TOP DOWN TO EQUALITY/INCLUSION

hierarchy: a classification or organization in which people, groups or things are ranked one above the other according to status, perceived importance, or authoritarian allocation of value. Those at the top of the hierarchy benefit from entitlement and privilege, and may exhibit a sense of superiority. Deference to hierarchy may be based on respect, habit or fear. Other terms for hierarchy: pecking order, chain of command, class, social status.

equality: inclusiveness without exception; the condition of being accorded the same value, respect, dignity, connection and humanity as all others without exception. At the level of our shared humanity, we are equal; anything that appears to be less is mere judgment. Other terms for equality: shared humanity, the same, equivalence, equitability, equilibrium, parallelism.

This equality honors the likeness of God or living spirit that dwells within each one of us. Different functions are performed by individuals serving in different roles based on skills and knowledge, but roles do not have entitlement, privilege or superiority attached to them. A role may come with a sense of belonging—it is how one serves the collective good —but a role does not define one's value or worth. A role is like a placeholder that one occupies for a period of time while one's mental, emotional and spiritual growth continues to be cultivated by the lessons the role teaches, and then one moves on.

PUNITIVE JUSTICE AND HIERARCHY

Hierarchy is an artificial classification that depends on a shared belief that those at the top are of greater value than others. Their elevated rank entitles them to special conditions and relieves them of certain obligations. The higher up the hierarchy one claims to be, the more privilege and entitlement one can demand. Hierarchy disregards community and our shared humanity in favor of self-interest.

Hierarchy, rules and punishment for violating the rules go together. Those at the pinnacle of the hierarchy generally write the rules and enforce them. The myth is that all rule violators are to be punished equally, as in the mantra "justice is blind." Of course, the hierarchy can grant exceptions to that rule; this is one of the privileges that comes with elevated status. Today's complex punitive system has many exceptions to the rules that those in control can apply when they so choose.

Hierarchy is a pervasive structure in our culture and has been in place for so long it is rarely questioned. Undoubtedly, many assume that we need a hierarchy for our institutions to function. After all, someone has to run the show and make the final decisions. Yes, but this does not require hierarchy because roles can be assigned duties without superiority and privilege being attached to the role.

The different duties and responsibilities associated with roles might be mistaken for a hierarchy but only at a superficial level. The difference between roles and hierarchy is important—hierarchy is not a role; it describes a relational structure. A role may be performed without distorting relational structures with privilege, entitlement or a sense of superiority.

We might think that hierarchy is essential to certain roles or functions, but this is not the case. As Abraham Lincoln demonstrated, the President of the United States is a role that can be carried out with humility and without a sense of superiority. Leadership of this caliber requires a strong moral compass, selfgovernance and character grounded in core values, like integrity, honesty, generosity, kindness and courage. A person who is conscious of our shared humanity can perform their role and still maintain equality as inclusion without exception.

Imagine if our U.S. Senators and state Governors routinely performed their roles believing that they are equal to their constituents. What if they carried out their duties with humility and demonstrated the courage needed to implement policies that strengthen the community? This is a quality of service that is beyond those who live in duality consciousness.

In our particular context—history, beliefs, customs, culture—some roles are now very hierarchical. The structure of the U.S. government, for example, enables elected leaders to turn their positions into a hierarchy that accords them special privileges. In a representative democracy, as it presently exists in the U.S., politics and hierarchy have become entwined for many (not all) legislators and executive branch officials.

Internal and external mechanisms for controlling abuse by those at the top are weak. Even when those who abuse their office are removed, the basic flaws in the system remain.

When we cast our ballots for elected officials, we want to trust that those whom we elect will look after our welfare, that they will serve us, not themselves. When they presume that their role accords them special privileges, our trust is violated. Dividing control among the three branches of government (legislative, executive and judicial) and between the federal and state levels of government diminishes the amount of control lodged in any one public official, but abuse and corruption can still occur.[1] The system works as well as it does because many elected officials are people of integrity who do not abuse the system.[2]

TEMPORARILY SUSPENDING HIERARCHY TO ADDRESS CRISES AND CONFLICTS

Hierarchy may be with us for a long time to come, but sometimes intentionally suspending it produces the best results. When a crisis arises, those at the top normally take control and make the decisions, but this can be an obstacle in getting to the facts and making the best decisions.

Subordinates may be afraid to challenge the authority of those in control, even in a life-or-death situation. When a conflict occurs, people often tell their superiors what they think their superiors want to hear or the story that helps those involved in the conflict avoid punishment. As a result, the people at the top often do not have accurate or complete information or the details needed to effectively address a crisis or a conflict—because of hierarchy.

The airline industry was perhaps the first to devise a process for temporarily suspending the hierarchy in order to permit those with the best information to make emergency decisions. Prior to the 1980s, crashes due to cockpit error were not uncommon. The problem presented by hierarchy became clear after the 1978 crash of United Airlines Flight 173. The captain was distracted by a landing gear problem and the crew was reluctant to tell him they were running out of fuel—that would violate the chain of command. The crew feared challenging the captain, even when they knew he was wrong. The plane crashed.

To address this problem, training procedures called "Crew Resource Management" (CRM) were adopted that temporarily replace hierarchical control with an inclusive process when an emergency occurs. Now, an emergency on a plane activates CRM and an authoritarian cockpit gives way to a process that empowers co-pilots and flight attendants to raise questions when they observe mistakes being made, including mistakes by the captain. Since the 1990s, CRM has become a global airline industry standard.[3]

Initially, there was resistance to CRM because it requires learning new communication skills and it changes interpersonal dynamics—CRM modified the established organizational structure. Yet when barriers to communication are removed, problems are efficiently solved, resulting in increased safety. The majority of crew errors are now well-managed and plane crashes are rare. While a number of factors in recent years have improved airline safety, CRM procedures that suspend the hierarchy are seen as a major factor in this improved safety record.[4]

CRM training concepts have been modified for application across a range of industries where critical decisions must be made. Air traffic control, ship handling, firefighting and medical operating rooms[5] are among the sectors where the hierarchical structure gives way to a process that empowers those with the most relevant information to engage in the decision-making process, at least when circumstances warrant doing so.[6] In the field of health care, a program similar to CRM called Team-STEPPS is used to improve communication and teamwork skills among health care professionals in order to improve patient health and safety.[7] If you are on the operating table, you want all decisions to be made based on the best information, not based on deference to hierarchy.

HIERARCHY IN THE SCHOOL SETTING

Wherever hierarchy exists, it is a barrier to discovering the truth. Schools are no exception. When students get into a fight, the students involved often do not feel safe telling school administrators what happened when they know the result will be punishment. The means generally used to get around this is to apply more punishment, as that is the only tool the hierarchy has to enforce compliance.

As the administrators are unable to determine who is guilty because they can't get to the truth, some schools have a policy of suspending all students involved in a fight, whether they started it or not. If a little punishment doesn't work, give them more. Apparently this is the remedy when they want to be sure those who are guilty do not escape punishment, but they are unable to determine who is guilty.

Below is an example of how one large school district used a "no contact contract" as punishment applied to all students in a fight. After a dispute, the students are separated and cannot speak to one another. This is necessary because the punitive system has no means of addressing the underlying conflict, so the students are likely to still be angry at one another. This enforced separation is a barrier to the communication needed for the students to resolve the issue. This required no-contact agreement is then enforced with yet another threat of suspension, expulsion, or even arrest—an example of how, when a little punishment does not work, the only remedy is to escalate the punitive consequences.

NO CONTACT CONTRACT

Date _____

I, _____, agree to have no verbal or physical contact with _____ for the remainder of this school year. I further understand that any contact could lead to my suspension from school and/or arrest by the Police Department.

_____   _____
Signature of Student   Signature of Witness

_____
Signature of Principal or Designee

After doing a number of circles in a school in this district, we realized that this contract actually made conflicts more numerous. The students learned they could instigate a fight between two or more students by telling one side that the other side wanted to fight. By going back and forth, pretending to be friends to both sides, they "boosted" the fight but would not get caught because after the fight, communication between the fighting students was prohibited. It became clear that this contract was a root cause of fights in the school, but the administrators had no way of seeing this underlying cause because the punitive system precluded getting to that information. In our circle processes, one of the first things the students in the fight figured out was who set them up for the fight.

Separation offers, at best, a short-term solution that leaves relationships broken and the root causes festering. But if the punitive system is all we know, we are unlikely to ask, "Is there a better way?"

EQUALITY AND CIRCLE PROCESSES

We can begin to introduce equality with circle processes. Temporarily suspending the hierarchy is what happens in a Unitive Justice Circle. The circle facilitators and those directly involved in the conflict come together and, by creating the interpersonal dynamics that make honesty and authenticity safe, the participants figure out what happened and the underlying brokenness out of which the conflict arose. When the process works well, they are present to their shared humanity, enabling the participants to achieve mutual understanding and a mutually beneficial resolution. An added benefit is that when those on the periphery of the conflict witness this outcome, it has a healing effect on everyone. This is Love in action.

Below is an agreement reached in a Unitive Justice Circle between two senior girls. One student had been gossiping about the other and a fight was imminent. The student who was the subject of the gossip came into the circle declaring that she was over the age of 18 and she knew she could go to jail if she got into a fight because she had previously been in trouble with the law. But she said that was what she was willing to do to stop the hurtful gossip.

AGREEMENT

On ___Oct 21___, 2011, the following people came together for a circle process:

The parties agreed as follows:

We agree to get along.

If we have a misunderstanding we will sit down in a private area and work it out.

We will keep contact with other.

We will set an example for other students about getting along.

Signatures:

In the circle process, the two students figured out that other students were "boosting" their conflict. (The no-contact-contract described above made this type of misconduct safe.) They had previously been friends and both wanted to repair that relationship. With this shared goal, they quickly saw what actions they could take together to do that. Those actions are reflected in their agreement.

The agreement the two students reached is mutually beneficial, neither of them had to lose and they got to the root cause of their conflict. They were even willing to share their experience with other students to help improve the school climate. Yes, the students became the solution!

Empowering students to initiate circles says to the students that we trust them and believe they can resolve their conflicts themselves when they have the necessary tools. In this environment built on trust, many students show that they can figure out what happened and how they can resolve it in a way that permits them to go forward together. As the administrators are not involved in the students' conflict, they can use that time to focus on what they were hired to do, educate.

Just as airline crashes are less common because those with the best knowledge—not only the captain—are involved in making the critical decisions, temporarily suspending the hierarchy in a school, a business or a family conflict can have a similar outcome. Bringing the people with the most relevant information together in a skillfully facilitated circle process increases the likelihood of a long-lasting resolution. This process may create stronger relationships among those in the conflict and strengthen the community as a whole.

EQUALITY AS INCLUSION WITHOUT EXCEPTION

Equality has different meanings in different contexts. To some, equality means a sort of material equivalency, as in my house is as big as your house. In Unitive Justice, equality means *inclusion* without exception. *Everyone* is valued, respected, and accorded dignity.

This concept of equality is found in many cultures and major spiritual traditions. It is found in the teaching, "love your neighbor as yourself" and in the Golden Rule, "do unto others as you would have them do unto you." It is reflected in the admonition to "love one another as I have loved you"[8] and in the commandment to love your enemies.[9] Inclusion without exception is found in the Muslim teaching of wishing for others what you wish for yourself. A similar urge to Unity and congeniality is expressed in the Hindu greeting, *Namaste*, meaning "the soul in me honors the soul in you,"[10] and in the Zulu greeting, *Sawbonna*, meaning "I see you." The ancient tradition of Ubuntu is grounded in the belief that my humanity is inextricably linked to your humanity—I am because you are. There is no exception to inclusion in any of these teachings.

How is inclusion without exception practiced? One way may be for structural control to be shared horizontally, regardless of community members' roles, when that is appropriate. This is what Crew Resource Management described earlier achieves. When equality—inclusion without exception—is present, different roles permit the community to function well without the forces of separation interfering. Equality means no one is given preferential treatment because they are valued—or feared—more than others.

Giving up preferential treatment based on hierarchy may be difficult, but it is commonly experienced in the Unitive Justice Circle; that is where I was first able to experience Unitive Justice in action. No role is accorded superiority or privilege. For this to work, creating a community system that supports this new way of engaging conflict can be the first step.

A 30-year member of an intentional community that is now utilizing this circle process reported one way in which the diminished reliance on hierarchy may be beneficial:

> It has changed us greatly for the good, and it has changed all of our relationships with the Director. He seems to have relaxed and become more accessible knowing that he no longer has to be the one to bring resolution to our community conflicts. More people are calling upon the community for the circle process and that allows the Director to be more of a friend than a judging authoritative presence. We all feel it and, as a result, are taking more pleasure in living together as a community.[11]

USING UNITIVE JUSTICE INSIGHT CIRCLES HELP TEACH INCLUSION

How do we teach inclusion without exception when people do not yet understand it and its structures? The Unitive Justice Insight Circle is one of our most important teaching tools. In workshops, we often offer UJ Insight Circles to give participants experiential learning about how Unitive Justice works. We begin with a real conflict that a person has not yet resolved and is willing to bring to a circle process. The other people in the conflict are role-played by other workshop participants.

I once heard a therapist describe the counseling process as an opportunity for those who experienced harm to revisit the past event in a safe place. By discussing and processing that event with one's therapist, its harmful impact is diminished. I immediately recognized why our UJ Insight Circles are so powerful. They provide an opportunity for those who experienced harm to revisit the event in a safe but simulated discussion *with those who caused the harm*. The person who brings their conflict often feels the sensation of actually speaking to the person who harmed them.

It seems that the person role-playing the one who caused the harm tends to connect with the underlying humanity that we share, and responds to this interaction in a heart-felt and realistic way. After these circles, those who brought the conflict frequently say that what the role-player said and shared was very close to what they would expect the person who caused the harm to say. Many report that this experience results in a deep level of healing.

We formerly called this a "practice circle," but the Insight Circle can provide an effective simulation of the actual experience of addressing the conflict. The person bringing their real conflict to the circle sometimes has a transformative experience because of the deep insight into the actual conflict that they gain. This is more than practice.

HOW DO WE RESPOND WHEN EQUALITY/INCLUSIVENESS IS ABUSED?

When a group chooses to live by the foundational principle of inclusion without exception, it comes with a vulnerability that must be taken into account. One example is when the inclusiveness of free speech—available to all and protected by the U.S. Constitution—is used to undermine free speech and even our democracy. We address this by placing limits on the right, defining circumstances in which it does not apply. Balancing the right to free speech and the right of all of us to be protected against the abuse of this right is an on-going challenge, with democracy sometimes hanging in the balance.

The Society of Friends (Quakers) faced this dilemma early on. The Friends hold a quiet space for people to share insights from the Holy Spirit. In the 1600s, some people who came to be known as "Ranters" [12] began to use the Quaker's space to speak in hoots and hollers, destroying the quiet space the Quakers sought to create. After struggling with how to respond in Love, the Quakers eventually resorted to a rule. It was resolved by authorizing each Friends Meeting to vote a person "not invited" to their meetings when necessary to protect and maintain the goal of the community.

We encounter a similar problem when we seek to go from rules to values in a circle process. Many come into the circle desiring revenge—they are not yet in the space of values. As a result, we begin a Unitive Justice Circle with one rule that all must follow in order to participate in the circle. The participants must use reflective listening until they can be present and fully listen to one another without using the scaffold reflective listening provides. Without this rule, the circle can bog down with participants stuck in their old patterns—talking over each other or even escalating the conflict in the circle space.

Reflective listening enables participants to be heard and accurately hear the other. It serves as a bridge for going from rules to values and from duality to Unity. This is how we move the circle process toward mutual understanding, which must occur before they can recognize their shared humanity. When the reflective listening rule is no longer needed to achieve the goal of the circle because the participants are present and listening to each one, it is dropped. The circle process only works when people come to the circle with the hope of resolving the conflict, and are willing to do the work. If a participant comes with an intent to prove the circle process does not work, it doesn't work for anyone.

When creating a unitive community, especially early in the process, someone may want to use its inclusion without exception to gain access, but then use that access to discredit the theory and the practices being taught. How do we address this and protect against it? The dilemma is that excluding those who cause disruption or take advantage of inclusion violates the principle of inclusion without exception. When seeking to introduce Unitive Justice in the midst of a punitive system, rules are sometimes required, but not for the purpose that rules serve in a punitive system. We are not seeking control, but rather to create a space to build, maintain and strengthen the bridge that carries us from duality consciousness to Unitive Consciousness. When Unitive Consciousness becomes the norm for a significant part of the population, the community will be strong enough to function without this special protection.

PROTECTING THE SAFE SPACE

Seeking to implement Unitive Justice at this point in time means we are necessarily working in the space between dualistic consciousness and Unitive Consciousness. There will be times when this is not easy and we will face difficult situations. I share my first experience of this in hopes it will give you some insight, should this happen to you.

Several years ago, I enthusiastically encouraged a man whom I believed had goals that were consistent with Unitive Justice to attend a five day UJ workshop—at no charge. He came, and on day one, before we even got to the first coffee break, he began thumping his chest and made an ugly and disparaging remark.

Before this, no one had even been rude in our many workshops; I had never experienced anything like this. In hindsight, I can see that I was in shock and traumatized. I felt no impulse to attack or respond in kind, but instead I became submissive and placating. One or two others also sought to smooth the waters, telling him they understood his pain. In my confusion, I was unable to access the Unitive Justice tools that I was teaching. I just recall being determined to not violate the principles of Unitive Justice. When we got to our first coffee break, one of the AUJ trainers was so distressed she was sobbing outside on the patio.

He stayed all five days of the workshop, continued to attack our work and sought to divide those who were attending. On day two or three he again made the same ugly, disparaging remark. At one point during a break, many attendees were outside the building and he called "his people" to come join him apart from others. A sense of division grew in the group.

One of the exercises was for us to break into small groups and practice the circle facilitation process. He and I and a third person who came with him attempted to use this time to do an actual circle, but it achieved nothing. No one challenged his behavior until the last day when one of the long-time AUJ members asked if she could share how she was feeling. She said she believed that his unwillingness to learn what I was teaching was a loss to him and he had diminished the opportunity for others to learn.

The tension in the room was intense as she spoke, so one of our facilitators offered to facilitate a circle between them. We broke for the pre-circles to be conducted. Shortly after the circle process began, he refused to participate in reflective listening. Instead, he stood up, threw the stress ball that he was holding against the wall and left the building. With time, why he came with the goal of discrediting our work became apparent.

It took time for me to recover from the experience, but it was a lesson I needed to learn. I would now first seek to engage in reflective listening, reflecting back what I heard him say and asking if that is what he wanted me to hear. If he persisted in being disruptive, I would perhaps consult with the community about how they would like to address it. Depending on the circumstances, I might invite him to leave. For example, if I felt someone in the group was actively being harmed by his presence, I might suggest that he was in the wrong place and must leave.

As we build space for this work, early on it will be fragile and may be undermined, so we must meet people where they are. On a deeper level, his action was clearly a cry for Love. Meeting a cry for Love with Love and not submission or anger when we feel personally attacked is definitely an advanced skill, an aspect of this journey that I continue to work on.

As we become more deeply grounded in Unitive Consciousness, I believe we will have the resources to handle a situation like this differently, in a way that does not include exclusion. The community will be able to circle him in Love and he may choose to stay in that space or leave if that energy is uncomfortable. But so long as this is new for us and we are still learning, I suggest we have a rule that helps us protect the space, just in case.

* * *

Invitation to Journal. Consider these questions:

   a. How do entitlement, privilege, and a sense of superiority show up in your life?
   b. How do entitlement and privilege impact your relationships with others?
   c. Are there some with whom the notion of equality—inclusion without exception—seems possible? Some with whom it seems impossible? What is the difference between the two?

d. How do you suggest we address the problem of offering inclusiveness without exception at the risk of opening a door to those who want to attack the new unitive system?

Suggested Viewing: A simple but poignant demonstration of how privilege gives some a head start is the video, *Life of Privilege Explained in a $100 Race*, available at https://www.youtube.com/watch?v=4K5fbQ1-zps (4 min.).

ARC 10: SAFETY
FROM PUNISHMENT TO CONNECTION

punishment: suffering, pain, or loss that serves as retribution.[1] Other terms for punishment: discipline, getting even, tit for tat, retribution, revenge.

connection: the state of being present to our shared humanity, a relationship that exists beyond our differences; the joining of individual minds within Unitive Consciousness. Other terms for connection: genuine mutual concern for one another, mutual trust, being present to our shared humanity, undivided whole, joined without limit.

PUNITIVE JUSTICE RELIES ON PUNISHMENT

Punishment is the bedrock of a punitive system. I learned in law school that three objectives justify using punishment: 1. to enforce compliance with the rules, 2. to achieve atonement or payback for rule violations and the harm done, and 3. to deter would-be wrongdoers by demonstrating that the consequence of violating a rule is painful or costly. I recall no mention of the cost to individuals and society of answering harm with more harm.

We are told that when punishment is used, its imposition will be fair because "justice is blind." A blindfolded Lady Justice embodies this myth. "Blind" justice is supposed to mean that the rules are enforced objectively and impartially, without preferential treatment for anyone based on wealth, race, gender or social status—or the bias of the judge. Blind justice implies that this no-exceptions harsh application makes punishment fair —*Dura lex, sed lex*. Even if a judge's relative is charged, the law is to be applied as though those administering justice cannot "see" the status of the accused.

When we look beyond the myth we find a different reality. If punishments were uniformly applied without the possibility of exceptions, the punitive system would be so harsh it would be rejected, especially by those in control. Exceptions are essential to make the system tolerable and make punitive justice work—another internal contradiction in this flawed system.

Those in control often get to decide who is punished, and who gets the benefit of leniency. Whom the police arrest and whom they let go is one example of extending an exception to one and not another. The specific charge the prosecutor levies against the accused or chooses not to levy is another. And this is what happens when a school principal suspends one student for several days but sends another student in similar circumstances to in-school suspension for the afternoon.

As I described earlier, for generations, neither civil nor criminal redress for child sexual abuse was available. Who did this broad exception protect? The adults who abused the children, including some legislators, judges, priests, ministers and youth organization leaders. From the beginning, the children were granted little protection.

Consider the failure to bring charges against a police officer who, with little reason, kills an unarmed Black man or woman—justice is hardly blind in that case. If policing were carried out in wealthy/white communities the way it is practiced in poor/minority communities, there would be an uproar. White-collar criminals are often given favorable treatment because of their privileged positions. Sitting in a courtroom as an observer will reveal many exceptions to the myth of blind justice.

Too often, those deemed inferior may expect justice to be blind, but only to their particular needs and circumstances. The rules of evidence in a trial are such that the needs of the marginalized remain out of sight; their individual circumstances and the societal/institutional conditions that foster crime are generally not considered in a court of law. Indeed, the punitive system must keep the larger context from being considered to maintain the myth that the system is fair. (See Arc 12, From Event to Context, for a discussion of this.)

> The suffering of pain and loss is often the result of violence. State-sanctioned punishment adds another layer of violence, and in

instances of state executions, the sanctioned punishment is death. We might not recognize the system's punishment as violence because of the claim it is motivated by the desire to stop violent crime, and because of our system blindness. Prisons are described as "secure custody institutions" and those in cages are "inmates." The criminal law process is cloaked in terms like "bringing people to justice," a legitimate enterprise because of its "deterrent effect."[2] If punishment effectively deterred crime, the recidivism rate—those who again commit crime—would not exceed the number who do not.

Punishment can be the means used to restrain, limit or hide violence, but not to end it. Because the structures of the punitive system undermine connection and trust while supporting separation and distrust, violence is perpetually experienced somewhere. During periods when violence is out of control, punishment is escalated to restore control.

Why does this pattern continue? Myths such as "justice is blind" and the "punishment fits the crime" permit us to overlook the contradictions, and they support other myths about our goodness and good intentions. Another reason the pattern continues is because checks and balances on those who would use punishment illegitimately are often weak and, when they exist, are hard to enforce. Fortunately, many judges and other officials act with integrity because they choose to do so, perhaps based more on their internal moral compass and not because the system has effective guard rails against abuse.

OUR NEW UNDERSTANDING OF CONNECTION

When interpersonal connections are strong, there is less need for punishment to enforce compliance with the rules. Recent research into how our brains are wired helps explain why this is so. A new field of neuroscience called "social intelligence" has found how important connection is to our wellbeing.

Daniel Goleman, author of *Wired to Connect*, writes, "The most fundamental discovery of this new science: We are wired to connect." In Goleman's book, "*Social Intelligence*," he writes:

> Neuroscience has discovered that our brain's very design makes it sociable, inexorably drawn into an intimate brain-to-brain linkup

whenever we engage with another person. That neural bridge lets us impact the brain — and so the body — of everyone we interact with, just as they do us.[3]

According to Goldman, the most potent exchanges occur with those people with whom we spend the greatest amount of time, especially those we care about the most. The neural linkups in our brains engage in an emotional tango, a dance of feelings.

These feelings have far-reaching consequences that ripple throughout our body, sending out cascades of hormones that regulate biological systems from our heart to immune cells. Our relationships mold not only our experience but our biology, as well! The brain-to-brain link that occurs in our strongest relationships shape us in ways as benign as whether we laugh at the same jokes or as profound as which genes are activated in the immune system's t-cells to fight bacteria and viruses.[4]

Connection is just as important at the community level. From the time we are born, our survival depends on it. Harm to another, including punishment, weakens connection. In the book, *The Spiritual Roots of Restorative Justice*, editor Mihael L. Hadley writes,

> When a harm is committed, something has happened that disrupts the harmony of the community. One response may be to resolve the resulting conflict. Another response is to punish the wrongdoer. We can teach our children the "Good Life," and their connection to the larger whole or teach them an adversarial approach to life by threatening them with punishment.[5]

Dr. Martin Luther King, Jr. understood how we are wired to connect long before it was confirmed by neuroscience. This is how he describes connection in his speech, *The American Dream*:

> And we are caught in an inescapable network of mutuality, tied in a single garment of destiny—whatever affects one directly, affects all indirectly. For some strange reason I can never be what I ought to be until you are what you ought to be, and you can never be what you ought to be until I am what I ought to be. This is the interrelated structure of reality.

The punitive system uses punishment as the framework for maintaining order. The unitive system uses connection to maintain safety, peace and harmony. That is true order.

CONNECTION IS THE BOND THAT HOLDS A UNITIVE SYSTEM TOGETHER

We are slowly waking up to the fact that we live in an interconnected world, which may be a new phenomenon for many in Western culture. In his seminal work, *The Ever-Present Origin*, philosopher Jean Gebser argues that human consciousness is an evolving process.[67] While some got there long ago, he argues that consciousness that affirms our interconnectedness on a scale wide enough to set humanity on a new course is only now occurring. It may be that Unitive Justice was not possible in an earlier era, but this is the time in our evolution when it is.

When we believe that we are each part of a larger whole, our reality changes. We see that our individual choices impact the whole, including us. What we do to another is like a sword with a 360-degree angle—when we harm others, we hurt ourselves in some way. It is the law of universal cause and effect—your thoughts, words and deeds become the cause that gives rise to specific effects that manifest and create your life as you know it.

What might the legal system be like if, instead of separation, those who practice law embraced connection? Integrative Lawyer Linda Alvarez[8] describes her rationale for emphasizing connection in her legal practice:

> I see my role as serving a human life within the context of a community of inter-dependent beings. It is my experience that there is no such thing as a discrete, finite response to conflict. Every word and deed generates some response because all of us are in relationship with one another -- and our lives together are ongoing conversations. Integrative practice, for me, is acting with conscious awareness about what sort of conversations, what types of 'cycles of response' I'd like to see grow in this world we share.

Linda is not alone. A growing number of lawyers are finding ways to continue to practice law in ways that are fully grounded in connection. British Barrister, Acting Solicitor and Mediator Amber Turner, who has practiced law in Gibraltar since 1998, opened Gibraltar's first Holistic Law firm in March 2013. During the pandemic in 2020, Amber set up a global platform so that law students, lawyers and clients could benefit from her unique wellbeing model of practicing law. Visiting Amber's website, www.AmberLaw.com, will introduce you to a revolutionary vision for practicing law.

Amber describes how she relates to her clients in terms I could not even imagine when I practiced law. When a new client came to me, I spent the first interview listening for points I could include in a winning theory of the case. Amber approaches the first client interview like this:

> I begin by becoming fully present for my client creating a safe space of non-judgment. I engage all my senses to take in what s/he is communicating non-verbally. What is their body language informing me about? What is the tone and pace of their speech? I am listening deeply with compassion. This all informs my questions and conclusions about my client and their case. I understand that my client's mental, emotional, physical and spiritual states are often colored by childhood trauma, and these states are intrinsic to the emergence of their legal problem.

Following her own 'holistic' approach, Amber has avoided contested hearings in many cases by using her system of connecting and referrals for professional support. Amber describes an exchange with the judge (addressed as "My Lord") in one of her court hearings as follows:

> One time, on attending at the Supreme Court the judge mentioned that I had not been before him for a while. I answered, "My Lord, I pride myself on such periods of absence. It means that we are sensibly and sensitively settling cases amicably. If attending before your Lordship, this means that sadly, both my learned colleague (for the 'other' side) and I have failed our clients. Court ought to always be the very last resort.

Perhaps this approach will eventually become typical. When we assume we are interconnected, terms that denote separation, like "victim" and "offender," become problematic. In some cases, the line between the victim and the offender may be clear—a drunk driver causing serious injury to a stranger in a road traffic accident is one example. But this is often not the case. When the parties are in a long-term relationship, such as a marriage or a business, who is the victim and offender might shift back and forth—the line between the two may not be as clear as the punitive system assumes.

No part of a system operates in isolation. When a crime occurs, discovering the underlying brokenness requires a community process. The one who broke the law cannot repair the underlying brokenness alone—the community must do that together. Without addressing the underlying brokenness out of which patterns of crime emerge, those patterns will continue. Connection opens the door to addressing root causes and finding lasting solutions—this is the path to reducing individual acts of harm.

Approaching the conflict without prejudging who is the offender and who is the victim does not negate the harm done or responsibility for it. It creates a space for discovering the complexity of the experience. As each participant recognizes they are connected and share power, they can harness that power to heal and transform. Drawing on the available resources, the conflict community discovers its ability to achieve a mutually beneficial resolution. A win-win resolution restores balance and may be personally transformative.

This is a significant difference between the punitive and unitive systems. In the punitive system, all but the "offender" are permitted to see themselves standing outside the event. In the unitive system, each participant considers the context from which the breakdown arose, the underlying conflict dynamic, and where each one stands in that larger dynamic.

This is not blaming the victim for what happened to them, as some mistakenly assume. Approaching the conflict as an opportunity for all to heal reflects a mindset outside the punitive mindset of narrowly focusing only on the offender. Those impacted by the conflict—the conflict community—may recognize that the harmful act was, in part, a function of their own beliefs and actions. Perhaps they see it as a function of systemic dysfunction at a deeper level. When participants begin to ask,

"What is my contribution to that systemic dysfunction?" a shift has occurred.

When the participants realize that they can shift from contributing to the breakdown to contributing to the healing, there is a giving and receiving that naturally arises. Connection must be present for this to be possible.

CAN WE DREAM OF A RETURN TO EDEN?

As I continually sought clues to help me understand the punitive-unitive dichotomy, I found an intriguing clue in the biblical story of the Garden of Eden. In Jewish and Christian theology, the fall of Adam and Eve (and all subsequent humans) was caused by them eating the "fruit of the tree of *knowledge of good and evil*." (Genesis 2-3; emphasis added). Many believe that eating the forbidden fruit, perhaps an apple or a pomegranate, caused them to be expelled from the Garden of Eden by God. This story, we are told, explains how we began our dualistic existence.

However, God told Adam and Eve, they could eat the fruit of every tree that yielded fruit *that had seeds* (Genesis 1:27–29). This means the forbidden fruit was not actual fruit—be it an apple or a pomegranate. Might this mean that the reference to eating the "fruit of the knowledge of good and evil" is actually a metaphor for taking unto oneself the *belief* in good versus evil? If so, this story becomes a profound message about our state of consciousness, not just an arbitrary rule imposed by God.

The concept of good versus evil denotes duality consciousness and separation. It undermines human connection; without connection, any semblance of Eden is impossible. Might it be that the "sin" of believing in separation, a belief that denies our inherent connection, is the cause of our being turned out of the Garden of Eden—our own doing, not punishment inflicted by God? Does this also mean that if we transcend separation and embrace our inherent Oneness, we may again experience the Garden of Eden?

Before Eve ate the forbidden fruit, we are told that the serpent tempted her to do so by telling her it would open her eyes and she would be as the gods, knowing good and evil. One might mistakenly think that having control over others is a god-like power. Instead, separation precludes us from experiencing our shared humanity and dooms us to conflict. I like to believe that the story of the Garden of Eden teaches that, so long as we believe in separation, we can never experience Eden—but it is a *choice that we have*. We can restore Eden if we stop believing that separation is reality, and instead embrace connection as the fundamental truth.

The good news is that connection was not lost; it remains within us, even if dormant. Recognizing our shared humanity is remembering what it is to be human, and when conditions are right, we do remember. We *can* do this.

I believe this is what Peter Gabel, a modern visionary, describes when he writes:

> When we fully enter into each other's presence, when we fully recognize each other in our sacred humanity, we actually experience the energetic flow that connects us. We emit an invisible but palpable radiance linking the poles of our Being as we come into connection and experience one another as here, together embraced in each other's sight. This kind of encounter—occurring sometimes in two-person encounters and ubiquitously in the "rising" period of liberatory social movements as this mutual recognition ricochets into a powerful social force—is inherently egalitarian. No one is experienced as above or underneath anyone else, but rather we all experience each other as fully present together in the same space, on the same solid ground of Being.[9]

Remembering this connection extinguishes our desire for retribution. When connected on this level, we do not want to harm our kindred spirits—they are an extension of ourself. Perhaps this is a step toward our return to the Garden of Eden.

* * *

Invitation to Journal. Reflect on your experience with punishment, whether you were punished or you punished someone else, then consider these questions:

a. Were there any instances that come to mind when you did not feel the punishment was fair?
b. What were the desired results? Did the punishment achieve the desired results?
c. Was the goal merely to achieve compliance? Was the goal something else—if so, what was it?
d. Can you imagine achieving the desired outcome by seeking a mutually beneficial outcome?

Suggested Viewing: *How Forgiveness Can be Used to Create a More Just Legal System.* In this Ted Talk, Martha Minow, a law professor for 40 years, shares her new awakening: our legal system needs a new philosophy of forgiveness! Available at https://www.ted.com/talks/martha_minow_how_forgiveness_can_create_a_more_just_legal_system?utm_source=newsletter_daily&utm_campaign=daily&utm_medium=email&utm_content=button__2020-04-24 (15 min.).

ARC 11: GOAL
FROM COMPLIANCE TO MUTUALLY BENEFICIAL ACTION/WHOLENESS

compliance: the act of obeying an order, rule, or request; doing what is demanded. Other terms for compliance: acquiescence, deference, resignation, submission, yielding, obedience.

mutually beneficial action: transformative action by two or more individuals in which conflict is transformed into unified goals and no one has to lose. Mutually beneficial action seeds increased social safety and wellbeing for all through honest communication, courageous vulnerability and the recognition of our shared humanity—from this, community harmony and wholeness emerge. Other terms for mutually beneficial action: harmonious resolution, balanced outcome, equity.

wholeness: the state of being unbroken, complete, a harmonious whole, Unity.

When addressing conflicts, the two systems of justice have different goals. Punitive justice seeks to achieve compliance using punishment and fear, while Unitive Justice seeks to achieve a mutually beneficial outcome by unifying conflicting goals; when this is achieved, no one has to lose.

Most of our language related to punitive justice tends to disguise or minimize the truth. While listening to a program about the history of Japan, I heard the commentator say that there had been an extended period of "peace" several centuries ago. Then the narrative went on to describe the brutality used to maintain what was called peace. It was not peace—it was forced compliance.

Compliance is not equivalent to consent. Even when people comply, they may not relinquish their agency. We are all participants in everything that affects us. Margaret Wheatley, an American management consultant who studies organizational behavior, notes, "[i]f leaders or task forces refuse to believe this, and go ahead and make plans for us, we don't ever just sit by passively and do what we're told. We still get involved. But we then act from the sidelines, from wherever we've been told to sit and wait."[1]

When people are not involved in decisions that impact them they can exercise their control by ignoring, resisting, or sabotaging the plans and directives that are imposed on them.[2] They may ultimately accept death over forced compliance. Forced compliance is, at best, a temporary fix.

Manipulation and coercion at the physical level may achieve control but they cannot achieve peace. Peace is a mental state that first exists within oneself before it manifests in one's outward actions; it cannot be imposed from without. Peace grows as it becomes a shared community value. Forced compliance is consistent with a punitive justice system, while peace is consistent with Unitive Justice. We should avoid calling forced compliance "peace."

PUNITIVE JUSTICE AIMS FOR COMPLIANCE

In the punitive justice system, punishment and fear are used to achieve compliance. From its inception in 11th and 12th century England through its implementation in the American colonies and up to the present day, the Western punitive system uses punishment to achieve compliance.

Punitive justice seems rational when one lives with the worldview of duality. In duality thinking, we believe we can build systems composed of independent parts and that people act in predetermined ways. When something is broken, we focus on fixing that part. If some are noncompliant, we seek to punish them until they do comply, like fixing a part, but people are not parts. People require connection to thrive; when harm occurs, it indicates that connection is broken.

Wheatley writes: "It's ironic to notice how our many attempts to impose order have created just the opposite effect, more disorder. And our continuing failures at trying to change people and organizations are teaching us that our mechanistic approaches are truly flawed."[3] She explains why this must change:

> [T]his 21st century world of complexity and turbulence is no place for the mechanistic thinking of the past. . . Nothing moves slowly enough for us to make sense of the world using any analytic process we were taught. . . We need a different worldview to guide us in this new world of continuous change and intimately connected systems that reach around the globe.[4]

Discovering the underlying conflict dynamic is essential. When we fail to understand how systemic forces influence events, it is easy to misinterpret certain behavior. If we don't understand the cause of non-compliance, we might apply more punishment only to get increased non-compliance. Misbehavior in schools is a good example. Research suggests that the rebellious acts of marginalized youth in public school settings are often acts of resistance rather than acts of behavioral deficit. They are often labeled as "at-risk," "damaged," and "emotionally and behaviorally disordered" and then treated as "Emotionally and Behaviorally Disordered" (EBD), compounding their sense of disrespect and exclusion. When they are punished they are further alienated.[5] Punishment is likely to be experienced as just another traumatic event to be endured.

As schools adopted zero-tolerance policies, resistive behavior increased and escalating the punishment became fuel for the school-to-prison pipeline.[6] However, my experience with circle processes based on Unitive Justice principles in a high school is this: when students are treated with respect and they are empowered, their best attributes often emerge.

Narrowly defining the goal as compliance excludes consideration of the whole—the whole person(s) and the whole context. We then fail to recognize institutional, systemic or societal conditions that fuel conflict and so we cannot address them. This renders peace unachievable.

UNITIVE JUSTICE AND MUTUALLY BENEFICIAL ACTION

One of the goals of Unitive Justice is mutually beneficial action. In a culture steeped in punitive justice, moving from the goal of compliance to mutually beneficial action involves a new understanding of how we engage with conflict. Unitive Justice sees conflict as a natural part of human activity and that, in the right environment, conflict naturally flows toward its resolution. Each of the fourteen Unitive Justice structures supports this outcome.

From the Unitive Justice perspective, conflict is an opportunity to learn, grow, heal, and even strengthen relationships. When a unitive system is in place, instead of fearing or trying to control conflict, we walk toward the conflict and engage with it. We seek to learn the information it contains about what is broken and, thus, is causing conflict. Until these root causes are addressed, conflict will continue to fester.

Conflict arises out of conflicting and often contradictory goals inherent in dualistic thinking. Not only do our goals clash with those of others, but we ourselves also hold contradictory goals. Walking toward the conflict allows us to discover the contours of the underlying brokenness out of which the conflict arises and where we stand in the brokenness. This often reveals how our connection to one another is broken. This tends to reveal our shared humanity and opens the door to healing.

Seeing where we stand in the underlying brokenness gives rise to a new understanding of accountability that is far more inclusive than the punitive system offers, accountability that is grounded in relationships and in community. In this view, accountability has multiple layers involving the one who caused the harm, the one who was harmed, and the community members where the harm occurred.

First, the one who caused the harm must answer to the person harmed and to contribute to that person's healing, including participation in the community healing that now needs to take place. There is also accountability to oneself, to achieve the self-healing needed to be a welcome and contributing community member. Taylor Paul and Prince Bunn are examples of such accountability, as they model how to go from being the problem to being the solution.

Second, members of the community are accountable for the conditions that persistently contribute to conflict and how they may contribute to those conditions. Community members are accountable to one another for creating a safe community and spaces for healing harm. There is a community responsibility to support the healing of those involved in and impacted by the conflict. Community accountability is a role that each of us have opportunities to step into in one way or another.

Third, the harmed individual needs to tell their truth, resolve their pain, and work on their own healing within the context of their community. There is accountability for doing the work needed to turn trauma into resilience. In some cases, the one harmed can find healing in sharing their own experience to bring attention to the systemic brokenness that allowed their harm to occur, using the harm they experienced as an example of why systemic change is needed. This is what I saw a group of adult survivors of childhood sexual abuse do as they achieved significant legislative changes that provided legal redress for other victims of this crime. The loss they experienced as children was given value by using it to protect other children from such abuse.

Dominic Barter, a leader in the Restorative Justice movement, describes accountability as "self-responsibility."[7] This new conversation permits those in the conflict community—everyone impacted—to create new goals that are aligned. This is the bridge to mutually beneficial action.

Over time, hopefully, people will come to embrace mutually beneficial action as the goal of justice. A vision of what this might produce in the future is depicted in the graph below, what we call the "Healing Decades," to reverse the data reflected in the Punishing Decades chart in Chapter Five, page 46. This vision sees our incarceration rate being turned upside down, diminishing just as quickly as it previously mushroomed.

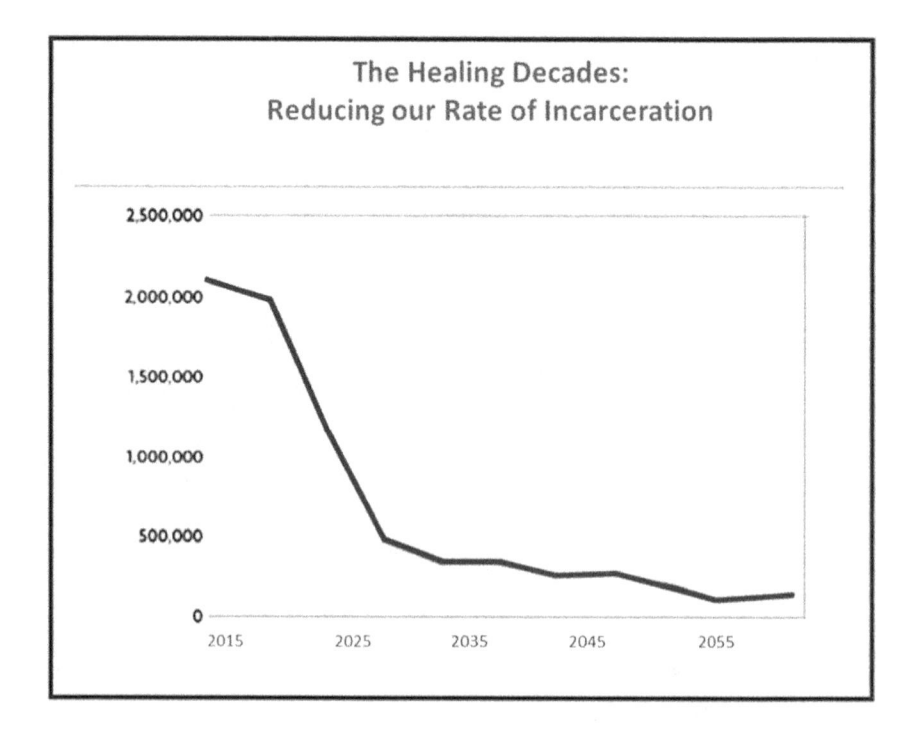

The Healing Decades: Reducing our Rate of Incarceration

Perhaps the day may come when enough of us live in Unitive Communities where Unitive Justice is practiced that this chart becomes a reality.

* * *

Invitation to Journal. When some people encounter the concept of Unitive Justice for the first time, they express fear that transitioning away from punitive justice and punishment will result in widespread non-compliance, disorder, perhaps even anarchy. With this in mind, please consider these questions:

> a. What was your initial response to the concept of Unitive Justice?
> b. Do you believe that the punitive system comes at an unnecessarily high cost, or do you believe the benefits outweigh the costs?
> c. Can you imagine Unitive Justice as a viable alternative to punitive justice?
> d. If so, what might your role in achieving the shift from punitive justice to Unitive Justice be?

Suggested Viewing: A prosecutor named Adam Foss shares his experience with punishment and his vision for a justice system that includes Love in the video, *A Prosecutor's Vision for a Better Justice System*, available at https://www.youtube.com/watch?v=H1fvr9rGgSg&t=16s (16 min.).

ARC 12: FOCUS
FROM EVENT TO CONTEXT

event: an incident, occurrence, a crime, the specific harm done. Other terms for event: conflict, wrongdoing, the act, the offense, the violation.

context: the interrelated conditions in which something exists or occurs; the circumstances that form the setting for an event, statement, or idea and in terms of which it can be fully understood and assessed;[1] the systemic conditions that give rise to individual, similar or repeated incidents and their particular consequences. Other terms for context: circumstances, conditions, situation, environment, setting, background.

TWO WAYS TO USE THE EVENT

In the criminal law system, a harmful act or crime is defined as a rule or a law that is broken. The event is used to determine who committed the crime, the offender's culpability and what punishment the offender will incur for this particular violation. The punitive system uses the event as the reason to arrest, charge, judge, convict and then punish the offender if found guilty.

Thus, the punitive system isolates responsibility, framing it narrowly as applying only to the "offender" because of their guilt. This narrow focus is achieved by making the *offender* the *object* of the punitive process and looking no further. Importantly, this narrow focus on individual guilt distracts attention from the role that political, social, and legal inputs play within the system.

In contrast, the Unitive Justice system uses the same event as the portal to discover the underlying conflict dynamic, the brokenness from which the harmful act arose. The *event and its context* are the *subject* of the unitive process. To heal and return to wholeness, we look to discover where wholeness was breached, both by individuals and by systemic forces.

Broadening the lens to encompass both the event and the context out of which that event arose is essential to address root causes and achieve lasting results. This is what leads to system change so that similar events do not continue to occur. This broader focus requires a different organizational design—unitive, not punitive.

THE PUNITIVE SYSTEM LIMITS ITS FOCUS TO THE EVENT

Punitive justice is designed to hold offenders accountable, period. This requires seeing only a few actors while excluding consideration of the context, including the systemic conditions in which the offender chose to act. In a criminal trial, rules of evidence systematically exclude consideration of the context, deeming that information to be "collateral" and irrelevant to the issue of offender guilt or innocence.

A side effect of this procedural rule is that it keeps the system's weaknesses from being revealed or addressed. Such a narrow focus can hide how the punitive system contributes to the underlying conflict dynamics and systemic injustice that fuel the very conflict the system is presumed to address. It keeps us from recognizing that the larger social and institutional structures that disadvantage certain groups may benefit more entitled groups. We should not be surprised that, although crimes are prosecuted and punished, things in the community often continue to be much the same as before the crime occurred.

This is an existential failure because it disregards the truth. In fact, an event does not happen in a vacuum. For every action taken, there is a chain of people and events that lead to particular consequences. Individuals and their environment are in constant interaction. The context of every harmful act manifests in a unique way—it has a certain conflict community that evolved over time, a particular distribution of control, resources and structural injustices unique to its place and time.[2] The context contains the information that tells us what needs to change to keep similar events from occurring in the future.

Focusing only on the events and not their context means we cannot get to the root causes. For example, stealing on Wall Street might involve inserting small hidden charges on a voluminous number of trades, while stealing in a public housing project might involve brandishing a gun in a corner grocery store. The same goal is accomplished—stealing someone else's money—even though the event's details may differ in each case. The thieves may be caught and punished in a punitive system that uses their acts as a reason to charge, convict and punish them. Still, so long as the context remains the same we can expect harmful events of a similar nature to continue.

In neither case, Wall Street or public housing is the thief alone responsible for the context in which the particular harm occurred. Do others who are responsible for setting up and maintaining the larger context, and who are perhaps benefitting from it, have some measure of culpability, as well?

Another side effect of this narrow focus in the court setting is that the community has no say or input regarding how or why the offense occurred and what needs to change for the harm to be healed. Moreover, the person directly harmed (the victim) is marginalized, made a witness for the state needed only to prove that the state's law was broken. The healing of those who actually experienced the harm is minimized or even ignored.

Maintaining the punitive system depends on this narrow focus. From a systems perspective, we find that all institutions that incorporate punitive justice structures, such as rules, hierarchy, judgment, punishment, etc., must also have a means of focusing on the event while ignoring the context. For example, in an educational institution where the punitive system is in effect, a narrow focus is maintained by limiting the focus of the research used to legitimize the system to students' test results,[3] while ignoring the larger context that impacts test results.

In the No Child Left Behind law that was implemented in 2002, students and also teachers are held responsible for test results and are punished for failing grades. This law, in effect, requires teachers to compensate for social conditions that are outside the teachers' control—homelessness, hunger, sustained trauma, etc. By focusing only on test results, discussion of these other factors is avoided.

In our economic system, the focus is limited to profit as the principal measure of success. When calculating profit, labor is reduced to a cost of production. To reduce costs, workers are laid off with no safety net if this increases profits. Collateral costs of doing business, such as damage to the environment, polluted air or water, are considered "externalities"[4] for which the polluter bears no responsibility and are not considered when calculating profit. Narrowly focusing on profit permits the conditions that promote economic disparity to remain unaddressed, even when the sustained harm is open and obvious.

In the "child welfare system," we focus blame on the parents for being irresponsible or abusive without considering systemic issues like poverty, trauma and other hardships. A 2021 article in Imprint News reports that a movement is growing to replace this long-established child welfare system with one that builds "the necessary community, financial and material supports for families to remain safe and healthy together, to ensure that power in decision-making rests with families and communities, and to dismantle policies and practices that disproportionately harm the safety and integrity of families."[5]

Focusing on the event while ignoring the context is reinforced by a widely accepted social theory—the "bootstrap" theory of individual accountability. Some argue that individual choice is determinative and the social context is irrelevant. This makes it easy for politicians to argue against considering the larger context. President Ronald Reagan promoted his "get tough on crime" policies by encouraging us to narrowly focus on the event, not the context when he said:

> We must reject the idea that every time a law's broken, society is guilty rather than the lawbreaker. It is time to restore the American precept that each individual is accountable for his actions.[6]

Reagan wanted us to see the issue of accountability as a binary choice, either-or, when both can be true: the lawbreaker is guilty *and* societal/institutional conditions play a role in what happened. Those who share Reagan's view must gloss over many societal injustices, including that some who are *not* guilty are nonetheless found guilty or choose to plead guilty to shorten the inescapable sentences they otherwise face.[7] Who bears accountability for that?

Many of the choices we make depend on our environment, our neighborhood, the educational opportunities we have, our work experience, the state of our health, our past experience of trauma, the daily difficulties that we face, and on the personal and communal beliefs that we hold. Structural injustices often play a role in shaping our choices. Bias and prejudice in many forms may be factors. A justice system that excludes consideration of structural and systemic factors while individualizing responsibility for the harm done will inevitably produce injustice.

Shifting our point of view to include the event *and* the context compels us to create ways to include both when we address conflict. Then we can address individual accountability, community responsibility and get to the root causes. This is the path to long-term resolutions and even system change that reduces on-going violence and conflict; this is a path to real peace.

THE EVENT: USING IT AS A PORTAL TO THE UNDERLYING CONFLICT DYNAMIC

Human relationships are complex and simple, epic and small. The punitive justice system avoids considering either this complexity or simplicity by keeping its inquiry superficial. Punitive justice timidly looks no farther than the surface level of the conflict.

In contrast, Unitive Justice is designed to hold the complexity—the myriad of diverse variables—of what it means to be human. Unitive Justice also reveals the simplicity of what is at the core of all conflict—separation crying for connection. When we recognize there is one problem—separation—we have one answer—to strengthen connection. This complexity and simplicity are both found in the context from which the particular event emerged.

The context of harmful events is not always obvious. Each person involved holds their own piece of the puzzle. To discover the context, there must be a means of bringing those involved together in a safe space for a process of discovery. This requires reframing the inquiry—not only "Who caused this harm?" but also, "What is the brokenness that is at the core of this event?" This shift in perspective creates a space for each person to consider how they may have contributed, directly or indirectly, intentionally or unintentionally, to what lies at the root of this particular harm—the underlying conflict dynamic. This is what the structures of Unitive Justice make it safe—and possible—to do. The Unitive Justice Circle provides a process to achieve this end. (Unitive Justice Circles are explained below in Arc 14.)

The context holds a wealth of information related to the event: how it happened, the unmet needs, the old wounds, the systemic dysfunction, the punitive beliefs that were triggered by the event and the fear that drives our daily life. The context includes the residue of choices made long ago, the hidden determinants, but their impact continues, like slavery, segregation or long-established religious beliefs. The context also holds shared negative beliefs about anyone who is different—beliefs about women, minorities, people who are not heterosexual, immigrants or people of one religion or another. Any given conflict leaves a footprint reflecting the context.

Culture is an important aspect of the context. We learn from our culture how to be kind. We also learn from our culture how to be violent and towards whom to direct our violence. Nazi Germany illustrates this point. When Jews in Germany were the object of Hitler's scurrilous remarks, Jews were attacked by neighbors who felt that Hitler's vitriol gave them license to do so. In today's Germany, such attacks on Jews are unacceptable—at least among most Germans.

It is important to note that the context can also reflect the energetic presence of lovingkindness, of many acts of generosity extended by one to another, reflecting a shared commitment to make the world a better place. We sometimes hear about one person—a teacher, a neighbor, a relative—who changed the trajectory of a person's life. The presence of that person changed the context.

For many of us, it is easy to think that the context is beyond our control or that we have no responsibility for it. However, as we expand our lens, there is a point at which we realize the context includes us—all of us. The context is where our connection manifests. With each choice we make, perhaps with each thought we hold, we impact the context in which our lives unfold.

When we lack information about all of the relevant factors at play and, thus, fail to include them in our considerations, we are sure to arrive at faulty conclusions. To escape this conundrum, Unitive Justice uses conflict as an opportunity for the conflict community—those who chose to do the harmful act and those impacted by it—to recognize how they are all entangled in the dysfunctional conflict dynamic. Resolving it involves all of them.

THE "OUT THERE" AND THE "IN HERE" ASPECTS OF THE CONTEXT

We generally think about conflict as something existing "out there," something someone else did to us or we did to them. But each dispute also has an "in here" aspect that places one's signature upon it and how the event's consequences unfold. This "in here" aspect shows up in how an individual reacts to an event, and it also constitutes an aspect of the larger breakdown dynamic.

As each individual processes the pain the event causes, it may bring up aspects of their personal history, and how they chose to react to prior experiences in their life. This important information, if uncovered, may provide a unique and valuable opportunity to heal the past, even if the event occurred long ago. Having an opportunity to heal past wounds may solve otherwise intractable problems in the present.

The "in here" aspect shows up sometime after the harmful act, perhaps immediately but it might be later. When something negative happens, we don't all show up in the same way. Despite the harsh environment, we sometimes hear someone who was in prison say that it was what they needed—it provided a much-needed time out or the opportunity for them to transform, as was the case with Taylor and Prince. Yet there are others in similar situations who are embittered and resentful. Similarly, conflicts impact us in dissimilar ways.

These different outcomes reflect our unique internal processing of the event. How we each respond to a situation is a choice we can consciously make, but more often, we react based on subconscious programming informed by our past experiences. The punitive law system routinely disregards this "in here" aspect of the conflict dynamic; this is an important lost opportunity.

How one reacts to a harmful event in the present can provide insight into how a past experience is still impacting one's life, even long after the event. The opportunity the present conflict presents to identify past wounds and to heal them now is an opportunity we can seize, especially if we are supported in doing so by a process designed for this purpose. As the past is healed, so is the present. The Unitive Justice Circle provides this opportunity.

I would like to share a personal experience that reflects one of my "in here" experiences. Because a circle process gave me an opportunity to recognize an old unhealed wound that continued to impact my life, I gained an important insight about myself.

I was teaching a college course, and cellphones in the classroom were an annoying problem. One day a good student who did not usually use his phone during class was doing so while we watched a video. I was upset so I walked over to him and, with my hands on my hips, angrily said, "Put that away and don't get it out again." The punitive system would treat his act as a violation of the university's no-cellphone policy and see me as the victim, thus, justified in my angry reaction. But I was embarrassed—I was teaching Unitive Justice principles and also how to facilitate circles.

After finishing the lesson, I said I would like to do a circle with the students in the class about this incident. In our circle process, we seek to get some insight into the "in here" aspect of the conflict during a pre-circle in preparation for doing the actual circle. In my pre-circle, the student facilitator sought to help me discover what this incident had triggered in me, my "in here" trigger. She asked if I felt disrespected by the student who used his cellphone in class. That was close, but I knew disrespect was not quite it.

I tried to connect with where the pain caused by this incident lay within me—this is a little like finding the right pitch on a tuning fork. In a moment or two, when tears welled in my eyes, I felt the energy align and I knew what it was. I felt *unappreciated*. When I connected with that old wound, I immediately recognized its source—I recalled being shamed as a child by my mother.

My mother grew up in the Old Order Brethren denomination, one that considers a little shaming to be good for you. (This was a root of my mother's life context, and it became a root in mine.) While she did not frequently do this, when she did, it was painful. I interpreted her behavior to mean that she did not appreciate me, and that was hurtful. For someone else, a similar experience might land differently.

My old wound was triggered by me reading this good student's conduct as evidence he did not appreciate me and that was hurtful. That wound was an aspect of the underlying brokenness out of which this conflict arose. If I did not have that wounded place in my subconscious, this conflict may not have occurred. This is why the punitive system's linear way of understanding conflict is so inadequate. The complexity of conflict reflects the complexity of human relationships. When we walk into the conflict and discover the underlying brokenness out of which the conflict arises, we can heal the broken relationship, create unified goals and go forward together.

What about the student who had violated the no-cellphone-in-class rule? In the circle that followed the pre-circles, I learned that he was on his phone because he was communicating with family members who had to decide where his dying grandmother would spend her final days. They wanted her to be as well cared for and as comfortable as possible. The family looked to their college-student son for advice.

I noticed that early in the class he had twice walked out of the room for a brief time. He shared that he did so to take their phone calls, but when he did that, he missed what was happening in class. He explained that he didn't want to miss anything, so he was trying to multitask—deal with the family crisis and learn what I was teaching. He did appreciate me!

While the use of his cellphone in class triggered my wound of believing I am unappreciated, I triggered his wound of believing he is disrespected—he felt disrespected by my curt reaction. I also learned that every student in the class felt disrespected by my outburst. (In circles with African Americans, the wound of disrespect, understandably, often comes up. This student was African American, as were all of the students in the class.) I felt remorseful.

Discovering that each of us experienced an old wound triggered by the action of the other is what often happens in the circle process as we get to the root causes of conflict. This is when circle participants tend to recognize their shared humanity.

I learned that the student did appreciate me, but without communicating with him, I misread his actions. And he misread my actions. I did respect him for the many positive attributes that he exhibited in class. If I knew what the student was dealing with, I would be happy to make an exception for him. Many conflicts arise from such misunderstandings, but we usually have no tools for uncovering these details or for experiencing the shared humanity that they reveal.

This conflict was resolved by the students offering to tell me when they need special consideration to deal with something that came up and I agreed to make exceptions in these cases. No one had to lose.

An added benefit was that I learned a lot about myself from that circle. Bringing my sensitivity to being unappreciated to my awareness made me more aware of the need to pause and consider my response. I wondered how often I had reacted from that old place of hurt in ways that hurt other relationships—with my husband, children, and possibly peers in my profession. Without this conflict with my student, I would not have seen the root cause and how it contributed to the breakdown. Missing that learning and the healing it provided would have been a lost opportunity for me to recognize and overcome that old wound.

When we discover the "in here" aspect of the conflict, we often see that we are a piece of the broken puzzle, even when we were not directly involved in the harmful act or event. That is when we begin to see new possibilities. Perhaps we see that not only do we have the power to forgive those whose harmful actions impacted us, they have the power to forgive us. In discovering these new possibilities, we discover a way to go forward together, even with those whom we previously perceived as adversaries.

Addressing the "out there" aspect of conflict is necessary, but that alone is not enough. The "in here" part shows us how we seek to impose control in the places we feel wounded, often without realizing that is what we are doing. Without this insight, we continue to act out of our past wounds and trauma, causing harm in ways we do not understand and do not intend.

This is why discovering the context is so important. The context shows us the particular underlying patterns of separation out of which the event arose and how its particular consequences unfold. This enables us to restore connection so that similar events are avoided in the future. When we are no longer afraid to look at the truth, all of it, we gain the insight needed to experience our shared humanity. Being present to our shared humanity changes everything.

The Unitive Justice Circle allows us to look "out there" *and* "in here" and thus discover the underlying conflict dynamic. This gives us the insight needed to recognize our interconnectedness and then reweave the fabric of our shared humanity, so no one has to lose. One circle at a time, we can heal the past and forge a stronger future.

Over time, the impact of repeatedly doing Unitive Justice Circles in a particular community will begin to reveal patterns of unmet needs and systemic conditions that impact certain—perhaps many—individuals in the community. I described earlier how doing circles in a troubled high school soon revealed how the "No Contact Contract" that students were required to sign after a fight set the stage for more fights. The students quickly learned that, when those in a fight could not speak to one another, they could set students up for a fight and never get caught.

Another pattern that might be revealed by doing repeated circles is that the rebellious acts of marginalized youth in a school setting are acts of resistance, not acts of behavioral deficit.[8]

When I facilitated circles in a troubled high school, some staff told me that nothing could be done about the misbehaving students because the parents were the real problem. Others believed that the school staff could not change the trajectory of these youths' lives because repeatedly punishing the disobedient students was futile. It was not uncommon to see adults yelling at these students in the hallways, threatening and sometimes belittling and demeaning them. My experience with some of the same non-compliant students in Unitive Justice Circles was that they *are* capable of behaving well. They are also able to resolve their conflicts when they have the tools to do so.

I observed how important it is for all students to feel seen and heard. I taught a class at the high school about Unitive Justice called "21st Century Justice." When a new student joined my class, we stopped and did a welcoming circle, a time to meet one another and offer to help when needed—to say, "we see you." Not once did I need to send a student to the principal's office or call security staff.

In some of the circles I facilitated, the generosity of spirit exhibited by students moved me to tears. I saw an assistant principal yell at one particular student who I will call Jaxsun, "You do that again and I will show you what I can do to you." To which Jaxsun replied, "Fuck you." He was, of course, punished. That same student was in one of the most poignant circles I facilitated—I learned why he fought.

This 9th-grade boy was cast as the "man in the house" because his father was in prison and he was the older of two boys. He believed that if he didn't fight, his little brother would be bullied or beaten up on the bus, and his family was more vulnerable to *another* robbery in their home. He believed that fighting, having a reputation for being tough, was the only way he could protect his mother and brother.

Jaxsun saw fighting as an act of bravery, an expression of Love and the only way to defend his family. For this he was punished, while the conditions he was dealing with the only way he knew how went unaddressed—generation after generation. How can a 9th-grade boy who faces such contradictions make sense of his world?

When we disclose the underlying conflict dynamic, we begin to see who and what is contributing to the trauma out of which the conflict emerges. This information can be transformative. It allows us to consider how we use our agency, and how we might do things differently going forward.

* * *

Invitation to Journal. Think of a recent time when you felt harmed by someone you love, then consider these questions:

> a. Rather than focusing on the "out there" aspect of the event (what was said or done that was hurtful and how you feel about the person who hurt you), focus instead on the "in here" aspect. What were you looking for at the moment the event impacted you?
> b. What need did you immediately seek to satisfy, or was it an old wound that was triggered? What were the origins of that need or that old wound?
> c. Do you still have that need or old wound? If so, how might it be met or released?
> d. If, at the time, you ignored the "in here" aspect of the event, was there a cost to you? If so, what was it?

Suggested Viewing: The TEDx video, *Context is Everything*, is a discussion of the impact of context in the field of medicine by Kerry Harling. Available at https://www.youtube.com/watch?v=wSV_YbUWQMk (16 min.).

ARC 13: ANIMATION
FROM OPPOSITION/CONFRONTATION TO SYNERGY

opposition/confrontation: hostile action or argument; an adversarial encounter. Other terms for opposition/confrontation: conflict, combat, challenge, resistance, antagonism, dissent, disapproval, criticism, defiance, obstruction, competition.

synergy: the uplifting energy present when individual components coalesce in a co-creative effort, producing an outcome that none could produce alone. Synergy permits separate parts to function as an integral, aggregate, whole system, although this is not a predictable attribute of their separate state.[1] Other terms for synergy: collaboration, teamwork, cooperation, co-creativity.

A PILLAR OF THE PUNITIVE SYSTEM IS OPPOSITION AND CONFRONTATION

Opposition and confrontation are an integral part of what happens in both civil and criminal courts in the U.S. Our courts are designed to be adversarial. In law school I was taught the theory that justifies this design: the truth is found through opposition and confrontation as a means of testing the truth of the witnesses. I find this theory to be unfounded—an adversarial environment too frequently brings self-interest and fear to the fore at the expense of the truth.

In both civil and criminal cases, this adversarial process involves each side presenting their evidence and each opponent having a right to challenge the truth and the relevance of that evidence. This includes the right to cross-examine the witnesses offered by the other side. Cross-examination can be traumatizing, especially when the stakes are high or when the questioning by the adverse attorney is brutal. Fear of facing "disclosure of their intimate, private life through requests for the contents of their phones and laptops" by the defendant's attorney reportedly deters half of all rape victims from pursuing criminal charges against the person who assaulted them.[2]

In the court process, the interest of each side is pitted against the other. Renowned 7th Circuit Judge Richard Posner contends that *the adver-*

sarial system does not work specifically because the lawyer's job is to press the client's case zealously, *not* to help find the truth.[3] These are not unified goals.

The adversaries also get to argue how the law applies to their version of the facts. However, case law supporting both sides often exists. The judge decides which law applies to which facts, a decision that may be influenced by the judge's bias. An imaginative judge can find some version of the law to justify even an unjust decision.

This happened to a client whose prior attorney had sex with her in his conference room the night before they appeared in federal court for the pre-trial conference in a case involving sexual harassment at work. She had been in the care of a therapist since long before this sexual event, making a defense of consent to this intimacy questionable, at best. Under the rules of evidence at the time, her past history of sexual activity, right up to the time she would testify at the sexual harassment trial, would be relevant evidence in the employment case, so the sexual encounter with her attorney was discoverable evidence (no attorney-client privilege for this). The next day, after having sex with her, the attorney pressured her to settle her case. This precluded her sexual history, including with her attorney, from being a subject of interrogation.

Based on these facts, I later represented the client in a suit for attorney malpractice against the offending attorney. Early in the case, the judge opined about his fear that if this woman prevailed against her attorney, many women would wrongfully charge their attorneys of having sex with them. When the judge issued his final judgment in the case, he ruled that sex with a client could not constitute attorney malpractice because when an attorney is having sex with his client, he is not practicing law! In his decision, the judge found a way to preclude any woman from winning a malpractice suit in these circumstances. An appeal to the Virginia Supreme Court upheld the trial court's ruling. In contrast, it is malpractice in Virginia for doctors to have sex with their patients.

Judge Posner points out that written laws rarely give precise direction about how a case should be decided,

> ... so judges 'fall back on their priors—the impulses, dispositions, attitudes, beliefs, and so on that they bring to a case,' before they look at the facts and at the law to be applied—and then use lingo

to obscure their actual grounds for deciding.[4]

Indeed, this is often the case. While we would like to think that the law is precise, there is tremen-dous leeway to go one way or another. Take the burden of proof, for example. In criminal cases, the government seeks to prove beyond a reasonable doubt (no room for doubt) that the accused is guilty as charged, while the accused seeks to show that there is at least some doubt regarding guilt. In civil cases, the adversaries are private parties seeking to prove their case, and there is a lower standard of proof—the plaintiff need only prevail by a preponderance of the evidence (at least 51%). In fact, both beyond a reasonable doubt and a preponderance of the evidence are imprecise measures, often decided by the imprecise process of opposition and confrontation and which side tells the more compelling story.

Because a criminal defendant faces the might of the state in the courtroom contest, criminal defendants have a right to an attorney protected by the U.S. Constitution.[5] In theory, if a criminal defendant faces incarceration and cannot them self afford an attorney, the government must provide legal representation at the public's expense. Guaranteeing there is an attorney for both sides means opposition and confrontation will be front and center in the trial. Without this confrontation, the system fails to provide even a semblance of due process or justice. Of course, they never get to the underlying causes.

The adversarial system that fails to recognize and address underlying causes is not limited to the legal system. It can also be the norm in other institutions—schools, businesses, churches, and families. Judge Posner's assessment that *the adversarial system does not work* is equally applicable whenever a punitive process is used to address conflict.

We can do better. Implementing the structures of Unitive Justice enables us to create a system that removes the need for opposition or confrontation.

THE UNITIVE SYSTEM IS SYNERGISTIC

Synergy is a special type of energy—an upward spiral of collective energy. It is positive and uplifting, present when creative work is being done. Connection, trust, lovingkindness and Unity are among the necessary ingredients for synergy to emerge. People working together in an integrated group achieve what none of them could produce, or perhaps even imagine, alone. Synergy is possible because of our interconnectedness. Synergy is not possible in an environment where opposition and confrontation are present.

We are capable of believing that we are separate and disconnected. We are also capable of believing that we are connected, interdependent, united in one purpose, and that each of us is equally essential to the mission. In a synergistic environment, breakdowns may still occur, but they will not result in one side being pitted against the other. Breakdowns, mistakes, and even conflict, are opportunities to find the places in need of healing.

As we create parallel, locally-initiated, unitive systems that embrace the Arcs to Unitive Justice as their blueprint for system change, synergy will naturally emerge. Synergy provides the flow that carries the mission forward and makes the whole greater than the sum of its parts.

* * *

Invitation to Journal. Consider these questions:

a. Do you work or live in an environment that is synergistic? If so, how did it become synergistic?
b. At this point in the book, how do you define justice?
c. How does this differ from your definition when you began reading this book?
d. What would you like our system of justice to achieve and how would you like it to operate?
e. What can you do to move this shift forward?

Suggested Viewing: In the video, *We Need to Talk About an Injustice*, Bryan Stevenson describes some of the injustices that arise in our adversarial justice system. Stevenson is the Executive Director of the Equal Justice Initiative (EJI). Available at https://www.youtube.com/watch?v=c2tOp7OxyQ8. (24 min.).

ARC 14: ENERGY/SPIRIT
FROM FEAR TO LOVE

fear: the negative emotion caused by the perpetual feeling of danger. Fear is heightened by the belief in separation and seeing the world divided between good and evil, us versus them. To the fearful mind, Love can seem inaccessible and idealistic. Other terms for fear: terror, fright, trepidation, panic, anxiety, angst, alarm, dread.

Love: the act of extending the vibration of positive, integrative energy. The more one extends the vibration of Love, the more one experiences the integrative nature of Love. To the loving mind, fear does not exist; the feeling of fear is recognized as the effect of separation. While we may experience fear, Love is our inherent nature. Other terms for Love: deep connection, devotion, profound fondness, heartfelt friendship, rapture.

NOTE ON FEAR AND LOVE

Within the "reality" of duality, actions flow in one direction—toward disconnection and fear that leads to harm and violence. Fear fuels a downward spiral. Within the reality of Unity, Love is present and actions flow toward connection, leading to healing and harmony. Love creates an upward spiral.

There are fundamentally two basic emotions: fear and Love. Punitive justice is grounded in fear, and Unitive justice is grounded in Love. Where Love is, fear is not—this is an ancient teaching.[1] These two emotions are the root of all other negative and positive emotions; both Love and fear are expressed in various ways.

The following are examples of how we express fear:

Revenge: the self-centered thinking that harming another will benefit oneself.
Hate: the self-centered thinking that the perceived differences between oneself and another make them despicable.
Greed: the self-centered thinking that there is never enough for oneself, so the craving for more is endless.

Jealousy: the self-centered thinking that one's self is diminished by the positive attributes of another or by what they have.

Here are some examples of how we express Love for one another.

Joy: the extension of Love and joy for another's breakthroughs and wellbeing or one's own breakthroughs and wellbeing.
Generosity: the extension of Love knowing that what is given with Love is not lost; it propagates within one's self and is always returned in some form.
Kindness: the extension of Love, good will and benevolence to another, while expecting no material gain.

Fear and Love are emotions, but they also impact our physical being. At the cellular level, fear signals to the cells that they must switch to protection mode, a state that precludes growth while survival is the focus. If this state exists for more than brief periods, the cells cease to grow or regenerate. When it occurs as a long-term strategy, this negative energy causes systemic breakdown that eventually manifests as disease of one sort or another.[2]

At the cellular level, the energy of Love signals to the cells that the environment is safe. This permits the cells to function in growth mode. Good health is maintained by the cells' continued growth and regeneration in this positive energy field. The wellness of individual cells is reflected in the wellbeing of the whole.[3]

FEAR FUELS PUNITIVE JUSTICE

In the fragmentation of duality consciousness, fear is inevitable. Each structure of a punitive system—control, judgment, deception, self-interest, hierarchy, punishment, confrontation, proportional revenge, etc.—is relied upon in an endless quest to address fear. The illusion that cause and effect are linear makes it seem reasonable to inflict punishment to secure compliance in order to feel secure and escape fear. In fact, using fear to undo fear is futile—the outcome always mirrors the means used to get there.

Moreover, because the experience of fear is felt in the body, it is easy to confuse this emotion with the body itself. To the fearful mind, attacking the source of fear is seen as necessary to protect the body. The only issue is whether to attack now or later, as the lack of action is seen as passivity, apathy, or cowardice. To actually forgive is misinterpreted as being weak, so the idea of forgiveness generates more anxiety.

We might seek physical remedies for our fear—food, drugs, weapons, punishment, armies, prisons and jails—but at best, they only mask the feeling and perhaps make it more tolerable. *Fear is a mental state*, not a physical one, so it cannot be healed on a physical level with medication or other physical means. Healing must occur on the level of the problem—the mind. It is Love that ends fear. But when we live in a state of fear, we cannot imagine the power of Love. In fear, "love" is conditional, given and withheld at will.

Fear is a state of believing we are subject to external conditions over which we have little or no control. In fact, it is thought that creates form; it is our fearful thoughts that give rise to a fearful world. We enslave ourselves while we, nonetheless, accept no responsibility for our condition. To maintain the illusions that sustain fear, we must avoid discovering the truth about ourselves or the truth about those whom we call our enemies. When we get to the truth, we find that we exist within our shared humanity—it is this truth that dispels our fear.

In our need for self-defense against what we fear, we answer harm with more harm, making the harm endless. We can see fear reflected in many of our public policies.

A tragic example of how fear played out on the world stage is the Treaty of Versailles at the end of WW I. Ignoring the complexity of human relations, this treaty reflected a "good versus evil" worldview. The treaty punished Germany, seen as evil, even though it had adopted democracy after the war, evidence of a desire for system change. Germany was forced to pay reparations to the "good" people for damage Germany caused them during the war. The treaty forbade Germany to have a military and paved the way for later French occupation of a portion of its land. The terms of the Treaty were grounded in vengeance, retribution and fear.

Implementing a policy that sought revenge further weakened Germany, demeaned the Germans and set the stage for WWII. The revenge of the WWI victors gave Hitler the platform he needed to use fear and hatred to mobilize Germans to seek their own retribution and conquest. Each side saw themselves as self-righteously justified in attacking the other. Unwittingly, the fearful thinking after WW I set the stage for the devastation of WWII. This was predictable—thought creates form. Frightened minds can only think of revenge and attack, all the while expecting the result to be compliance and peace.

Fortunately, the Allied nations did not make the same mistake at the end of WWII. I previously mentioned the Marshall Plan created by the U.S. after the war. Instead of retribution, the U.S. provided aid to rebuild the allied nations of Europe, but the *aid was extended to friend and foe alike*. Germany and Japan, both former enemies, received aid, as well. This policy sought to heal all of the war-torn nations, including those that had done their best to defeat us. These policies created strong allies and an enduring era of peace with Germany, Japan, and much of the world. William Wohlforth, an international relations expert at Dartmouth College, noted, "We can't find another period with a shift in conflict trends that compares,"[4]—a beautiful example of how Love conquers fear.

Unfortunately, the leaders of the Eastern Bloc nations dominated by the Soviet Union chose not to participate in the peace plan. How much better it would have been for their people (and their place in history) if they had.

Nineteen years after the end of WWII, I spent my sophomore year of college in Paris, France. During Easter break, my classmates and I flew into West Berlin, an isolated enclave under American, British and French control surrounded by communist territory. One day during our visit we went into East Berlin by passing through "Check Point Charlie" in the newly-built Berlin wall, a barrier designed to stop the thousands of East Berliners who were escaping into West Berlin. The East Berlin guards counted how much money we had on us as we entered. This soviet sector of Berlin showed the strains on the East German economy from the heavy war reparations being extracted by the Soviet Union.

As we walked the streets, we saw people who were terrified of their own government. There were still bullet holes in the walls of many buildings. A classmate and I had lunch in a restaurant and the fear was palpable. The waiter gave us a paper receipt for the cost of our meal. He didn't speak English, but he made it clear that we had to have it when we exited East Berlin so we could account for why we had less money than when we entered, and to prove we had not given cash to a citizen of East Berlin.

In contrast, by then most of Western Europe was rebuilt, its people were free and Americans were admired. Several French people told me that Americans are naïve, but they are good, honorable people to whom the people of Europe extended much gratitude. I was proud to be a citizen of a nation that, in such a significant moment in world history, was recognized for the courage, integrity and generosity of its people.

I was sorrowful when I learned of the U.S. soldiers who committed hideous acts of torture and abuse of the prisoners under their control at Iraq's Abu Ghraib prison in 2004. I knew the sacrifice of many Americans during WWII that earned the respect and love of people around the world was cast aside, tarnished and trampled on. The Marshall Plan versus Abu Ghraib—what more precise demonstration of the differences between justice based on lovingkindness and justice based on vengeance can one nation give the world?

We have not put an end to the forces out of which war emerges. After a period of being the world's lone superpower and a fairly reliable model for democratic values, the U.S. slid back into a retributive mode with two failed wars in Iraq and Afghanistan. When President George W. Bush launched the war in Iraq, there were reports of White House staff talking of how the U.S. was the "new Rome," a prophetic prediction, but not in the way they intended.

While this was happening, Russia and China became more formidable powers by taking punitive means to greater extremes. The time will come when their fear-based house of cards will fall, but how or when is far from known. What we can do now is have a serious conversation about what America's norms and values will be going forward—the world's future depends on it.

What can we learn from these decades of experience with fear and Love? When people's minds are full of fear, they are attracted to those with authoritarian ambitions, politicians who manipulate their fear by promising to destroy first one "enemy" and then another. Fearful individuals purchase assault weapons designed for mass killing, which can now be done as easily as going to their local Walmart where assault weapons can be purchased not far from the baby diapers.

This is all the more reason to build our local systems of Unitive Justice as quickly as possible and to seek allies in doing so among our policy makers. We need laws that regulate gun possession and use for the wellbeing of all, but we can do even more. We can create a culture in which assault weapons, even if available, are not used against school children, one's fellow employees, random people at an event or anyone else. There is more reason now than ever to work for Unitive Justice.

LOVE IMBUES UNITIVE JUSTICE

Love is an unconditional, integrative force, the spiritual embrace of Oneness that is essential to Unity. Healing is Love made visible. It is the source of power, girded with wholeness, vision, and light, extending into infinity. Anything outside of Love is an illusion. Harmful acts do occur, but they are recognized as a call for Love.

Seeing a wrong as a call for Love may be a challenge for many. Thich Nhat Hanh, a Vietnamese Buddhist monk and global spiritual leader, explained the logic for doing so as "Interbeing," or the interdependence of all beings. In the preface to his poem *Call Me by My True Names*, he told of a young girl who threw herself into the ocean after being raped by a pirate, then he explained why one should not be too quick to judge the pirate.[5]

> When you first learn of something like that, you get angry at the pirate. You naturally take the side of the girl. As you look more deeply you will see it differently. If you take the side of the little girl, then it is easy. You only have to take a gun and shoot the pirate. But we cannot do that. In my meditation I saw that if I had been born in the village of the pirate and raised in the same conditions as he was, there is a great likelihood that I would become a pirate. I cannot condemn myself so easily…. If you or I were born today in those fishing villages, we may become sea pirates in twenty-five years. If you take a gun and shoot the pirate, you shoot all of us, because all of us are to some extent responsible for this state of affairs.

The monk points out the need to consider context before judging.

What he suggests may be a level of accountability that many find difficult to imagine—while in duality consciousness. Seeing a wrong as a call for Love requires a shift in consciousness from duality to Unity. A first step might be to realize that vengeance and what serves our best interests are irreconcilable, contradictory goals.

As we understand that the underlying conflict dynamic encompasses us all, laying blame is replaced with addressing human needs and solving problems. Hence, the underlying dynamic becomes one that fosters healing. I concede that, when I am upset and feeling fear or anger at some harm that I just experienced, it is challenging to be in that mindset. Being hard does not make it untrue. Transcending fear and anger so I can be present to another possibility is something I seek to master.

In the abstract, the idea that we can reconcile Love with hurtful, destructive acts seems unrealistic and irrational. In a punitive system that only supports retribution and revenge, it is impossible to reconcile Love with destructive acts. And yet, when it is no longer an abstract idea but instead is a lived experience, our understanding can shift. This is yet another invaluable lesson that Taylor Paul and Prince Bunn have to teach us.

I didn't know Taylor and Prince when they were living "on the side of wrong." We met after they experienced a remarkable transformation and after they figured out how to be present to Unity. In their previous lives, they sank to the lowest depths, but through courage, insight, commitment and so much more, they became amazing human beings, men I would trust with my life.

This is the irony of their transformation—had they not gone to the depths of their prior life, it is unlikely they would have achieved the level of transformation they now model for the rest of us! It is their lived experience of crime in the past that now makes them such compelling messengers for Justice as Love. They are touching the lives of many people. Unitive Consciousness seems to be filled with such ironies, what we might call "miracles." In Unitive Consciousness, they are normal.

Taylor and Prince now say that everyday their actions are motivated by their commitment to make amends for what they did, to earn forgiveness for the loss of life that they caused. Their present work is how they honor those lost lives and the members of their victims' families. They created a training program for incarcerated men and women called

Unitive Prison Culture Change. It has the potential of changing how our penal institutions operate and touch the lives of many people, both in and out of prison. And this is just one thing they are doing to make the world a better place.

It is hard for me to condemn Taylor and Prince for their prior acts when those acts became the genesis of lovingkindness on a level beyond what many of us experience. If it is possible to earn forgiveness, in my estimation they have done so. I realize that this turns everything we are taught about retribution and revenge upside down, but I know this new learning to be more true than those old lessons. In the midst of sorrowful loss, being present to Love is a regenerative energy that can be harnessed for good. This brings to mind the mythical phoenix bird rising from the ashes as a symbol of resurrection after loss; she resurrects more beautifully than before.

As humans, we can exercise free will. We can choose to sin—sin (*hamartia* in Greek) means to miss the mark and wander from the path of honor. Everyone at times misses the mark. In the consciousness of Love, the shift to seeing a wrong as a cry for Love results in us giving the Love that is sought.

Suppose we offer an opportunity for those who cause harm to choose a path of transformation and we support them in that choice—while they are incarcerated. This is what the Unitive Prison Culture Change training for jails and prisons is designed to do. (*See* www.unitiveprisons.com.) In that case, we are giving the Love they seek and we will reap the reward many times over, without jeopardizing our own safety.

Instead of the mental slavery that fear fosters, Love offers freedom. Recognizing I am the creator of the life I experience, I am free to exercise my power to liberate myself. When I hold thoughts tied to strong emotions, Love or fear, they are like seeds and will bear a harvest that reflects their inherent nature. In negative thought (fear), I am my jailer; in positive thought (Love), I am my liberator. As I determine what thoughts I will hold, no one can set me free but me. This is the gift of the creative power that is an aspect of our shared humanity, a gift given to each of us to pass on to others. This is not altruism. It is a new form of self-interest —what is good for oneself *and* others is good for all of us.

Perhaps we will only see glimmers of this possibility during our lifetime. Still, we can plant the seeds through Unitive Justice and by creating

Unitive Communities that consciously seek to live by one standard of morality—do unto others as you would have them do unto you, and other similar spiritual teachings. We transition from fear to Love by letting go of the voice of fear, not by fighting it. As Love is extended to one individual at a time, over and over, it grows until a positive, exponential change is achieved. So be it!

EXPERIENCING UNITIVE JUSTICE IN A UNITIVE JUSTICE CIRCLE PROCESS

I found it difficult to imagine replacing the punitive system with Unitive Justice until I experienced the difference. With that experience, I know there is only one choice: Justice as Love.

There are many varieties of circle processes, but I have only found one that provides an opportunity to experience Unitive Justice on a reasonably regular basis. This is the facilitated Restorative Circle process for addressing conflict taught by Dominic Barter. (More information about this process is at www.RestorativeCicles.org.)

When we teach how to facilitate Barter's circle process in combination with Unitive Justice theory, the two align in a way that seems to deepen one's understanding of how justice and Love are interrelated. To denote the difference that arises when the two are taught together, we call these circles "Unitive Justice Circles."[6] I have already described the outcomes of several of these circles. This is how the circle process unfolds.

A Unitive Justice Circle begins with one identified event that resulted in harm. If the parties have a long-term relationship, they may have many harmful acts to choose from, but the circle facilitator helps identify just one that is presently "alive" for those involved. This event is not used to prosecute and punish, as in the punitive process, but as a portal to access the underlying brokenness out of which this harmful event arose so that the parties to the conflict can address it.

Reflective listening is used to ensure that those who speak are accurately heard and those listening understand what the speaker said. This is the pattern of the conversation:

Circle facilitator to Participant 1: "*What do you want known about how you are now with the event and its consequences?*"
When Participant 1 answers, the facilitator asks Participant 2: "*What did you hear him say?*"
When Participant 2 reflects back to Participant 1 what was heard, the facilitator asks Participant 1: "*Is that what you wanted her to hear?*" This continues repeatedly as the questions go deeper, and until each person who speaks is accurately heard. Repetition and consistency are important elements in creating a safe environment.

STAGE ONE OF THE CIRCLE PROCESS: ACHIEVING MUTUAL UNDERSTANDING

Stage one of the circle process seeks to achieve mutual understanding. Participants come to understand why others saw things as they did and how they see them now. This stage explores the "out there" aspect of the conflict (what happened and why). The consistent and repetitive process of asking and answering questions as described above is changing the participants' thinking. They are beginning to dissolve the beliefs they hold about the other that give rise to fear and separation.

On a deeper level, the consistency and repetition of the questions is helping the participants move from the lower brain where fear and the desire for retribution are active, to the cortex where executive function lives in our brain.[7] This paves the way for stage two of the circle.

STAGE TWO OF THE CIRCLE PROCESS: SHARED POWER AND CONNECTION

We describe stage two as where our shared power and connection tend to emerge. The objective is for each participant to recognize where they stand in the larger conflict dynamic—how their participation, directly or indirectly, and their reaction to the conflict are part of the larger whole. As mutual understanding gives rise to appreciation, appreciation tends to give rise to a sense of connection.

This is the stage where self-responsibility comes into play. As the circle participants realize how they used their agency and sought to exercise control, they tend to see what they did failed to serve them well. This opens the possibility of seeing how each participant might choose differently as they go forward. This arises, not by being judged by others, but by each individual discerning their own responsibility introspectively.

The second stage of the circle process can also give rise to a moment of transformation, a significant shift that occurs when participants recognize their shared humanity—they connect at a level beyond their differences. When they genuinely connect at this level, any desire for retribution or revenge disappears. They do not want to harm someone with whom they have this level of connection. Even when they do not experience their shared humanity, healing often occurs.

The one who directly caused the harm tends to reach the point of self-responsibility with the realization that their choices have an impact and that they do have agency. This might come with the concurrent realization that causing harm does not serve one's own interests. The logic that guided the decision to cause harm no longer makes sense. They may realize this is not how they want to show up.

The circle process also gives the person who experienced the harm an opportunity to access healing. In addition to processing in a positive way some of the fear they retain from the event, the circle is an opportunity for the one harmed to consider how they responded or reacted to the harm. This can provide a window into a past wound that continues to distort their experience of life, or perhaps an unmet need that they realize can now be met. This evolution in thinking can help dissolve some of the thought forms that keep the conflict alive.

In some cases, the one harmed might see how the harm to them arose out of a larger systemic pattern that impacts many people. They may be empowered to bring attention to this systemic harm using what happened to them as an example of why systemic change is needed. As I previously described, I saw this happen when I was trying child sexual abuse cases. The opportunity to be truthful in public about what happened was empowering. Sharing their poignant personal experiences led to the reform of Virginia's laws[8] relating to the statute of limitations for cases of child sexual abuse and removed one hurdle to seeking redress.

In addition to the person who caused harm and the one harmed finding healing in a circle process, community members may experience healing, as well. Those who are indirectly involved in the event may discover their self-responsibility when the context is considered and the underlying brokenness is discovered. They might recognize some way that each of them contributed to the underlying brokenness out of which the harmful event arose, perhaps through inaction or lack of concern for others, even putting their self-interest first.

The second stage of the circle is when participants might consider what they can do differently to avoid this outcome in the future for themselves and others. This may include relinquishing the belief that it is not their problem and that it does not affect them—realizing that we are all connected. As concrete steps are identified that each participant may undertake, it tends to result in increased social safety and wellbeing[9] among participants, and perhaps the larger community, as well.

THE THIRD STAGE OF THE CIRCLE PROCESS: MUTUALLY BENEFICIAL ACTION

The third stage of the circle process, called "mutually beneficial action," is when giving and receiving begin to flow between and among those in the conflict. When we seek only to address the harm done by the "offender" we are locked in the past. How the past might be healed is never asked in the punitive process and we lose the opportunity to achieve this deeper and broader healing.

The third stage of the circle is when those impacted, directly and indirectly, come to an agreement about how they can go forward together. With real healing, they see the past differently and can now join in unified goals. This may lead to a return to balance that was lost at some earlier point, perhaps long ago. With real healing, we can make the present and the future different from the past.

John Lash, the Executive Director of the Georgia Conflict Center, describes his experience of engaging with conflict instead of running from it, as occurs in Barter's circle process, as follows:

> First, it depersonalizes whatever unpleasantness I am experiencing. I can view conflict as not so much about me as about the way that I am in relation to the rest of the system. I can try to discern what the feedback is telling me and make an appropriate adjust-

ment or series of adjustments. [Second], it enables me to approach the conflict with curiosity instead of anger or fear. This is known in academic circles as a 'positive orientation to conflict' and points to the idea that conflicts are actually opportunities.[10]

The benefits of the circle process do not end when the circle ends. After seeing how the simple questions asked in the circle work and being guided in using reflective listening, participants are often able to use these techniques on their own. A number of my students who learned this process reported that when a conflict arose with their mother or a friend, they could now resolve it on their own. Instead of responding defensively to an accusation, they simply asked, "What do you want me to know about this?" When the person replied, the student reflected back what they heard and asked if that was what the one who accused them wanted them to hear. Some students reported, "We had one of our best conversations ever." Using this process enabled them to hear one another at a deeper level and to connect. Having the tools to address one's own conflict is empowering.

In the Restorative Justice program based on Unitive Justice principles implemented at Armstrong High School in Richmond, Virginia, students and staff who experienced this circle process when conflicts arose shared the following experiences with a researcher.[11]

> "I noticed that some fights, some arguments, some fights get talked out more, instead of just suspension, instead of just suspending somebody from school, where they get away from their education for like five days, they don't learn nothing for that whole five days. Instead of doing that [suspensions] you could do a circle and they do the circle they sign the paper, then they go to class, and they become friends again, or they leave each other alone." −11th grade female

> "Me and my friend were playing around in class, and we actually solved [a conflict using] the Circle. It was fun, but it was serious too, and we did it all by ourself. Cause my friend that used to be in the facilitator circle training, me and her we was just playing at first but my other friend, the girl I'll call my friend and the girl I'll

call my sister, they was arguing about something or whatever. So me and X said, 'let's have a circle,' and then we was playing—we was playing though, and then it actually solved their problem. Now, they talk. So we actually did a Circle, all by ourselves."
—12th grade female

"It's just really been helpful for me with my friends and things. Like, recently I had a problem with my friends and I just pulled it to the side, I was like, 'why this, why that, how come this going on?'" —9th grade male

"I've only participated in one circle, and it was arguably the most revolutionary thing I've ever seen. I mean these girls couldn't walk within 50 feet of each other without, 'I can't believe she's, you know, and then, now, they talk, they say 'hi' to each other. I mean, they literally would walk down the hall and 'I'm gonna hit her, I'm gonna you know,' and it was just a complete turn around [after the Circle]. I think the Circle gave them an opportunity to voice their opinion, and then the other heard and voiced their opinion. Then they came to this epiphany that they're actually more alike than they are different." —School Counselor

How did the availability of these circle processes impact the larger school community? Evidence may be found in the Safe Schools Information available on the Virginia Department of Education website. While this information does not indicate the cause of the reduction, reports for the decade 2010–2020 (the year before the Armstrong program began through seven years after) uniformly indicate that *the lowest number of incidents at Armstrong were reported during 2012-2013*. (See the graph on the next page.) That was the second year and last year of our Restorative Justice Program at Armstrong. These results are consistent with the testimonials cited above.

Armstrong High School
No. of Incidents Per Year

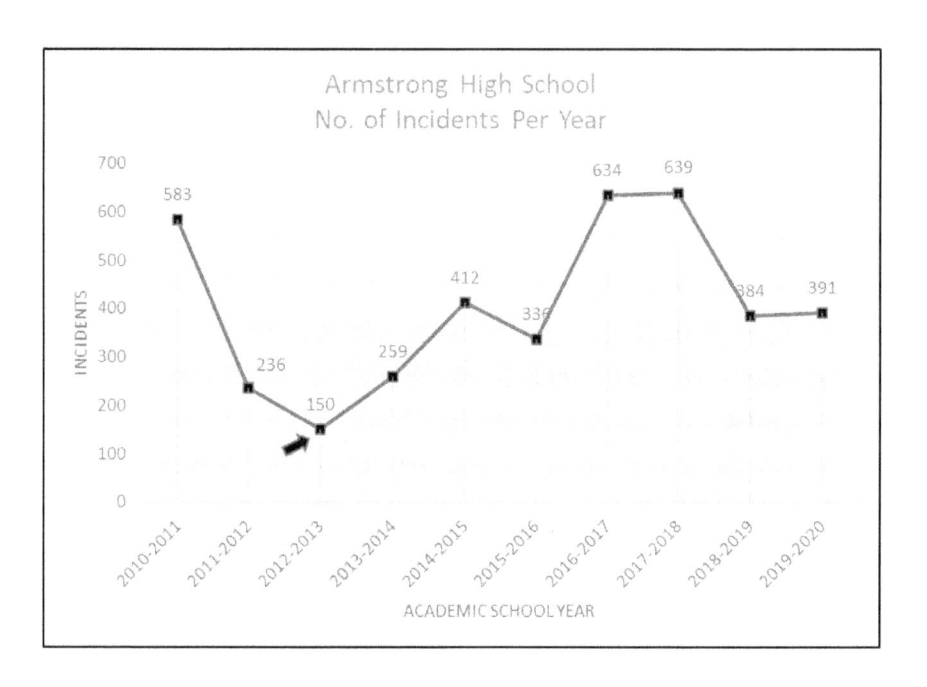

Academic School Year	Incidents
2010-2011	583
2011-2012	236
2012-2013	150
2013-2014	259
2014-2015	412
2015-2016	336
2016-2017	634
2017-2018	639
2018-2019	384
2019-2020	391

Even though we are talking about major systemic change, it is not necessary to fight the existing system. Instead, as Unitive Justice Circles are offered and a new system begins to emerge, people come to see its benefits and are drawn to it. With time, the result is fewer conflicts, more students in class instead of being suspended, and fewer are arrested and in jail.

As Unitive Justice Circles usually involve relatively few people, their organized use will often happen in a defined community that has adopted this process as its means of addressing conflicts, such as a school, church, business, prison, detention center, neighborhood, or even a city. This approach is growing, but admittedly, it may be our children or grandchildren who finally enjoy the benefit of a widespread application of Unitive Justice principles—if we begin to create those systems where and when an opening arises.

As you journey into this new paradigm, perhaps you will have the opportunity to attend Unitive Justice training that makes experiential learning more easily accessible. Please visit the Alliance for Unitive Justice website at www.a4uj.org for more information about training opportunities. By joining the AUJ group, UJ Accelerators, you may also connect with others who are now implementing Unitive Justice in their location.

* * *

Invitation to Journal. Consider these questions:

a. How do you feel about responding to the commission of a crime as a cry for Love?
b. If this seems like a reasonable concept, how might you overcome any conditioning or reflex that you have to respond to harm with judgment and retribution?
c. Think of a time when you harmed someone. Can you think of any way that your harmful act was a cry for Love on your part?
d. Think of a time when someone harmed you. Can you think of any way their harmful act was a cry for Love on their part?
e. If at some time in the future we are to treat a crime, such as robbery, as a cry for Love, how might we create a policy response to the crime that also addresses the needs of the person who was robbed?

Suggested Viewing: If you have the time, a relevant video is *Bruce Lipton - Fear vs Love State and Stress's Effect on Your Body*, available at https://www.youtube.com/watch?v=Nro0wlXIwd4 (51.38 min.). The books of Bruce Lipton were among the sources from which I learned in the early days of this journey.

CHAPTER TEN
NEW INFORMATION THAT COMPELS SYSTEM CHANGE

Sometimes we are confronted with information so compelling that it cannot be ignored. We now have scientific research that brings into question the reasoning behind public policies involving crime and violence, whether it is committed by youth or adults. It raises important questions about what we consider to be good practices.

When an eye-for-an-eye justice was codified in the Code of Hammurabi 1700 years before the common era, modern science was in the distant future. What the new science teaches us about human thinking and how the mind works undermines the notion that punishment is a good way to address conflict or achieve compliance. I will highlight two areas of modern research that we find especially useful in our Unitive Justice training, but there is now a lot of research that confirms these findings.

OUR MENTAL STATE DICTATES BEHAVIOR

I begin with the research of Dr. Bruce Perry, MD, a psychiatrist who has worked with trauma-impacted children who experienced the Branch Davidian Compound siege in Waco, the Oklahoma bombing, Sandy Hook, and other horrific situations. His research has led to the Neurosequential Model that gives a graphic illustration and description of what happens in our brains when any outside stimuli occurs.[1]

Every stimulus that our body processes starts in the brain stem where our "automatic" responses occur, such as breathing, heart beating, etc. This is also where the fight or flight response is triggered. The information then travels up to the midbrain that controls appetite/satiety, sleep/wake, arousal/attention, and motor regulation. The next stop is the limbic system which controls memory, pleasure/reward, sexual behavior, attachment and bonding, and emotional reactivity. People whose thinking processes are operating in the brainstem, midbrain, or limbic parts of the brain are not functioning from the reasoning center of their brain, the cortex.[2] These lower parts of the brain are no doubt where a lot of duality thinking occurs.

The Path to Cognitive Thinking

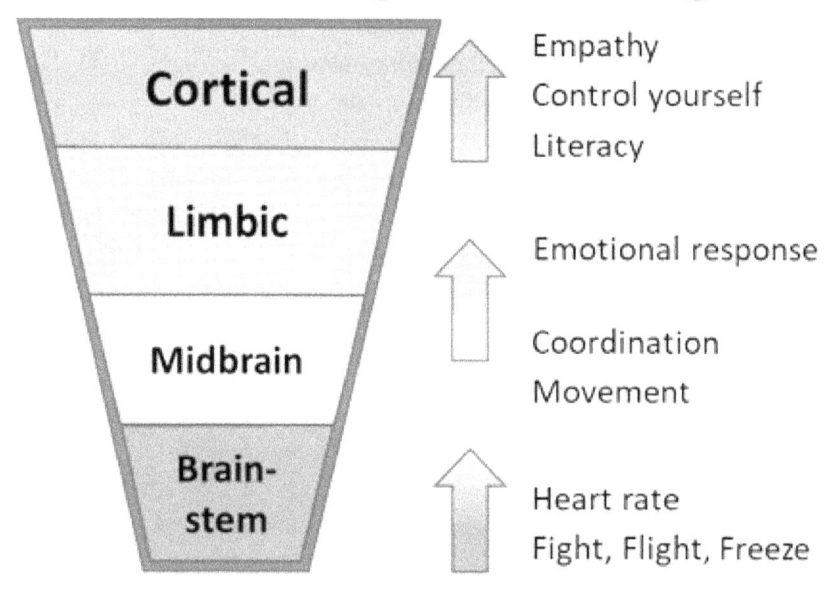

Cortical	⬆	Empathy Control yourself Literacy
Limbic	⬆	Emotional response
Midbrain	⬆	Coordination Movement
Brain-stem	⬆	Heart rate Fight, Flight, Freeze

The cortex is the last area of the brain impacted by thoughts, events, and other stimuli, and where the executive function occurs. Our creativity, sense of time/past and future, speech and language, hopes, aspirations, planning and thinking, and values and belief systems come from the cortex. *Learning and creativity occur in this part of the brain.*[3] The cortex is also where we absorb the accumulated and distilled experiences of thousands of previous generations,[4] hidden determinants from the past.

These mental processes happen in an instant. Which part of the brain responds to a stimulus depends on the mental state of the individual at that moment. Because toxic stress shuts down the cortex, people who suffer from toxic stress may react to events in irrational ways. Their responses do not come from the reasoning center of their brain. Their response might be hyperarousal, increased vigilance, and resistance moving to defiance and then aggression. Alternatively, there may be a dissociative response that may appear as disinterest or disconnection and might show up as rocking or sitting. The response of dissociation could be as extreme as entering a "daydreamlike" state.[5] *A student who is suffering from toxic stress is incapable of learning, regardless of how skilled or experienced the teacher may be.* This also raises a critical question about how consideration of toxic stress should be reflected in our criminal law policies?

While different types of stress may affect cognitive processing, healing from trauma does not require eliminating all stress. A tolerable level of stress can support emotional growth and the processing of events in a healthy way, but this will not happen overnight. In an educational setting, if a student experiences a traumatic event, the teacher may be the person who has the first opportunity to establish a sense of safety, a normal routine and the ability to access the cortex. This sense of safety is achieved through consistency, routine and familiarity, conditions that create a "therapeutic web" that is the key to dealing with any traumatic event.[6] These are the conditions that Unitive Justice Circles tend to provide and help explain how they support the healing process. How can these conditions be made a part of our response to reports of crime?

Dr. Perry teaches us that students who suffer from toxic stress need to learn to trust before they can change. This is a time consuming process and cannot be hurried.[7] When a child misbehaves, the disruptive behavior needs to be addressed, but a more effective way may be crouching down to the student's level and speaking softly but firmly about the behavior. Approaching the child in a way that triggers or exacerbates a fight or flight response is counterproductive. The goal is to make the child feel safe and better able to cope with the stressful situation.

How should we respond to adults who are being disruptive or violent? If the subject's behavior comes from the brainstem, midbrain or limbic part of the brain, applying more force may make things worse. If they are not operating from their cortex, aggression on the part of law enforcement is likely to exacerbate the situation. It might be that when the police confront the violator, they may also shift into their lower brain functioning, then the confrontation could come down to brute force.

This new understanding must be considered in our approach to adults and youth who commit crime and who react in irrational ways. How do we incorporate these scientific findings into our criminal law theory?

PUNISHMENT IS YET ANOTHER ADVERSE CHILDHOOD EXPERIENCE

Our beliefs about punishment have deep roots. Punishment is embedded in beliefs about how to discipline children, how punishment makes them good people, and how we teach them that it is the adults who are in control. Most of us believe it is ethical and reasonable to punish a child who commits a wrong, so long as the punishment is in proportion to the misconduct being punished. Who decides how much? The punishment might range from sitting in a corner to a severe whipping, depending on the state of mind of the adult administering the punishment. The expected outcome is compliance, but we know the response to punishment is often noncompliance and recidivism.

Without critical analysis, we continue to plant the belief that punishment is justice in the minds of our children from one generation to the next. Research now tells us that what is learned from punishment in childhood is not as linear—punishment to compliance—as we may believe. Punishment may be just one more traumatic, adverse childhood experience to be endured using whatever coping strategies the child can muster.

The second area of research that I address involves Adverse Childhood Experiences (ACEs). These are traumatic events that occur in childhood that can have an immediate and lifelong impact. What we now know about ACEs demands a new assessment of the relationship between justice and punishment.[8] We know that punishment, the foundation of punitive justice, often fails to produce the intended results. ACEs may help us understand why this is the case. The Adverse Childhood Experiences Study (ACE Study) is a research project conducted by the American health maintenance organization Kaiser Permanente and the Centers for Disease Control and Prevention.

The project's original intent was to study obesity, but the researchers found a link to childhood trauma. In the 1980s, the dropout rate of participants at Kaiser Permanente's obesity clinic in San Diego, California, was about 50%, even though all of the dropouts successfully lost weight while in the program. Interviews with people who had left the program showed that a majority of the 286 people interviewed had experienced childhood sexual abuse. The interview findings suggested to the researchers that weight gain might be a coping mechanism for depression, anxiety and fear.

The research continued until the childhood trauma experiences of over 17,000 Kaiser Permanente patient volunteers were surveyed. About half were female; 74.8% were white; the average age was 57; 75.2% had attended college; all had jobs and good health care because they were members of the Kaiser health maintenance organization. Participants were asked about different types of childhood trauma, including:

1. physical abuse
2. sexual abuse
3. emotional abuse
4. exposure to domestic violence
5. household substance abuse
6. household mental illness
7. parental separation or divorce
8. incarcerated household member
9. physical neglect
10. emotional neglect

Additional research indicates that food insecurity should be added to this list.[9]

This study prompted additional research that raised more questions about trauma, findings that now compel us to reconsider how we use punishment in any setting. In fact, spanking may alter the child's brain response in ways that are similar to severe maltreatment, potentially impacting brain development, changing biology, and leading to lasting consequences. Recent research shows that spanking a child may be just one more traumatic event on top of many others. [10]

This research indicates that spanking preschool and school-age children can cause them to be more likely to develop anxiety and depression disorders or have more difficulties engaging positively in schools and acquiring skills of regulation. This makes them less likely to be successful in educational settings.

The stress from trauma doesn't magically disappear. If it is ignored or not effectively processed, it is either somaticized (shows up as physical symptoms or disease—such as obesity) or it is acted out in destructive ways. Other than the mitigating factors considered in the penalty stage of potential death sentence cases, the punitive justice system has *no* tools for processing trauma—indeed, punishment can, in some cases, cause trauma or be re-traumatizing.

We now know that punishment can be yet another traumatic event. This fact makes the argument for Unitive Justice system change even more urgent than before. We now know that security is a keystone of trauma resiliency and healing. The structures of Unitive Justice create an environment that provides safety for everyone. Unitive Justice offers spaces where it is safe to be honest and vulnerable so insight and mutual understanding are achieved and trust is strengthened. This helps heal past wounds and diminishes the effects of trauma. Unitive Justice does not reinforce negative self-perceptions or project judgment based on misperceptions, both conditions that perpetuate trauma.

Trauma-informed care—using knowledge about trauma and its manifestation to facilitate resilience and recovery—dictates that we find means other than punishment to address noncompliance, harm and violence. Unitive Justice is a model of justice with no punitive elements— just what the doctor ordered!

POSITIVE CHILDHOOD EXPERIENCES (PCES, UNITIVE JUSTICE AND HEALING

We now have decades of experience and research on Adverse Childhood Experiences. A more recent development is the new research on *Positive Childhood Experiences* (PCEs). It provides equally compelling evidence supporting Unitive Justice as a much-needed and long-overdue system change.

In a John Hopkins University study that involved over 6,000 women and men over the age of 18, it was discovered that adults who self-report more positive childhood experiences tend to have a lower likelihood of clinical depression or poor adult mental health.[11] Even if someone had a high ACE score, if they also had a relatively high PCE score, these positive factors seemed to minimize the psychological toll of ACEs.[12]

What are the PCEs that account for these positive results? Seven were identified on the PCE psychometric analysis. All questions relate to experiences before the age of 18.

1. Able to talk with my family about my feelings.
2. Felt that my family stood by me during difficult times.
3. Enjoyed participating in community traditions.
4. Felt a sense of belonging in high school.
5. Felt supported by friends.
6. Had at least two non-parent adults who took a genuine interest in me.
7. Felt safe and protected by an adult in my home.

According to the researchers, the new positive-childhood-experiences measure showed a dose-response relationship between how many positive experiences adults reported and their mental and relational health. Cumulative positive childhood experiences measure a "cumulative positive" impact in the same way adverse childhood experiences measure "cumulative risk." Simply put, more PCEs mean better mental and physical health short term and long term.

The PCEs research indicates that children and adults can thrive despite an accumulation of negative childhood experiences *if* they also had positive childhood experiences.[13] This indicates a two-pronged approach is needed:

1. Boost positive childhood experiences.
2. Reduce adverse childhood experiences.[14]

The research found that it is common for people reporting fewer ACEs to still have poorer mental and relational health outcomes if they did not also report having had positive childhood experiences.[15] It appears that positive childhood experiences are the keystone of good mental health as adults. The structures of Unitive Justice create a culture in which positive experiences, for children and adults alike, are the norm.

Recovering from trauma and neglect is about relationships, rebuilding trust, regaining confidence, returning to a sense of security—it is about *connection*. It is imperative to develop lasting, caring relationships. For students, it can be with a bus driver, a teacher, the principal or another adult who cares,[16] as well as parents and family members. In order for a child to become kind, giving and empathetic, they need to be treated that way.[17]

Programs and resources used in schools may need to be updated to remove the punishment, deprivation, and force that traumatizes children, many of whom may already be traumatized.[18] The teacher plays a key role in setting the tone and relaying to the student that they won't be allowed to upset the others in the class, and at the same time, signifying that the student's inherent worth and dignity will not be violated. To do this, the adult must be present, fair and calm, but not afraid.[19] This conduct comes from operating in the cortex.

Dr. Perry and his colleagues have discovered ways to "normalize" the toxic stress response by using *consistent, predictable, repetitive, moderate, and controllable stressors.* We require an environment where we feel safe and in control to access the cortex. In a Unitive Justice Circle, this appears to be the internal process that permits participants to go from the goal of retribution and revenge to mutual understanding and the ability to create a mutually beneficial outcome.[20] This change in perspective can only happen when thinking moves from the lower brain to the cortex.

How do we cultivate environments that support a shift in our mental processes? Unitive Justice is one way.

* * *

Invitation to Journal. Consider these questions:

> a. Did the research on ACEs provide insight into your own past experiences? If so, what is that insight?
> b. Does Dr. Perry's research and the ACEs study change how you view punishment? If so, in what way?
> c. Will this research change how you respond to disruptive behavior? If so, in what way?

Suggested Viewing: An informative video that explains more about Adverse Childhood Experiences, called *How Childhood Trauma Affects Health Across a Lifetime,* by Nadine Burke Harris is available on YouTube.com at https://www.youtube.com/watch?v=95ovIJ3dsNk (16 min.).

On a more positive note, it is suggested that you watch the video, "Dr. Bruce Perry on How to Transform Pain Into Power." He explains how to transform the experience of post-traumatic stress into power and wisdom on the path toward healing. https://www.youtube.com/watch?v=XmQ09RkiF8o (2.16 min.).

You can get a measure of your own experience with childhood trauma by taking the ACE quiz. A user-friendly friendly and anonymous version is available on the Compassion Prison Project website at https://compassionprisonproject.org/take-the-ace-quiz/.

CHAPTER ELEVEN
UNITIVE JUSTICE AND LOVINGKINDNESS IN ACTION

This book begins with a description of the punitive legal system. In this final chapter, we consider how to apply Unitive Justice theory and practice to achieving peace in today's world. We delve into the practical implications of crossing the bridge from punitive justice to Unitive Justice.

Our justice system's problems are apparent—its track record of failure speaks for itself. However, even if you are convinced that we need justice system reform, you may still not see that Unitive Justice is the answer. Justice as Love/Unitive Justice is a foreign concept to many, and some might feel it is a far stretch. That is where I began, as well. Now I am prepared to answer the question, is Unitive Justice possible? Unitive Justice is not only achievable, it is imperative.

Think of the change required for fish to go from living in water to living on land—a system change of enormous magnitude, yet it happened. For us to go from justice as revenge to Justice as Love might seem as unlikely as fish transitioning from living in water to living on land. And yet, for some, the transition to Justice as Love has already occurred. The question is, will it become universal before humans self-destruct, the path we may now be on?

Some things are clear. First, the task is not to tear down or disrupt the existing system; that is nothing more than a continuation of dualistic thinking. Moreover, until a new system is in place and begins to impact outcomes, we still need the control imposed by the punitive system to maintain a semblance of order—it is better than nothing while we plant the seeds of genuine system change. This is not a quick fix.

Second, our approach must be outside the present paradigm, yet implemented by people who are still in it. Our work is to change the system in which, in many ways, we are still embedded. We will approach our dualistic circumstances with a Unitive mindset. We will essentially do what Taylor and Prince did to transform the prison that confined them—they lived into lovingkindness while in the punitive system. In whatever system we are in, that is what we will do, as well. Exactly how this will be done will vary from system to system, depending on the variables present in each.

UNITIVE JUSTICE IN SPIRITUALITY/RELIGION

I begin with the application of Unitive Justice in spirituality and religion. Unitive Justice Spirituality is an important aspect of the Unitive Justice movement. Some major faith traditions have focused on eye-for-an eye justice, a teaching that gives moral legitimacy to retributive, punitive justice. However, those same traditions also have messages about forgiveness, mercy, and Love that give moral legitimacy to Unitive Justice and Justice as Love. Spiritual and religious teachings that are grounded in Love have a major role to play in achieving system transformation in the justice system and in the culture at large.

We have many ways, including religious and spiritual teachings, and also Unitive Justice, to teach morality, ethics and values inclusively. The opportunity for inclusivity exists in the principle of what is called the Golden Rule in Christianity, do unto others as you would have them do unto you, but is taught in some version by many faith traditions. Numerous other teachings also connect diverse spiritual and religious traditions.

Writing in the Jewish magazine, *Tikkun*, Judge Bruce Petersen sets out several visions of Unity found in different traditions. He cites Chief Luther Standing Bear, a Sioux chief in the late 1800s, who describes a unifying life force as follows:

> From Wakan Tanka, the Great Spirit, there came a great unifying life force that flowed in and through all things—the flowers of the plains, blowing winds, rocks, trees, birds, animals—and was the same force that had been breathed into the first man. Thus all things were kindred, and were brought together by the same Great Mystery.

Petersen also quotes Kabir, a 15th century Sufi poet, who said:

> In your veins, and in mine, there is only one blood, the same life that animates us all! Since one unique mother earth begat us all, where did we learn to divide ourselves?

And from the Buddha:

He who experiences the Unity of life sees his own Self in all beings, and all beings in his own Self, and looks on everything with an impartial eye.[1]

The moral measure of lovingkindness is found in all major sacred texts and philosophies. Our digital encyclopedia, Wikipedia,[2] listed examples of major spiritual traditions that teach lovingkindness, including:

Judaism: "Loving-kindness" is the English translation of the Hebrew word חסד ("chesed"). In the book of Psalms this term refers to acts of kindness motivated by love. Psalm 107, verse 43: "Whoso is wise, and will observe these things, even they shall understand the loving-kindness of the LORD." In Pirkei Avot: "The world stands on three things: Torah, the service of God, and deeds of loving-kindness." (1:2)

Hinduism: "Priti" (Sanskrit: प्रीति) means lovingkindness in Hindu traditions, and refers to "amity, kindness, friendly disposition, love, affection, harmony, peacefulness." in texts such as Grhya Sutras, the Mahabharata and the Puranas. "Maitri" is another term found in Hindu literature that means lovingkindness, especially in Hindu Yoga-related literature. "Mettā," a Pali word given the association of lovingkindness and friendliness, is related to the Sanskrit word "maitri."

Buddhism: "Mettā," as described in the Metta Sutta of the Pali Canon's Sutta Nipata (Sn 1.8) and Khuddakapatha (Khp 9), is equivalent to the English term, "lovingkindness.

Christianity: The term lovingkindness is translated from the Hebrew root word for lovingkindness, "chesed" (חסד) and is found in The King James Version, the New King James Version, the American Standard Version, and the New American Standard Bible (NASB1995). Other versions of the Bible also translate references to "chesed" as "lovingkindness."

"Agape," (Ancient Greek ἀγάπη, agápē) is a Greco-Christian term referring to "love: the highest form of love, charity", and "the love of God for man and of man for God."

Despite how universal the teaching of lovingkindness is, our system blindness is also virtually universal. It shows up in all of the institutions we are immersed in, including religion. It is not unusual to find duality consciousness reflected in religious texts when they are describing the presence of a vengeful god. This tends to negate our ability to see the world and our role in it through the lens of a loving God.

In our culture, we are taught lessons about a vengeful god from childhood. I experienced this when a neighbor girl returned from her Bible School class and told me that I could not go to heaven because I was Catholic—Jesus did not die for my sins the way He died for hers. Separation. Hierarchy. Judgment. Punishment. This doctrine reflects a belief in a retributive god. A loving God is free of punitive characteristics, as is Justice as Love.

I have spent some time seeking to understand the death of Jesus through the lens of a loving God. This is where that search led me.

Leading up to His death, Jesus intentionally walked into, and even helped provoke, a tumultuous situation that He knew would cause the authorities to react. This may have been because He sought an opportunity to demonstrate for us what it looks like to extend unconditional Love to others, without exception, even someone who is torturing and may kill us. Perhaps He was modeling for us how to consistently walk in the footsteps of a loving God, without judgment or a desire for retribution, knowing that a nonviolent response is far more powerful than a violent attack. He demonstrated endurance, despite the pain and suffering being inflicted. He was showing us what it means to extend Love to those who are crying for Love, those who, in their state of duality consciousness, know not what they do.

To extend Love, even when being harmed, is a tall order, but still possible. It was demonstrated many times during the Civil Rights Movement, as recorded in photos and videos of the time: a column of silent protesters kneeling at the Edmund Pettus Bridge as Sheriff Jim Clark, in his white helmet, wielded his cattle prod; a young John Lewis in a trench coat being beaten over the head.[3]

When civil rights leader C.T. Vivian was a young man in seminary in Nashville, he met nonviolence advocate Jim Lawson and trained alongside other future leaders such as John Lewis and Diane Nash. He later became a lieutenant in Martin Luther King, Jr.'s Southern Christian Leadership Conference (SCLC).[4] Understanding how powerful a nonviolent response to a violent attack can be, Vivian intentionally walked into a tumultuous situation, intending to provoke a violent attack against himself. In his memoir he wrote:

And let's be honest: Selma was home to a virulent, racist sheriff, Jim Clark ... [who] was almost certain to respond less than peacefully to our peaceful initiatives. We needed a conflict that would demonstrate our plight. . . . Such a response, we hoped, would sicken Northerners as Birmingham had and motivate an already sympathetic President Johnson to expedite voting rights legislation.[5]

Small skirmishes had produced no change. Then on Feb. 15, 1965, Vivian led a group of prospective voters to the courthouse steps where Clark again blocked them. This time, there were television cameras present. Vivian taunted Clark, "What do you tell your wife at night? What do you tell your children?"

Eventually Sheriff Clark ordered the cameramen to turn off their cameras and his deputies began to push the crowd back. Clark punched Vivian in the face, sending him falling back against the courthouse steps. Vivian writes that he was hurting but brushed himself off and got up. "I remembered the training I'd received from Jim Lawson in Nashville. We can never allow violence to defeat nonviolence. You have to resist the impulse to turn in the other direction and leave. You have to stay."[6]

One cameraman had kept his camera on. Soon, the footage was on the evening news and then the whole world was watching. Civil rights leader and diplomat Andrew Young later said: "No one gave C.T. any instructions to do that. It took a lot of courage to get in Jim Clark's face. But if he had not taken that blow in Selma, we would not have had the Voting Rights Act."[7] A nonviolent response is more powerful than a violent attack.

Because both retributive justice and Justice as Love are found in major religious texts, religion can take us in one direction or another. On one hand, it provides a powerful tool for transformation and recognizing our shared humanity. On the other hand, it can be divisive and destroy connection. It can be unitive or it can be dualistic.

As a child, I learned about how religion can separate us, even when that is not the intent. The majority of the population of about 4500 in the small Colorado farming community where I grew up were white protestants. A growing Hispanic population was mostly Catholic. A small number of Japanese people came to Colorado during WWII when their families were interned in a camp in the fertile Arkansas Valley. When the war ended and they were released, some became farmers in our community. Those who were older included some Buddhists, but the younger generation mostly became protestant. There was only one Jewish family in our community.

In this community, my Catholic upbringing made me a minority. I had my first encounter with religious divisiveness when I attended a public grade school. Each morning before our classwork began, we were required to recite the Lord's Prayer—the protestant version of the prayer. A moral conflict ensued for me, because as a Catholic, I was taught that the protestant ending of the prayer, "for thine is the kingdom, the power and the glory, for ever and ever," was written by a scribe and was not what Jesus said; this made reciting that part of the prayer a sin for which I could end up in purgatory or hell.

To this day, I still recall the discomfort I experienced each time I felt the need to remain silent while my protestant classmates finished the prayer—in order to be saved from damnation. I felt like I had spots that marked me as "different." There were no Jewish children in my class, but I understand that in some schools the Jewish children left the room while this prayer was recited. This is not an experience our children in public schools should have.

I was glad when, in 1962, the U.S. Supreme Court declared prayer in public schools to be unconstitutional.[8] This meant that students could not be pressured, explicitly or implicitly, to conform to the religious teachings of one denomination or another, or be ostracized for being different. Freedom of religion is an essential right, but it comes with a responsibility to others who do not share your religious beliefs. Religion is personal, making it easy to use as a weapon to divide.

In a 2022 decision, the U.S. Supreme Court reversed the prior ruling that prohibited prayer in public schools, and now this division can again occur.[9] Based on the prior established ruling, a public high school football coach who persistently prayed on the 50-yard line following football games was violating the Constitution. The reasoning was that the First Amendment protects private citizens, not those who are employees of the government and therefore are agents of the state, as public school teachers are. The newly constituted Supreme Court held that state agents have a First Amendment right to pray in our public, tax-supported spaces.

Katy Joseph, the director of policy and advocacy at Interfaith Alliance, said the decision that again permitted school prayer "dismantles decades of progress."

> Exploiting his position of authority, coach Joseph Kennedy pushed players to participate in prayer in the middle of the field immediately after games. This was no private expression of devotion, as he and his lawyers claim. Instead, Mr. Kennedy forced students to choose between their religious freedom and being part of the team — an agonizing decision that no student should ever be forced to confront.[10]

In her dissenting opinion, Supreme Court Justice Sotomayer wrote:

> Today's decision is particularly misguided because it elevates the religious rights of a school official, who voluntarily accepted public employment and the limits that public employment entails, over those of his students, who are required to attend school and who this Court has long recognized are particularly vulnerable and deserving of protection. . . In doing so, the Court sets us further down a perilous path in forcing States to entangle themselves with religion, with all of our rights hanging in the balance.[11]

Based on my childhood experience, I am drawn to the logic of Justice Sotomayor's argument. Reinstating prayer in public schools will give rise to conflict that is unnecessary.

We can create inclusion and connection by teaching Justice as Love across different faith and spiritual walks. We are not separate, we are One. My aspiration for Unitive Justice is that it supports traditional religions and many versions of spirituality in being unitive, in teaching that connection is our essential nature. In your veins, and in mine, there is only one blood; the same life force animates us all!

UNITIVE JUSTICE IN EDUCATION – UJED

The education of our youth is critically important to the wellbeing of our nation. Unfortunately, beginning in the 1980s, the U.S. began a "get-tough" approach to crime that eventually spread to our schools in the form of zero-tolerance discipline. Predictably, as force escalated, more force was needed. Surveillance cameras, metal detectors, drug-sniffing dogs, and School Resource Officers, who are often active-duty police stationed within the school building, all became punitive-focused measures used to maintain control of the school environment. Now, a fight on school grounds that formerly was dealt with by the principal becomes a criminal charge for assault and battery.

Zero tolerance uses "exclusionary discipline" that separates the offending students from the rest of the school community. According to the U.S. Department of Education Office of Civil Rights, during the 2011-2012 school year, 3.5 million students were suspended in school; 3.45 million were suspended out of school and 130,000 were expelled, out of 49 million students enrolled in U.S. schools.[12] Various means achieved this end: mandatory penalties, such as 5 or 10-day suspensions or expelling the students for the remainder of the school year, referrals to alternative schools, referrals to law enforcement, and school-based arrests —for breaking school rules.

As punishment escalates, the time spent learning in school diminishes. One collateral damage is that the educators are not fulfilling their duty to educate the expelled students. These policies and practices blur the line between the education and criminal law systems. These strong-arm tactics fuel a breakdown of trust in the community. The result is a school-to-prison pipeline that funnels youth from the school system to the courts and penal institutions.

Zero tolerance discipline instituted the schoolhouse version of "what crime was committed, who committed it and what is their punishment to be?" The adverse childhood experiences that students experience due to zero tolerance no doubt contribute to negative health outcomes now and into their adulthood, plus the attendant costs. Our present knowledge about ACEs and PCEs makes a compelling case for Unitive Justice in education.

Unitive Justice in Education (UJEd) is based on Unitive Justice theory and the 14 Arcs. This provides a school environment with the tools needed to create system change, where participating in community traditions will naturally occur as a strong community is created. Students will feel a sense of belonging because the culture is designed to be inclusive. The feeling of being supported by friends naturally flows from building strong relationships and more non-parent adults take a genuine interest in them. UJEd provides a school environment that is positive and trauma-informed. Our schools are a perfect place to begin to give our children a new experience of justice—unitive, not punitive.

In the description of Arc 14, I described the success of the Restorative Justice program based on Unitive Justice principles at Armstrong High School in Richmond, VA, in 2011-2013. An improved version of UJEd, called the UJEd Whole School Program, now trains a UJEd Leadership Team of approximately ten staff members in a school to create and sustain culture change using Unitive Justice principles and processes. This team provides the critical mass needed for school culture change to be sustainable.

The first opportunity we had to implement this new approach was in the high school and middle school in Hopewell, Virginia, a yearlong program that began in January 2023. The number of reported disciplinary incidents in the high school went from 213 for the quarter just before the program began to only 100 incidents for the third quarter of the program—a decrease of over 50% in less than a year! In the middle school, the reported disciplinary incidents went from 200 in September 2022 before the UJEd program began to only 101 in September 2023.

Simultaneously, a UJEd Whole School Program was initiated at Trey Junior School in Najjemba Village in the Wakiso District in Uganda. The school in Uganda was built specifically to be a Unitive Justice school. In Uganda, we are told that children and youth are regularly caned (beaten with canes) because of a belief that this is what makes them good people. To date, no student in Trey Junior School has been punished, and the students are thriving and have good grades. Conflicts are resolved using circles. A number of people in the vicinity of the school stop by to ask what they are doing to have such well-behaved students. The belief that punishment is correction is another myth that helps sustain the punitive system. Unitive Justice theory and practice are proving to be highly successful in creating school culture change, in the U.S. and abroad.

For students who come into the school environment having experienced adverse childhood experiences, UJEd provides an ideal setting for supporting their healing and enhancing their chance of favorable emotional and physical health outcomes as children and into adulthood. Students who are fortunate enough to mainly have positive childhood experiences will have an even greater chance of positive health outcomes in a unitive school environment. No one has to lose.

We unconsciously pass the moral inconsistencies of punitive discipline on to our children. Teaching children to punish harm with more harm models for them our adversarial approach to justice. We have a choice to instruct our youth differently. We can give them a safe learning environment without sacrificing fairness and order.

We can teach them to resolve conflict by coming together, by restoring connection, beginning at the micro level—at home, at school, and in the neighborhood. Perhaps, when they are adults, they will find ways to apply this same inclusive approach on the macro level, perhaps even on the world stage.

The Alliance for Unitive Justice offers training in the UJEd Whole School Program in courses taught online and in workshops that are taught in person. For more information about the UJEd Whole School Program, please visit the AUJ website at www.a4uj.org. The time for UJEd in our schools, public and private, has come.

UJED FOR YOUTH IN DETENTION: ENDING THE PIPELINE TO PRISON

Building on the work Prince Bunn does with youth in detention, the Alliance for Unitive Justice created a program that teaches Unitive Justice principles to troubled youth. In ten lessons, it provides a foundation for turning youth confinement into youth excellence and empowerment. Because these youth are already immersed in the punitive system, they need only look at their circumstances to understand why implementing Unitive Justice and achieving system change is important.

If the youth are in short-term detention, this program is given in a few weeks and helps fill the void that might be left by sparse programming while youth await their court date or, if they are convicted, their transfer to long-term facilities. When they are in long-term detention, some serving their early years of incarceration as a juvenile before a sentence of years or decades as an adult begins, the program is expanded over more time and provides in-depth work.

UJEd for Youth in Detention gives the youth life skills that will serve them long into the future: selfgovernance, an understanding of values, and the experience of equality and inclusion without exception. These then foster connection, trust and a safe environment. Social emotional learning is cultivated through experiential learning and all aspects of this program meet the standard of trauma informed care.

This program has been modified for use with groups of troubled youth in the school setting, for students who share a common issue such as bullying, absenteeism, food insecurity, gangs and the like. This program is called UJEd Youth Leadership Circles. It teaches these youth some of the Unitive Justice Arcs and then supports them in becoming leaders in school culture change—it is asset-focused, not deficit-focused. If conflicts among the youth in these groups is reduced, there will be a positive ripple effect throughout the school. We are also teaching this Youth Leadership Circle process to school staff so they can then teach it to the student population at large, empowering all students to be leaders in school culture change.

The UJEd Youth Leadership Circles program is also available to youth in programs such as Boys and Girls Clubs, or wherever youth come together to learn values and life skills. Being asset-focused, it uplifts everyone in the program, despite their backgrounds.

To paraphrase Martin Luther King, Jr., every child and young adult is an heir to the legacy of dignity and worth. This program offers youth a new model of justice, not one based on getting even, but one that is instead based on lovingkindness.

THE UNITIVE PRISON CULTURE CHANGE TRAINING PROGRAM (UPCC)

How do we free ourselves of the misplaced blame, scapegoating and mass incarceration that plague the criminal law system? When they were convicted, Taylor and Prince were seen as the problem and a threat to society, as reflected in their life plus 26 and life plus 80-year sentences. That could have been the end of the story; they could have merely become two more incarcerated men without a future, but they had a different plan. Their severe prison sentences provided a crucible that gave them the time they needed to look within, knowing that the answers that exist elsewhere did not work. Upon their release, Taylor and Prince committed to teaching others how to achieve transformation during their incarceration, just as they had done.

Over the course of three years, from 2020 to 2023, Taylor Paul and Prince Bunn, with the assistance of filmmaker Patrick Gregory and me, created a training program for those who are incarcerated called Unitive Prison Culture Change (UPCC), a training program for jails and prisons.[13] Six of the 14 Arcs to Unitive Justice are used as the framework for teaching how to achieve the transformation that Taylor and Prince realized before they ever heard of Unitive Justice.

An important aspect of UPCC is that it offers the perfect antidote to the punitive system's hidden internal engine, i.e., blaming criminals for the dysfunction within the larger system, thus keeping the deeper problems from being addressed. We are told they are inherently flawed, irredeemable, and that is why the criminal law system continually fails at its job of corrections. Showing that many, if not most, of those convicted of crime can use their time in jail or prison to achieve personal transformation directly refutes the scapegoating message that they are inherently evil and beyond redemption. Inmates who prove themselves able to transcend the punitive system, even while in it, tend to delegitimize the essential scapegoating aspect of the criminal law system. Not all inmates will achieve this level of transformation, but if even a small number do so, that is the beginning of significant system change.

WHAT OUTCOMES CAN THE UNITIVE PRISON CULTURE CHANGE PROGRAM ACHIEVE?

One of the first outcomes the UPCC program is expected to achieve is a new perspective on individual accountability and the role our internal moral compass plays in being accountable. Prince talks about his long walk to the mirror and not just to look for blemishes—he took the long walk to the mirror to come to terms with himself. This was essential for him to achieve his personal freedom, and he did not need any authority telling him to do it. With this, he embraced selfgovernance and began a journey of transformation.

Prince explains an outcome that he observed:

> As we both [Prince and Taylor] modeled selfgovernance in our pod, others saw the power in it and began to follow our lead to find their own personal freedom. No compulsion or coercion was needed. By the power of attraction to what is good, the environment in one cell and then another changed, then the environment in the cells to the right and the left changed. The pod took on a different culture, and then the change showed up out on the yard.

In the same way, inmates who receive the UPCC training and begin to embrace this new way of being will give rise to a cadre of inmates who understand how to handle their own affairs. Inmates exercising selfgovernance through their own initiative changes the culture inside the prison walls. It begins to diminish the punitive culture and emphasizes radical tenderness, connection and mutual benefit. This results in a more effective outcome than we might expect.

Taylor describes the nature of this change as follows:

> Eventually, this approach leaves the infraction book on the shelf, no longer needed on a regular basis. The "kangaroo courts" used to address internal infractions disappear. Correctional officers can facilitate more programming, have time to receive upgraded training and experience less "compassion fatigue" as they make fewer rounds and have fewer negative interactions with inmates who are governing their own affairs. How is this achieved? Because *this is who we, the inmates, truly are—our inherent goodness is waiting to be recognized and empowered.* Then new people begin to enter our lives and with that, the seeds of culture change spread far and wide. We know from experience this is what happens.

This program guides inmates in finding their personal freedom, but it doesn't stop there. This culture change can help everyone in the system find their own freedom, from the warden to the line staff. As fewer infractions are committed, there is less paperwork and less time managing unruly inmates in dangerous situations. Staff get to go home on time—this means lower operating costs. Correction staff have time to help support the inmates in their growth. The family and friends left back home will benefit, as well, as their incarcerated family members and cohorts show up in ways they are proud of.

Beginning with the first UPCC course that I taught, our expectations were confirmed. In the first class they were asked to share their understanding of justice. Uniformly, they shared that punitive justice was essential. I asked if it works, why do we still have so much crime? They all seemed to agree it was because people need to understand the consequences and that will stop the violations. One suggested the punishment should happen in public to be sure people understand the consequences. I asked why more people who have been incarcerated—so they understand the consequences—are rearrested after their release than those who are not? They were not aware that was the case, but many of them have been in jail and prison previously. It was clear that punitive justice was the only possibility they could imagine, and they wanted it to work.

As the twenty-class course progressed, I could see the transformation happening. At the last class they were asked to share what their main takeaway from the class was. A number of them said it was that they now know there is an alternative to punitive justice. As that class came to an end, one of the men said that things do not work at the prison, and everyone agrees they don't work. He said that the efforts to fix them don't make any difference. Then he said, "If things are going to change, *we* have to change them, and we know what we have to do."

Each of the classes has one or more videos by Taylor and Prince in which they talk about and model how they changed the prison culture during their incarceration. Indeed, by the end of the course, the participants know what they can do to change the prison culture.

The system change that the Unitive Prison Culture Change training program seeks to achieve is a prison community that embodies what J. A. Faris describes as "compassion, sharing, reciprocity, upholding the dignity of personhood, individual responsibility to others, and interdependence by recognizing a common and shared humanity."[14] Taylor and Prince assert, "We know this is possible—we did it."

INTRODUCING UNITIVE JUSTICE CRIMINOLOGY THEORY

There is a growing movement to humanize incarceration loosely organized under the designation of "humanist criminology" or "positive criminology." This encompasses new approaches, including peacemaking criminology, social acceptance, crime desistance, restorative justice and other theories that focus on the positive factors and strengths that help individuals to rehabilitate and successfully integrate into the community.[15] I was generally aware of this movement as I worked on the UPCC program with Taylor, Prince and Patrick.

My part in developing the Unitive Prison Culture Change training program included designing the curriculum based on six Unitive Justice Arcs, helping to edit the course videos and writing materials for the course handbook. In this deep immersion, I began to see a theory for implementing unitive structures in the prison and jail setting. Not just a general outline, but a clear distinction between what I understood to be offered by new positive criminology theories and what Taylor and Prince did while they were in prison. This led to Unitive Justice Criminology theory, a theory that predicts the conditions in which those who were the problem become the solution.

Unitive Justice Criminology theory guides us in implementing Unitive Justice principles and practices within our correctional institutions to achieve system change from within. UJ Criminology provides inmates isolated from the outside world opportunities to experience transformative practices. Their period of incarceration is when they have time to do this inner work. To deny them this opportunity because we want their punishment to be harsh and painful hurts the rest of us as much as them —and it wastes taxpayer dollars.

How can inmate transformation be achieved? UJ Criminology addresses *both* the individual brokenness that manifests in acts of crime *and* the systemic brokenness that fuels crime and perpetuates unsafe communities. Some of the key elements of the UJ Criminology approach include the following, all of which are consistent with the 14 Arcs to Unitive Justice:

1. Selfgovernance becomes the norm, so hierarchical control is less frequently needed.

2. Strengthening values permits rules to be relied on less frequently.
3. Peer-to-peer is emphasized, increasing the sense of inclusion and equality and diminishing the need for hierarchical control.
4. Making it safe to be honest reduces the prevalence of deception.
5. Honesty promotes trust, diminishing the distrust that undermines relationships.
6. Strengthening community bonds reduces the negative attraction of self-serving acts.
7. Providing opportunities to acquire insight reduces the negative impact of projecting judgment that is informed by misperceptions, prejudice and projections.
8. As a sense of connection grows, there is less need for punishment—community wellbeing increasingly lies in connection.
9. As synergy grows, an environment of opposition and confrontation is replaced by creative interaction.
10. Unitive Consciousness grows as duality consciousness dissipates.

As this journey unfolds, those who were branded as the problem because of past criminal activity have an opportunity to become part of the solution, to be players in achieving system change. If their transformation is deep enough, they will take their learning about the model of justice that has no punitive elements to the communities to which they return. This may become a factor in helping us change the course of the punitive system. Perhaps the time will come when former convicts teach the rest of us about "Justice as Love." Might this be the ultimate way *the problem becomes the solution?*

When I compare UJ Criminology to what other positive criminology theories offer, I see two common elements. Both are asset-focused, not deficit-focused as is often the current norm, and both emphasize connection. I also see a significant difference. While all of the new theories I reviewed seek better and more humane ways to "fix those people," none of them see "those people" as the fix, as Taylor and Prince do in their program. Perhaps their unique experience and perspective as inmates permitted them to envision a possibility that academicians and corrections staff could not see.

Unitive Justice Criminology is asset-focused but to a new degree. UJ criminology assumes that most inmates are inherently good and in a carefully-created environment, they are capable of developing new habits of mind and of making significantly different choices. The deep divide between the citizens at large who feel threatened by crime and those convicted of crime is addressed by using our investment in incarceration as an inmate "reset" opportunity, a path to their transformation if they so choose. This is exactly what Taylor and Prince achieved during their incarceration. This is the cornerstone of Unitive Justice Criminology theory: it suggests that the transformation achieved by Taylor and Prince is *replicable*.

UJ Criminology theory demonstrates how, in Unitive Consciousness, attacking those whom we see as our enemies is replaced with working alongside them to achieve unified goals. This gives rise to a new vision and mission for our penal institutions, without requiring change to the larger criminal law system. We can continue to prosecute, convict and isolate those who commit crime as punishment for their wrongdoing and to protect the public. This addresses the need for offender accountability and a sense of safety in the community. But now, the goal of how time in jail and prison is used is to give those who are incarcerated an opportunity to achieve a personal transformation. The next step will be for them to demonstrate they are not a threat by becoming the solution to the problems they previously caused.

A shift in our corrections policy can make the time that inmates spend in prisons and jails at the taxpayers' expense an opportunity to experience the same type of transformative learning experience that Taylor and Prince achieved. They need time to engage in this training in order to achieve transformation, and time is what jail and prison provides. Those who are being punished for committing crime become co-producers and active participants in creating the new justice model that helps us address specific acts of crime *and* the systemic injustices of the old system. They return home with new tools that change their relationship with the punitive system and their role in the community in a positive way.

Unitive Justice Criminology provides what criminologists Anastasia Chamberlen and Henrique Carvalho recommend: "strive to strike a careful—and admittedly difficult—balance between addressing systemic and structural injustices on the one hand while incorporating an intimate, relational and antiessentialist[16]—and therefore transformative—approach to justice on the other."[17] UJ Criminology also fosters an environment where "a different sense of justice can be lived and felt in a concretely embodied manner . . . " just as Chamberlen and Carvalho describe in their writings.[18]

This policy change from dehumanizing to humanizing those whom we incarcerate, provides an antidote to the unjust scapegoating of those charged with crime. UJ Criminology dispels the us/them dichotomy. This opens the opportunity to consider and address the underlying brokenness that perpetuates violence in our communities.

UNITIVE JUSTICE IN THE REALM OF POLITICS

What might a Unitive Justice system of politics look like? It is the process by which we choose decision-makers who lead us from a punitive to a unitive system. It begins when some citizens blessed with the courage and commitment to run for public office lead us in manifesting the dream of a more perfect union.

Government is a distinct sector because it is "owned" by the people. Politicians are empowered in a way others are not: they are accorded a place on the stage of public discourse to voice their ideas and seek voter support. Access to the political stage is a powerful tool for bringing Unitive Justice principles to the public's awareness.

Unitive Politics includes recruiting candidates for public office who, once elected, help bend the arc of history toward unitive government. Once elected, they are public servant decision-makers committed to implementing policies that enhance the social safety and general wellbeing of all people, regardless of their circumstances. To serve in this role is a unique civic duty.

How would these politicians be different from those who serve their own interests? Twelve characteristics of public servants guided by Unitive Justice principles are as follows:

1. They model selfgovernance. This helps forge a path toward less hierarchical control.
2. They model core values, so rules become the secondary means of securing our communities because our shared values are primary.
3. They see themselves as equal to others, performing their role without a sense of entitlement, privilege or superiority.
4. They are honest, open and transparent. They make deception unacceptable.
5. They are trustworthy, diminishing the distrust that undermines relationships.
6. They work to create strong communities where self-serving acts are not condoned.
7. They seek insight to inform their decisions, thus avoiding the negative impact of projecting judgment.
8. They foster and support connection so that, as connection grows, the need for punishment is diminished.
9. They generate synergy in their working relationships, diminishing opposition and confrontation.
10. They are courageous, overcoming the self-doubt that could undermine their conviction and commitment.
11. They are grounded in lovingkindness and radical tenderness, thus warding off fear.
12. They work toward unified goals and mutually beneficial policies, modeling how to avoid chaos and revenge.

How does one run as a Unitive Justice candidate? I can share what I did when I ran for statewide office in 1994 and again in 2001. I was a neophyte, not only in politics but it was also early in my understanding of Unitive Justice. I was motivated to run by a desire to offer voters some policy possibilities that align with the Unitive Justice principles that I was discerning and to see if there was a constituency for this message.

In running for office, I learned a lot about the political process and interacting with voters as a way to create change. I didn't know what was needed to win an election, and I still had supporters willing to work hard on my behalf. I didn't win either election but I learned that many believed in the message behind Unitive Justice. There is a craving for a unitive approach to public policy, although that is not the language used by the voters—yet. I am not alone in seeing this possibility.

A recent article titled "Support political parties that embrace unitive Consciousness" encourages voters to vote for candidates who exhibit this quality—in Malaysia! The author, Ronald Benjamin, wrote: "It is through unitive consciousness that we are able to see the beauty and goodness in others in a sustained manner."[19] Agreed!

Perhaps the most disheartening aspect of my experience running for public office was seeing what some candidates are willing to do to win an election. I learned how common it is for candidates to justify their lack of honesty/integrity on the grounds of expediency, thinking they must be dishonest to be elected and that the end justifies the means.

My opponents in the Democratic primary were good men whom I knew meant well. I was perplexed when I heard them state their commitment to defend the NRA's interpretation of the Second Amendment because that was what it took to get elected, even when they knew it is bad public policy. Many politicians have done so. The resulting lax regulation of guns gives us headlines like these: "Heavily Armed Protesters Gather Again at Michigan Capitol to Decry Stay-At-Home Order,"[20] and "Gun Stocks Soared as a Pro-Trump Mob Invaded the US Capitol Hill."[21] Democracy cannot survive with invaders carrying guns in the halls of our legislative bodies where public policy is made.

Even more tragic are headlines like this: "Homicide is a leading cause of death in kids, and rates are rising, study finds."[22] Guns were the most common weapon used in children's deaths in 2022, according to the study. Political inputs designed to shape policy and the resulting policy outputs are inseparable.

In Unitive Politics, the primary goal is to achieve enduring system change that transcends the dualistic, punitive world we inherited. This cannot happen if deception and self-interest are the means used to win. We must use unitive means to win—the means we use become the end we achieve.

Ultimately, the goal is to elect officials who will work to strengthen our communities with well-resourced schools, accessible health care, safe streets, police who act with integrity, and leaders who serve the common good. They model how to be a citizen of integrity—honest and loving—we especially need this as an example for our youth. Losing an election must not discourage our candidates or their supporters in a mission as important as this.

We can again learn from Taylor Paul and Prince Bunn. They were highly motivated to change the prison culture to prove they were worthy of returning to society—to be free. Parole was the door to their freedom, yet each man was denied this opportunity on multiple occasions, even while they were teaching the prison's re-entry courses to men who were going home. Taylor describes how he dealt with repeatedly losing his bid for parole as follows:

> So, they turned me down ten times, and each time, I wrote them a letter saying thank you for the opportunity of being seen, and I'll continue to put my best foot forward. The last turn down I received, I said all of the above, but at the end I wrote PS: Next year, I'm going to make it even more difficult for you to tell me no."

We are so deeply immersed in our punitive culture that, to transcend it, will be challenging. When a candidate runs on a Unitive Justice platform, they need the commitment and determination that Taylor demonstrated in his quest for freedom. When their best-laid plans fail, they persist. They learn their lessons, make adjustments, and when they return, they make it even more difficult for the voters to tell them no.

UNITIVE JUSTICE IN THE REALM OF GOVERNMENT

Now is the time to use our laws and public policies as tools for creating the world we want to experience. At this time in human history, we are charged with re-envisioning the institutions that carry out human engagement and enterprise. This section considers how we create institutions of government that are based on unitive principles. These terms are important to the discussion.

politics: the interaction between citizens and those who serve them in public office. Two major aspects of politics include 1. electing those who serve in the role of representatives of the people in exercising governmental power and control and 2. the process by which the governed and those who govern consider and collaborate on the design of public policy.

government: the exercise of power and control over the public domain, collectively of the people, by the people and for the people.

democracy: a system of government where the decision-makers are elected by the majority of voters. Policies are grounded in connection and guided by unified goals that lead to mutually beneficial policies.

autocracy: a system of government that serves the self-interest of one person with ultimate authority and his inner circle of minions, at the expense of all others. Closely related terms include dictatorship, despotism, monarchy, totalitarian government, tyranny, absolutism and oppression.

Our nation is unique because its founding documents plant the seeds for a more perfect union. The Declaration of Independence is a document written with great deliberation at a time of transformation, the moment the British colonists declared themselves to no longer be subjects of the British king. It sets forth guiding principles that speak to our highest aspirations for humanity. This principle remains just as compelling today as it was then.

> *We hold these truths to be self-evident, that all men are created equal, that they are endowed by their Creator with certain unalienable Rights, that among these are Life, Liberty and the pursuit of Happiness.--That to secure these rights, Governments are instituted among Men, deriving their just powers from the consent of the governed . . .*

Likewise, the preamble to the Constitution of the United States declares a vision of what we can achieve if we relinquish our attachment to separation and retribution.

> *We the People of the United States, in Order to form a more perfect Union, establish Justice, insure domestic Tranquility, provide for the common defense, promote the general Welfare, and secure the Blessings of Liberty to ourselves and our Posterity, do ordain and establish this Constitution for the United States of America.*

In his speech, *The American Dream*, Dr. Martin Luther King, Jr. reflects on how the U.S. Declaration of Independence offers a dream of Unity, but how dualistic thinking stands in the way. King's message is as profound now as when it was delivered in 1964.

> It wouldn't take us long to discover the substance of that [American] dream. It is found in those majestic words of the Declaration of Independence, words lifted to cosmic proportions: "We hold these truths to be self-evident, that all men are created equal, that they are endowed by God, Creator, with certain inalienable Rights, that among these are Life, Liberty, and the pursuit of Happiness." This is a dream. It's a great dream.
> The first saying we notice in this dream is an amazing universalism. It doesn't say "some men," it says "all men." It doesn't say "all white men," it says "all men," which includes black men. It does not say "all Gentiles," it says "all men," which includes Jews. It doesn't say "all Protestants," it says "all men," which includes Catholics. (Yes, sir) It doesn't even say "all theists and believers," it says "all men," which includes humanists and agnostics.
> Then that dream goes on to say another thing that ultimately distinguishes our nation and our form of government from any totalitarian system in the world. It says that each of us has certain basic rights that are neither derived from or conferred by the state. In order to discover where they came from, it is necessary to move back behind the dim mist of eternity. They are God-given, gifts from His hands.
> Never before in the history of the world has a sociopolitical document expressed in such profound, eloquent, and unequivocal language the dignity and the worth of human personality. The American dream reminds us, and we should think about it anew on this Independence Day, that every man is an heir of the legacy of dignity and worth.
> Now ever since the founding fathers of our nation dreamed this dream in all of its magnificence—to use a big word that the psychiatrists use—America has been something of a schizophrenic personality, tragically divided against herself. On the one hand we have proudly professed the great principles of democracy, but on the other hand we have sadly practiced the very opposite of those principles.

All I'm saying is simply this, that all life is interrelated. And we are caught in an inescapable network of mutuality, tied in a single garment of destiny—whatever affects one directly, affects all indirectly. For some strange reason I can never be what I ought to be until you are what you ought to be, and you can never be what you ought to be until I am what I ought to be. This is the interrelated structure of reality. John Donne caught it years ago and placed it in graphic terms, "No man is an island entire of itself; every man is a piece of the continent, a part of the main."[23]

King acclaims the vision of democracy but also acknowledges we are not there yet. We have set upon this journey, but we must remain committed. A unique attribute of our democratic system is that we have a wide-open door at the grassroots level for all adults to exercise their right to participate in their government by exercising their right to vote. But to be meaningful, our votes must be informed by honest information and we must have candidates to vote for who are people of integrity—and our votes must be counted.

The laws written by our legislators are an important way that we, as a people, show Love for our neighbor. Our public policies are how we, as a people, shall be known by our acts of Love and our courage. We must strengthen our faith that things can be different. We begin by first seeing what can be in order for it to become what is. History is on our side—history proves that the trajectory of this nation is forever toward connection and Unity.

HOW CAN UNITIVE PRINCIPLES HELP ADDRESS THE CRISIS DEMOCRACY FACES?

When there is breakdown in the governmental fabric of a nation, attacking those who are involved will not secure a lasting solution. It is more likely to perpetuate the conflict or cause it to take different forms. If attack does not work, what do we do? When the problem is separation, there is only one solution—connection.

At the time this book is being written, our democracy faces a crisis. There are some who seem willing to destroy democracy and replace it with authoritarianism, not realizing they will be further diminished in such a regime. What is a Unitive Justice response to this crisis? It is not to attack, it is to offer a viable alternative and draw supporters by attraction. Success is more likely if we offer those who are angry, alienated and fearful of the "other" what they want—connection, respect, dignity, and to be recognized for their inherent goodness and the humanity they share with others.

Where do we begin? A place to begin might be in local city and county political committees. Those who are familiar with the inner structure of these groups may see opportunities to make changes from within, one activity at a time. If the official committees are too hostile to be safe, perhaps those who support change can begin a parallel group that offers to serve the functions of building connection and recruiting candidates for office who believe in democracy for the people and by the people. Then the task is to work hard for their election. This is not a time to accept defeat or give up hope. Our future, the future of our children and grandchildren depends on us. We are each responsible for the world we create and what we leave to future generations.

Justice does not require harm to others, not even our "enemies." If we are to leave our children a better world, we must create the means to address our conflicts, not by destroying each other, but by discovering the places where we can open the portal to healing and transformation.

UNITIVE JUSTICE TRANSCENDS OUR DIFFERENCES

Separation is deep within our culture. Some think the solution is to write a rule against it, as though it is a problem that exists at the material level. Organizations are sometimes asked about their anti-racism policy. And do they have anti-sexual harassment training, and how about anti-bullying? Anti-policies run the risk of merely temporarily reorganizing parts of the system, serving as a band-aid on the brokenness within, while judgment and separation continue. How does Unitive Justice deal with this issue?

Unitive Justice is grounded in the principle that the equality and inclusion of all cannot exist so long as hierarchy or the dominance of one over another exists, so it eliminates the need for anti-policies by fostering change at the level of the heart and mind, by creating connection at the level of our shared humanity. Unitive Justice *transcends* our differences.

This is a positive and empowering way to address discrimination and prejudice, regardless of who the author or receiver may be.

Taylor and Prince were perhaps my most important teachers of how to transcend our differences, as this is what they did in order to transform the prison culture during their many years of incarceration. I described in various of the Arcs how they interacted with the men in their pod by being fully present and loving toward them, especially gang members. Taylor describes this as "showing them that we saw their humanity so they themselves could see their humanity," a process he calls "radical tenderness."

Instituting one measure for how we interact with everyone—our shared humanity—eliminates the need for a multitude of anti-policies to address the many ways we discriminate against and are hurtful toward one another. Out of this came the Unitive Justice theory and practices that address discrimination and prejudice by creating connection at the level of our shared humanity. This transcends our differences, however they manifest.

I recently taught a Unitive Prison Culture Change class in a Virginia prison. There were eleven Black men and one white man in the class, all of whom had no reason to trust me—I knew I had to earn their trust. So, from the moment I began teaching the class, I was fully present to the humanity that we all shared. I was intentionally present to their inherent goodness, their dignity and their personhood. Before long, trust was established. Our differences did not disappear, but they were no longer a reason for judgment or separation. There is a collateral benefit of connecting at the level of our shared humanity: we discover that our differences are actually assets. The prison course I taught is one example of how this can manifest.

I was in the prison teaching this twenty-lesson course because I and other UJ practitioners recognize the enormous potential many people behind bars have to be credible messengers for Justice as Love. Taylor and Prince prove this to be the case, not in spite of their past and their incarceration, but *because of it*. But those who are incarcerated often need to learn how to assume this role. We need their help with this work and, as the men in the class began to learn about Unitive Justice, most seemed to be inspired to answer this call. This provides an opportunity for us to go from asking what they did wrong, and to even go beyond asking them what happened. Instead, we ask what is the best they can be and how can we help them be that. This helps us meet our goal and our mission of teaching Justice as Love, while at the same time, it affirms their inherent worth. These are unified goals and no one has to lose.

Another example of transcending our differences to achieve more together than we can do alone is Trey Junior School in Wakiso District, Uganda. One of our instructors, Sara Daves, is a white woman who went to Uganda for six months. Despite significant cultural differences, implementing UJ theory and practices in a Ugandan school populated with only Black children and teachers was soon achieved. This is the first school in the world to be certified by the Alliance for Unitive Justice as a Unitive Justice School. All school staff are trained in Unitive Justice theory and circle facilitation and the traditional practice of caning the students is never used. Conflicts are resolved early on before they escalate using Unitive Justice Circles. This successful school is evidence that, because Unitive Justice is grounded in our shared humanity, it is universal and applicable in any culture.

In our Unitive Justice training materials, we don't mention race, but every class we teach is about transcending our differences—that includes race, but also religion, gender, age, sexual orientation and all our other differences. This is possible as we discover our shared humanity. It gets easier with practice.

EMBRACING A UNITIVE PERSPECTIVE TO HEAL THE PAST

To achieve system change, we must find a way to release attachment to the past. Dwelling on past grievances and judging how others victimized us and how we will get revenge destroys all possibility of experiencing peace. When we experience toxic stress, which dwelling on past wrongs can trigger, our response might be hyperarousal, increased vigilance, resistance or outright defiance and then aggression. Stewing in retribution and revenge is not only unhealthy for us, but it is also the cause of much of the suffering in the world.

We can choose instead to control our thoughts and not let every stressful event or situation that comes to mind take over. We can achieve this by creating a sense of safety through consistency, routine and familiarity, conditions that create a "therapeutic web" that is the key to dealing with any traumatic event.[24]

We are now immersed in a toxic political environment that can easily overwhelm us—if we let it. When being free becomes more important than revenge for what happened in the past, these are steps we can take to remain centered. First, it is true that duality thinking leads to harmful acts—we can see these acts are their cry for love. Forgive them, for they know not what they do.[25] If they are functioning in the lower parts of the brain, they are not thinking clearly. Ask how we can respond with lovingkindness, as did the Amish I described in the section on Arc 7: Guiding Moral Principle.

Second, if we let harmful, hateful acts of one political actor or another take over the real estate in our minds, the sensations that arise in the body are not good. Stress and various degrees of trauma can leave us feeling depressed and disempowered.

Prince Bunn sometimes says, "My hole got a rope." I will share the rope I use to pull myself out of the political morass we are in. My practice is to swim for an hour every other day, when possible. To occupy my mind as I do the routine of back and forth in the pool, I do a series of mantras. One series of mantras involves those who upset me or have caused me harm. I affirm the humanity I share with them. For example, "I am present to the humanity I share with Donald Trump." Or I might recite: "I am present to the humanity I share with my estranged friend, Reba Brown," and so on, down the list. This returns me to my center. There is a second reason to maintain this practice.

I know Donald Trump wants desperately to be loved. Somewhere along his journey, he may have gotten love and attention confused. He is a master at getting attention in ways that often generate animosity and anger. But I have learned that those who live on the dark side are capable of seeing the light if the conditions for that arise. I also know that those who have dwelled in darkness can experience a transformation and become voices for Justice as Love. For my good and theirs, I'm not willing to give up on anyone. Likewise, I hope others will not give up on me when I lapse back into duality—I know I must be willing to give what I hope to receive.

Being present to the humanity I share with those who cause harm as they cry out for Love keeps a spark of hope alive that a transformation is possible. There is always the possibility they will realize that being on the side of right is not so bad after all. We are living in deeply divided times. This is how I choose to respond in order to get through challenging times healthy and whole, and to avoid lapsing into the darkness of duality myself. It permits me to accept what is and still continue on with commitment.

This journey is easier if you find like-minded people who share your desire to create in Unitive Consciousness. They will be your teachers and you theirs. The 14 Arcs provide a guide for the process and practice as you manifest this new community, and other guides exist, as well.

You can begin in the system you are presently in. Taylor and Prince found it in a prison pod with over 80 other inmates. Different points of entry might be available to the prison staff. It might be the warden or top prison administrators who initiate the change. Where is the entry point in the system you are now in? Can you change the culture of a department or even an entire business? Or is your entry point your relationship with the person in the cubicle next to yours?

Schools and college environments are ripe for building systems based on Unitive Justice to promote and support harmonious and trusting learning communities. Business organizations can create workplace cultures and systems based on lovingkindness. This culture then becomes instilled in employees who, in turn, take those practices to clients, customers and others with whom they interact in the work community, and home to their families. Many religious institutions already teach Love and are perfect places to support a Unitive Justice system. We can build on the foundations that exist.

There are also people we know who, in their daily lives, extend lovingkindness and are fully present to those in need. We saw many examples of this during the covid-19 pandemic in 2020 and 2021, especially among healthcare workers who risked their lives to serve others. Those who selflessly offered aid and comfort after the 9/11 attacks are another example of our greater goodness. Many others extend lovingkindness but go unnoticed in the cacophony of voices calling for revenge. We can begin to notice. We can begin right where we are to transcend the environment we are in, one choice at a time.

We can choose to nurture hate, but we may also choose to nurture and sustain Love. Because the values that sustain Unitive Justice are lived through selfgovernance, not external control, we don't need permission from those in control to begin creating loving communities. We just do it, as Taylor and Prince did in prison and continue to do now. While this may only occur one micro change at a time, bending the arc of justice toward Love is within our power.

Releasing attachment to the past does *not* mean that we ignore criminal acts or permit murderers and rapists to run loose on our streets. The criminal law system will continue to work as it does now as we build unitive systems from the ground up. As unitive structures grow, punitive justice will be needed less; it will diminish in size and importance until Unitive Justice becomes the norm—at some time in the future.

You may have read the letter that was allegedly written by Albert Einstein to his daughter, Lieserl, about the Universal force of Love. Perhaps Einstein was not the actual source,[26] but the sentiment it expressed is relevant to our time in history. In part, it reads:

> After the failure of humanity in the use and control of the other forces of the universe that have turned against us, it is urgent that we nourish ourselves with another kind of energy…
>
> If we want our species to survive, if we are to find meaning in life, if we want to save the world and every sentient being that inhabits it, love is the one and only answer.
>
> Perhaps we are not yet ready to make a bomb of love, a device powerful enough to entirely destroy the hate, selfishness and greed that devastate the planet.
>
> However, each individual carries within them a small but powerful generator of love whose energy is waiting to be released. When we learn to give and receive this universal energy, dear Lieserl, we will have affirmed that love conquers all, is able to transcend everything and anything, because love is the quintessence of life.

The energy of Love does conquer all. Just a note of caution along with the optimism. Beware of the propensity for attachment to a unitive system to become a new religion with the pitfalls of control and judgment that come with it. Freedom is the goal, not a new version of duality thinking. Our commitment to lovingkindness will light the path.

CONCLUSION

The journey to Unitive Justice will be challenging. The punitive justice system will not disappear overnight, but we know where its weaknesses lie and what needs to change. We can now measure any system designed to deliver justice by the degree to which it embodies the structures of Unitive Justice. When we silence mental chaos and disorder, we will realize we have sufficient knowledge to make Justice as Love the legacy we leave for future generations.

We will face difficulties in changing long-standing structures that support duality, but we have a plan. Using the 14 Arcs to Unitive Justice as a roadmap, we design institutional structures that are unitive—in our justice system, in education, business, how we practice religion, on our spiritual path, how we run jails and prisons and so much more. Slowly, in place of the old punitive structures, we create unitive systems. The stage of history is set—the moment is ours to seize.

Carl Sagan observed, "Our species is young, and curious and brave and shows much promise." Let us begin to fulfill the promise of who we truly are.

* * *

Invitation to Journal. Think about where you were when you began reading this book, your understanding of justice and your vision for humanity, then consider these questions:

> a. Where do you see yourself on the spectrum from duality consciousness to Unitive Consciousness?
> b. Are you satisfied with where you are?
> c. Where would you like to be in a month, in a year, in a decade from now?
> d. What legacy would you like to leave for future generations?
> e. What can you do today or tomorrow that you have never done before, something that represents the flutter of your wings that can cause the butterfly effect, here and perhaps even abroad?
>
> **Suggested Viewing:** This short video puts it all in perspective, *Carl*

Sagan - Pale Blue Dot. Available at https://www.youtube.com/watch?v=wupToqz1e2g (3.30 min.).

A second suggested viewing. In 2002, psychotherapist Jenny Phillips began offering intensive meditation retreats for inmates at a maximum-security prison in rural Alabama. The 10-day retreats are conducted mostly in silence. The documentary, *The Dhamma Brothers: East Meets West in the Deep South*, explores the experience of four convicted murderers who participated in the retreat. It is available for rent at https://vimeo.com/ondemand/dhammabrothers. A trailer (2.2 min.) for the documentary is available at https://www.youtube.com/watch?v=zA8XFEyeMi8.

This is the meditation practice that I began to learn in 2021 and have now practiced for over twenty years. It has been a pillar of insight and strength for my Unitive Justice journey.

ACKNOWLEDGMENTS

I'm grateful to the village of family, friends, and professionals who, over the past decade, supported me in writing this book. Always there for me, my husband Eric, children Andrea, Weston, and Danielle, and grandchildren, Sam, Mae, Laina, Finn, Grace, and Evelyn. Lumi Dragulescu edited an early version with a different title; my good friends Misha Hendrickson, Jodi Clark and Susanne Shilling provided feedback on that version, as well. Former AUJ board members, Donna Chewning and Shelly Jost Brady, also reviewed one of the early versions. I hosted a "book club" online with friends who gave me suggestions: Addilynn Holloman, Helen Landry, Dulaney Collins, Molly Soeby, Ruth Micklem, and Sarah Vogt. That was Molly Soeby's first reading of the manuscript; she has now read it at least three times, including being one of two people to go through the final manuscript and assist with endnotes. Tami Sober, friend and professional colleague, provided important feedback for several sections. Law Professors, Ann Freedman and her husband, Rand Rosenblatt, provided advice and guidance with critical sections. John Montgomery's writing on the "Discovery Doctrine" provided the basis for my section on that topic. Kim Eley and KWE Publishing supported the process by having Bethany Good provide valuable editorial guidance, Taylor Mills do a final proofread, and Michelle Fairbanks create the cover design.

I am grateful for the training I received from Dominic Barter in a circle process that provided experiential learning in Justice as Love and justice system change. Anyone who reads this book will know that Taylor Paul and Weldon "Prince" Bunn are among my fellow travelers on this life-changing journey. Why and how they were able to implement Justice as Love in a prison environment by drawing on their inner wisdom took my understanding of Unitive Justice to a new level. It also led me to see that, when conditions are right, what they did is replicable and that led to Unitive Justice Criminology theory. As my understanding of the work of Taylor and Prince deepened, it also led to the inclusion of two additional Unitive Justice Arcs, from control to selfgovernance and from self-doubt to courage. Patrick Gregory and the years we spent editing the videos for the Unitive Prison Culture Change training program also contributed to this deeper understanding. Susan Barker York has consistently been a companion on this journey, and our work together continues.

I am grateful for the contributions of all of those whom I named and so many more who were supportive who are not named.

ABOUT THE AUTHOR

Sylvia Clute brings twenty-eight years as a trial attorney to the task of discerning a model of justice with no punitive elements—what she now calls Unitive Justice. This epoch in her life began in 1987 when her spiritual journey and her work in the courtroom collided, but she had important tools in her toolbox for what lay ahead. A law degree from Boston Univ. and graduate degrees in public policy from the Harvard Kennedy School of Government and the Univ. of California/Berkeley bring practical knowledge to her work on cutting-edge policy reform. She learned of diverse approaches to public policy when she studied in Paris, France two decades after WWII and served two years in a remote Nepali village during her Peace Corps service. She now serves as President and Exec. Director of the Alliance of Unitive Justice, a nonprofit that offers training and programs on Unitive Justice theory and practice. (www.a4uj.org) Unitive Justice is applicable in education, corrections, politics and government, spirituality/religion and leadership—everywhere people come together in community. It is being taught in law schools and grass-root groups are creating new ways of applying Unitive Justice in diverse settings worldwide.

Sylvia is the author of *Beyond Vengeance, Beyond Duality: A Call for a Compassionate Revolution*, and a novel, *Destiny Unveiled*. This book is her seminal work on Unitive Justice theory and practice, the product of thirty-six years, and counting, of inquiry, research and writing, leading to a practical theory of Justice as Love. Find out more on www.sylviaclute.com and www.unitivejustice.com.

ENDNOTES

CHAPTER ONE

1. Stephenson, Alice, "Why Do Law Firms Overlook Women for Partnership?" *Forbes*, Oct 4, 2021, accessed Mar. 13, 2023. https://www.forbes.com/sites/forbesbusinesscouncil/2021/10/04/why-do-law-firms-overlook-women-for-partnerships/?sh=79c280e528fc.
2. Nils Christie, "Conflicts as Property," *The British Journal of Criminology*, Vol. 17, No. 1, (Jan. 1977).
3. Christie, "Conflicts as Property," 4.
4. *Ibid.*
5. *Ibid.*, 5.
6. *Ibid.*
7. Elahe Izadi, "The powerful words of forgiveness delivered to Dylann Roof by victims' relatives," *Washington Post*, June 19, 2015, accessed May 4, 2023, https://www.washingtonpost.com/news/post-nation/wp/2015/06/19/hate-wont-wn-the-powerful-words-delivered-to-dylann-roof-by-victims-relatives/?utm_term=.26b0ea46dde7.

CHAPTER TWO

1. Dana Greene, "Repeat performance: is restorative justice another good reform gone bad?," *Contemporary Justice Review: Issues in Criminal, Social, and Restorative Justice*, Vol 16, No. 3, (2013) 360, accessed May 4, 2023, https://www.tandfonline.com/doi/abs/10.1080/10282580.2013.828912.
2. *See* "Test, punish, and push out: How 'zero tolerance' and high-stakes testing funnel youth into the school-to-prison pipeline," *Advancement Project*, Washington, D.C., (Jan. 20, 2010).
3. "Quotes from Rev. Dr. King's Last Years: 'A Revolution of Values,'" *Kairos*, January 15, 2017, accessed September 18, 2022, https://kairoscenter.org/quotes-from-rev-dr-kings-last-years/.

CHAPTER THREE

1. *Encyclopædia Britannica*, s.v. "Code of Hammurabi," accessed March 5, 2020, http://www.britannica.com/EBchecked/topic/253710/Code-of-Hammurabi.
2. *Encyclopædia Britannica*, s.v. "Lex talionis," accessed March 5, 2020, http://www.britannica.com/topic/talion.
3. *Wikipedia*, s.v. "An eye for an eye," accessed March 5, 2020, https://en.wikipedia.org/wiki/Eye_for_an_eye.
4. John Montgomery, "Beyond Neoliberalism – The Dawn of a New Civilisation," *The*

Conscious Lawyer, (August 2020), accessed on Sept. 19, 2022, https://www.thecon sciouslawyer.co.uk/beyond-neoliberalism/. Montgomery is among those working to transform our traditional system of justice, work that began after he realized that the traditional corporation's lack of a comprehensive conscience is detrimental to stockholders, society, and the environment.

5. Elisabetta Povoledo, "Vatican Repudiates 'Doctrine of Discovery,' Used as Justification for Colonization," *New York Times*, Mar. 30, 2023, accessed April 10, 2023, https://www.nytimes.com/2023/03/30/world/europe/vatican-repudiates-doctrine-of-discovery-colonization.html?smid=nytcore-ios-share&referringSource=article Share.
6. Thom Hartmann, *Unequal Protection: The Rise of Corporate Dominance and the Theft of Human Rights*, (U.S., Rodale, Inc. 2002), 101.
7. *Austin v. Michigan State Chamber of Commerce*, 856 F.2d 783 (6th Cir. 1988), rev'd, 494 U.S. 652, 110 S. Ct. 1391 (1990).
8. ACIM, (Foundation for Inner Peace, 1989), 49.
9. See *Wikipedia*, s.v. "Just war theory," accessed May 19, 2023, https://en.wikipedia.org/wiki/Just_war_theory.
10. Later versions of this doctrine added additional conditions and some variations.
11. Catholic doctrine provides that the responsibility for determining if these conditions are met belongs to "the prudential judgment of those who have responsibility for the common good," reported St. Charles Borromeo Catholic Church, Picayune, MS., accessed August 12, 2022, http://www.scborromeo.org/ccc/para/2309.htm.
12. See *Wikipedia*, s.v. "Just war theory."
13. Ishaan Tharoor, "The Christian nationalism behind Putin's war," *Washington Post*, April 19, 2022, accessed May 4, 2023 https://www.washingtonpost.com//world/2022/04/19/patriarch-kirill-orthodox-church-russia-ukraine/?utm_campaign= wp_todays_worldview&utm_medium=email&utm_source=newsletter&wpisrc=nl_to dayworld&carta-url=https%3A%2F%2Fs2.washingtonpost.com%2Fcar-ln-tr%2F369e4d9%2F625e353b64253a7f343be2fb%2F5972846c9bbc0f1cdce5cca5%2F20%2F72%2F625e353b64253a7f343be2fb,.
14. Nicole Winfield, "Pope urges peace, not politics in call to Russian patriarch," *AP News*, March 16, 2022, accessed May 4, 2023, https://apnews.com/article/russia-ukraine-pope-francis-europe-lifestyle-religion-b474a5a67ba5c1be26aedf343b7c8eb9.
15. "The Golden Rule is Common to All Religions," *Norman Rockwell Museum*, (undated), accessed May 4, 2023, https://www.nrm.org/2018/03/golden-rule-common-religions/.
16. Ben Johnson, "Timeline of Roman Britain," *Historic UK*, accessed Sept. 18, 2022, https://www.historic-uk.com/HistoryUK/HistoryofBritain/Timeline-of-Roman-Britain/.
17. *University of Houston, Department of History*, accessed Jan. 8, 2015, http://vi.uh.edu/pages/bob/elhone/comcrts.html. No longer available.
18. "The Common Law and Civil Law Traditions," The Robbins Collection, *School of Law, University of California at Berkeley*, accessed March 5, 2020, https://www.law.berkeley.edu/library/robbins/CommonLawCivilLawTraditions.html.
19. Rupert Ross, *Return to the Teachings: Exploring Aboriginal Justice*, (Toronto, Ontario: Penguin Books Canada, Ltd., 1996), 92.
20. Author's note: Laws known as "gerrymandering" are one example of laws that benefit the lawmakers, not the citizens they serve. These laws draw district boundaries in ways that support the re-election of the incumbent legislators.

CHAPTER FOUR

1. Joe McGinniss, *The Selling of the President*, (New York: Penguin Books, *1968*).
   Comments on the book at "Portfolio," a New York University journalism online site, include the following (at http://journalism.nyu.edu/publishing/archives/portfolio/books/book293.html, accessed May 17, 2020):
   "Mcguiness (sic) looks at propaganda and its role in American politics through Richard Nixon's media campaign of 1968. It describes how Richard Nixon, in order to "sell" the public his image of the 'new Nixon' utilized television propaganda. Nixon knew that he could not rely on the press to give him a positive image. He ends up relying on television "the way a polio victim relied on an iron lung." *Id.* at 38.
   "Mcguiness looks in detail at each of Nixon's media consultants. . . It discusses how each of these people helped craft a media friendly Nixon. Treleaven, for example, went to "work on Nixon's personality" and sense of humor.
   "The book is shocking because it shows how every public can be manipulated. Nixon's campaign was built around television shows where Nixon would answer live questions. McGinniss points out "Nixon could get through the campaign with a dozen or so carefully worded responses that would cover all the problems of America in 1968" (p. 63). The careful grooming of his image causes even Nixon to remark:
   "It's a shame a man has to use gimmicks like this to get elected." This book is helpful for anyone interested in propaganda and how publics can be manipulated. Hopefully, for journalists, it will provide guidance for how to read the reality behind the image."
2. Dov Grohsgal and Kevin M. Kruse, "How the Republican Majority Emerged," *The Atlantic*, Aug. 6, 2019, accessed May 8, 2023, https://www.theatlantic.com/ideas/archive/2019/08/emerging-republican-majority/595504/.
3. Author's note: Dixiecrats were southern Democrats dedicated to states' rights and segregation and who opposed the civil rights programs supported by the national Democratic Party.
4. Peter Suciu, "Social Media Remains A Source For News And A Breeding Ground For Pandemic Conspiracies," *Forbes*, Sep 3, 2021, accessed May 8, 2023, https://www.forbes.com/sites/petersuciu/2021/09/03/social-media-remains-a-source-for-news-and-a-breeding-ground-for-pandemic-conspiracies/?sh=fe54c45cb221.
5. Suciu, "Social Media Remains A Source For News And A Breeding Ground For Pandemic Conspiracies."
6. David Harvey, *A Brief History of Neoliberalism*, (Oxford University Press, 2005), 2.
7. Susan George, 1999 speech, "A Short History of Neoliberalism," *The Transnational Institute*, March 24, 1999, accessed Dec. 22, 2022, https://www.tni.org/en/article/short-history-neoliberalism.
8. Heather Cox Richardson, "Letters from an American," March 18, 2023, accessed March 19, 2023, heathercoxrichardson@substack.co.
9. Montgomery, "Beyond Neoliberalism – The Dawn of a New Civilisation."
10. George, 1999 speech, "A Short History of Neoliberalism."
11. Melinda Cooper, *Family Values, Between Neoliberalism and the New Social Conservatism*, (New York: Zone Books, 2017), 21, 313.
12. Nancy MacLean, *Democracy in Chains, The Deep History of the Radical Right's Stealth Plan for America*, (New York: Penguin Random House, 2017), 151.

13. MacLean, *Democracy in Chains, The Deep History of the Radical Right's Stealth Plan for America*, 234.
14. David Corn, *American Psychosis, A Historical Investigation of How the Republican Party Went Crazy*, (New York: Hatchett Book Group, 2022), 288.
15. Professor Deborah J. Lucas, MIT Sloan distinguished professor of finance and director of the MIT Golub Center for Finance and Policy, pegs the cost of the 2008-09 bailouts at $498 billion. Tam Harbert, "Here's how much the 2008 bailouts really cost," *MIT Management*, Feb. 21, 2019, accessed Dec. 20, 2022, https://mitsloan.mit.edu/ideas-made-to-matter/heres-how-much-2008-bailouts-really-cost.
16. Brendan Ballou, "Private Equity Is Gutting America — and Getting Away With It," *New York Times*, April 28, 2023, accessed May 7, 2023, https://www.nytimes.com/2023/04/28/opinion/private-equity.html.
17. Harvey, *A Brief History of Neoliberalism*, 48-50.
18. Corn, *American Psychosis, A Historical Investigation of How the Republican Party Went Crazy*, 319, 323.
19. Schmidt's appearance on the MSNBC Lawrence O'Donnell show, Feb. 8, 2022.
20. Ishaan Tharoor, "Trump's personality cult and the erosion of U.S. democracy," *Washington Post*, Aug. 19, 2022, accessed May 8, 2023, https://www.washingtonpost.com/world/2022/08/19/trump-cult-of-personality-democracy-erosion-united-states/.

CHAPTER FIVE

1. "Corrections - Report of The National Advisory Commission On Criminal Justice Standards and Goals, 1973," U.S. Dept. of Justice, Office of Justice Programs, NCJ Number 10865, written by the National Advisory Commission on Criminal Justice Standards and Goals, January 23, 1973, Foreword, accessed Sept. 19, 2022, https://www.ncjrs.gov/App/Publications/abstract.aspx?ID=10865.
2. "Corrections - Report of The National Advisory Commission On Criminal Justice Standards and Goals, 1973," U.S. Dept. of Justice, Office of Justice Programs, 1.
3. "Corrections - Report of The National Advisory Commission On Criminal Justice Standards and Goals, 1973," U.S. Dept. of Justice, Office of Justice Programs, NCJ Number 10865, written by the National Advisory Commission on Criminal Justice Standards and Goals, January 23, 1973, accessed Sept. 19, 2022, https://www.ncjrs.gov/App/Publications/abstract.aspx?ID=10865.
4. "Corrections - Report of The National Advisory Commission On Criminal Justice Standards and Goals, 1973," U.S. Dept. of Justice, Office of Justice Programs, 1.
5. "Corrections - Report of The National Advisory Commission On Criminal Justice Standards and Goals, 1973," 597.
6. "The Criminal Justice Standards and Goals of the National Advisory Commission, Digested from a National Strategy to Reduce Crime," Penn. Committee for Criminal Justice Standards and Goals, (1973), 45 – 51.
7. "The Criminal Justice Standards and Goals of the National Advisory Commission, Digested from a National Strategy to Reduce Crime," Penn. Committee for Criminal Justice Standards and Goals, 596.
8. The rate of incarceration has slowed since 2010, at least temporarily. "The combined state and federal imprisonment rate (the number of persons sentenced to more than one year in state or federal prison, per 100,000 U.S. residents) for 2020

(358 prisoners per 100,000 U.S. residents) represented a decrease of 15% from 2019 (419 per 100,000 U.S. residents) and a decrease of 28% from 2010 (500 per 100,000 U.S. residents)." Source: E. Ann Carson, "Prisoners in 2020 – Statistical Tables, Summary" *DOJ, Bureau of Justice Statistics,* (Dec. 2021), 1, accessed May 4, 2023, https://bjs.ojp.gov/library/publications/prisoners-2020-statistical-tables.
9. "Too many laws, too many prisoners: Never in the civilised world have so many been locked up for so little," *The Economist,* July 22, 2010, accessed May 4, 2023, http://www.economist.com/node/16636027. "Justice is harsher in America than in any other rich country."
10. Anthony Zurcher, "Report: US prison rates an 'injustice'," *BBC News,* May 2, 2014, accessed May 4, 2023, http://www.bbc.com/news/blogs-echochambers-27260073. "In 1973 the number of Americans in prison was around 200,000. By 2009 that number had grown to 1.5 million. An additional 750,000 Americans are held daily in local jails."
11. An American Society of Criminology report concludes that in 1980, in addition to an expanding prison population, there were another 600,000 people in jail, nearly 3.8 million on probation, and nearly 713,000 on parole—6.3 million adults–about one of every 31 adults–under some form of correctional supervision, a ratio of one of every 91 adults. Plus, there were 106,000 children in juvenile facilities (public and private), nearly 2,300 adults held by the military, 18,000 in U.S. Territories, and 1,600 in Native American jails and detention facilities. An additional several hundred thousand juveniles were on probation or parole, plus the same number of adults and juveniles on some form of pretrial supervision. Over seven million Americans were caught up in one of several correctional systems on any given day, making the correctional system one of the largest and most pervasive social control systems in the United States.
12. Rachael Bedard, Joshua Vaughn and Angela Silletti Murolo, "Elderly, Detained, and Justice-Involved: The Most Incarcerated Generation," City University of New York Law Review, Vol. 25, Issue 1, (Winter 2022) 162, accessed May 4, 2023, https://academicworks.cuny.edu/clr/vol25/iss1/15.
13. "Pew Report Finds More Than One in 100 Adults Are Behind Bars," Pew Center on the States press release, Washington, DC, Feb. 28, 2008. Based on 2006 statistics.
14. *See* Michelle Alexander, *The New Jim Crow: Mass Incarceration in the Age of Colorblindness* (New York, N.Y.: *The New Press,* 2010).
15. *The Sentencing Project,* "New Incarceration Figures: Thirty-Three Consecutive Years of Growth", (undated) accessed May 17, 2020, https://big.assets.huffingtonpost.com/incarcerationrates.pdf.
16. Deborah J. Vagins and Jesselyn McCurdy, "Cracks in the System: 20 Years of the Unjust Federal Crack Cocaine Law," *ACLU,* Oct. 2006, 1-2, accessed May 4, 2023, https://www.aclu.org/other/cracks-system-20-years-unjust-federal-crack-cocainelaw.
17. Vagins and McCurdy, "Cracks in the System."
18. In Virginia, Black people constituted 20% of state residents, but 43% of people jail (2015 figures) and 53% of people in prison (2017 figures). Source: "Incarceration Trends in Virginia," *Vera Institute of Justice,* Dec. 2019, accessed May 4, 2023, https://www.vera.org/downloads/pdfdownloads/state-incarceration-trends-virginia.pdf.
19. Alisa Roth, "The Truth About Deinstitutionalization," *The Atlantic,* May 25, 2021, accessed Aug. 17, 2022, https://www.theatlantic.com/health/archive/2021/05/truth-about-deinstitutionalization/618986/.

20. Alisa Roth, "The Truth About Deinstitutionalization."
21. Liji Thomas, "Prisoner Post Traumatic Stress," *News Medical*, Feb 27, 2019, accessed Oct. 30, 2022, https://www.news-medical.net/health/Prisoner-Post-Traumatic-Stress.aspx.
22. "Florida Mortality Study - Florida State FOP," a study conducted for the Florida legislature in 2011, accessed May 20, 2023, https://pdf4pro.com/view/floridamortality-study-florida-state-fop-1ca76b.html.
23. *The Compassion Prison Project*, https://compassionprisonproject.org/, accessed June 12, 2021.
24. Jeffrey Toobin, "The Mitigator: A new way of looking at the death penalty," *The New Yorker*, May 9, 2011, accessed May 4, 2023, http://www.newyorker.com/magazine/2011/05/09/the-mitigator.
25. "Incarceration and Reentry," *The Assistant Secretary for Planning and Evaluation* (ASPE), accessed May 19, 2023, https://aspe.hhs.gov/topics/human-services/incarcerationreentry-0.
26. Lauren-Brooke Eisen and Oliver Roeder, "America's Faulty Perception of Crime Rates," the *Brennan Center*, March 16, 2015, accessed May 4, 2023, https://www.brennancenter.org/our-work/analysis-opinion/americas-faulty-perception-crime-rates.
27. "What Caused the Crime Decline?" *National Institute of Corrections, U.S. Department of Justice*, Accession Number: 029758, 2015, accessed Sept. 12, 2022, https://nicic.gov/what-caused-crime-decline.
28. "Kentucky Passes Legislation to Address Out-of-Control Corrections Costs," *Right on Crime*, April 29, 2011, accessed May 4, 2023, https://rightoncrime.com/kentucky passes-legislation-to-address-out-of-control-corrections-costs/.
29. Christopher Hartney, "US Rates of Incarceration: A Global Perspective," *Evident Change*, formerly the *National Council on Crime and Delinquency*, Nov. 8, 2006, accessed May 19, 2023, https://evidentchange.org/publication/us-rates-of-incarceration-aglobal-perspective-focus/.
30. Steven Hawkins, "Education vs. Incarceration," *The American Prospect*, Dec. 6, 2010, accessed May 4, 2023, https://prospect.org/special-report/education-vs.-incarceration/. "Our penchant for punishment has come at a cost. We spend almost $70 billion annually to place adults in prison and jails, to confine youth in detention centers, and to supervise 7.3 million individuals on probation and parole. Indeed, confinement costs have claimed an increasing share of state and local government spending.
31. *The Sentencing Project*, "New Incarceration Figures: Thirty-Three Consecutive Years of Growth", (undated) accessed May 17, 2020, https://big.assets.huffingtonpost.com/incarcerationrates.pdf.
32. "State and Local Expenditures on Corrections and Education," *U.S. Dept. of Education, Policy and Program Studies Service*, July, 2016, accessed on Sept. 19, 2022, https://www2.ed.gov › rschstat › eval › other › expenditures-corrections-education› brief.pdf.
33. "State and Local Expenditures on Corrections and Education," *U.S. Dept. of Education*.
34. Jenni Gainsborough and Marc Mauer, "Diminishing Returns: Crime and Incarceration in the 1990s," *The Sentencing Project*, Sept. 2000, 3, accessed May 19, 2023, https://www.prisonpolicy.org › scans › sp › DimRet.pdf.
35. Matthew R. Durose, Alexia D. Cooper and Howard N. Snyder, "Recidivism of Prisoners Released In 30 States In 2005: Patterns From 2005 To 2010 – Update", *Bureau*

of *Justice Statistics*, Apr, 22, 2014, NCJ 244205, accessed May 4, 2023, https://www.bjs.gov/index.cfm?ty=pbdetail&iid=4986.
36. Mariel Alper, Matthew R. Durose and Joshua Markman, "2018 Update on Prisoner Recidivism: A 9-Year Follow-Up Period (2005-2014)," *Bureau of Justice Statistics*, May 23, 2018, accessed May 4, 2023, https://www.bjs.gov/index.cfm?ty=pbdetail&iid=6266.
37. Anastasia Chamberlen and Henrique Carvalho, "Feeling the Absence of Justice: Notes on our pathological reliance on punitive justice," *The Howard Journal of Crime and Justice*, Special Issue, first published March 22, 2022, 8, accessed May 4, 2023, https://doi.org/10.1111/hojo.12458.
38. Lauren-Brooke Eisen and Oliver Roeder, "America's Faulty Perception of Crime Rates," the *Brennan Center*, March 16, 2015, accessed May 4, 2023, https://www.brennancenter.org/our-work/analysis-opinion/americas-faulty-perception-crime-rates.
39. "What Caused the Crime Decline?" *National Institute of Corrections, U.S. Department of Justice*, Accession Number: 029758, 2015, accessed Sept. 12, 2022, https://nicic.gov/what-caused-crime-decline.
40. *Ibid.*
41. Chamberlen and Carvalho, "Feeling the Absence of Justice: Notes on our pathological reliance on punitive justice," 10.
42. Chamberlen and Carvalho, "Feeling the Absence of Justice: Notes on our pathological reliance on punitive justice," 9-10.
43. William J. Sabol and Thaddeus L. Johnson, "Justice System Disparities: Black-White National Imprisonment Trends, 2000 to 2020," *Council on Criminal Justice*, Sept. 2022, accessed Oct. 31, 2022, https://counciloncj.foleon.com/reports/racial-disparities/national-trends?campaign_id=9&emc=edit_nn_20221031&instance_id=76126&nl=the-morning&regi_id=48638959&segment_id=111572&te=1&user_id=23d568496d7dde089d8b5f2509703917. "In 2020, responses to the COVID-19 pandemic led to an unprecedented 15% drop in state prison populations, but that historic decline did not result in a change in Black-White imprisonment disparities."
44. Sabol and Johnson, "Justice System Disparities: Black-White National Imprisonment Trends."
45. *Ibid.*
46. *Ibid.*

CHAPTER SIX

1. *See* Vipassana as taught by S. N. Goenka in the tradition of Sayagyi U Ba Khin at https://www.dhamma.org/.
2. Bruce Perry and M. Szalavitz, *The Boy Who Was Raised as a Dog: and other stories from a child psychiatrist's notebook; what traumatized children can teach us about loss, love and healing.* (NY: Hachette Book Group, 2017), 364.
3. Luke 23:34 (KJV).
4. Margaret Wheatley, "Bringing Schools Back to Life: Schools as Living Systems," in *Creating Successful School Systems: Voices from the University, the Field, and the Community*, 3, edited by Francis Duffy and Jack D. Dale, (Norwood, MA.: Christopher-Gordon Publishers, September 1999). Wheatley's article is also available at http://www.margaretwheatley.com/articles/lifetoschools.html.

CHAPTER SEVEN

1. "April 4, 2020: A Day of Prophetic Mourning & Action," *Poor People's Campaign*, accessed May 17, 2020, https://www.poorpeoplescampaign.org/a-day-of-prophetic-mourning-action/.
2. John Stuart Mill, *On Liberty* (1859).
3. Author's note: The fourteen structures that I describe are not definitive; more could be added, but fourteen provides an in-depth analysis and is manageable. Other comparisons might include, for example, "from hypocrisy to integrity." Hypocrisy is prevalent in a punitive system because of the contradictions in its design. Those in control justify its harshness as fair because "justice is blind" (i.e., applied equally to all) while they apply exceptions when they deem it appropriate—many exceptions. In contrast, the unitive system depends on integrity for its existence; because of its consistency exceptions are not required.
4. David Bohm, *Wholeness and the Implicate Order*, (New York: Routledge, 1980), 17.
5. Ross London, *Crime, Punishment and Restorative Justice: From the Margins to the Mainstream*, (Eugene, OR.: Wipf & Stock, 2014), 315.
6. Mikhail Lyubansky, Dominic Barter, "Restorative Justice in Schools: Theory, Implementation, and Realistic Expectations," in: M.G.C. Njoku, L.A. Jason, R.B. Johnson (eds) *The Psychology of Peace Promotion. Peace Psychology Book Series*, (2019) 313. Springer, Cham. https://doi.org/10.1007/978-3-030-14943-7_19.
7. Jeff Latimer, Craig Dowden, and Danielle Muise, *The Effectiveness of Restorative Justice Practices: A Meta-Analysis*, The Prison Journal, Vol. 85, No. 2, June 2005 128. DOI: 10.1177/0032885505276969. A subscription is required to access.
8. John Braithwaite, *Restorative Justice and Responsive Regulation* (Oxford: Oxford University Press, 2002) 73.
9. Washington Post Editorial Board, "Virginia finally curbs solitary confinement—but not enough," *The Washington Post*, Mar. 10, 2023, accessed Mar. 12, 2023, https://www.washingtonpost.com/opinions/2023/03/10/virginia-solitary-confinement-prisons-bill/?wpisrc=nl_headlines&carta-url=https%3A%2F%2Fs2.washingtonpost.com%2Fcar-ln-tr%2F395cbc7%2F640c5f57d8b4d160754ae2a8%2F5972846c9bbc0f1cdce5cca5%2F35%2F58%2F640c5f57d8b4d160754ae2a8&wp_cu=fda45995c71a214e4d3bf226449e9287%7C4345BC5E037B29C2E0530100007F2828.

ARC 1: SECURITY/ORDER

1. *AZ Quotes*, citing R. Buckminster Fuller (1982), "Critical Path," p. 62, Estate of R. Buckminster Fuller, accessed May 18, 202, https://www.azquotes.com/quote/1039737.
2. David L. Hudson, Jr., "Is Cyberbullying Free Speech?", quoting Justin W. Patchin, *ABAJournal.com*, Nov. 1, 2016, accessed May 4, 2023, http://www.abajournal.com/magazine/article/is_cyberbullying_free_speech.
3. Paul Gowder, "The Rule of Law is for Controlling Power, Not Keeping Order," *Niskanen Center*, October 31, 2018, accessed May 4, 2023, https://www.niskanencenter.org/the-rule-of-law-is-for-controlling-power-not-keeping-order/.

4. "Auschwitz, Nazis and the Rule of Law," *Michigan State University College of Law, Institute for Comparative Law and Jurisprudence*, July 11, 2012, updated February 22, 2013, accessed May 4, 2023, https://msulawpolandprogram.wordpress.com/2012/07/11/auschwitz-nazis-and-the-rule-of-law-4-2/.
5. Arifa Akbar, "Mao's Great Leap Forward 'killed 45 million in four years,'" *Independent*, Sept. 17, 2010, accessed May 4, 2023, https://www.independent.co.uk/arts-entertainment/books/news/maos-great-leap-forward-killed-45-million-in-four-years-2081630.html.
6. Aysha Pamukcu, "10 Local Laws That May Be Doing More Harm Than Good," *ChangeLab Solutions*, Mar 26, 2018, accessed May 2, 2021, https://medium.com/changelab-solutions/10-local-laws-that-may-be-doing-more-harm-than-good-68c8ee8005c5.
7. Author's note: As a private citizen, I worked for and against various laws in Virginia for a number of years. It was during the time when many people acknowledged that Virginia's laws relating to adultery had become obsolete, even hypocritical, but the attempts to change them were met with the charge that the sponsor of the legislation was promoting adultery and was, therefore, immoral. Politics trumped good policy making.
8. J. A. Faris, "African Dispute Resolution: Reclaiming the Commons for a Culture of Harmony," a paper delivered at the Lawyers as Peacemakers and Healers: Cutting Edge Law Conference held at the Phoenix School of Law, Phoenix, Arizona, Feb. 22-24, 2013, 3.

ARC 2: GOVERNANCE

1. In contrast, the Inuit have over 50 words to describe snow and reportedly the Sanskrit language has hundreds of words for various states of consciousness, indicating the importance of snow and states of consciousness in those respective cultures. David Robson, "There really are 50 Inuit words for 'snow'," *Washington Post*, Jan. 14, 2013, accessed May 4, 2023, http://www.washingtonpost.com/national/health-science/there-really-are-50-eskimo-words-for-snow/2013/01/14/e0e3f4e0-59a0-11e2-beee-6e38f5215402_story.html, and David Gersten, *Are you Getting Enlightened or Losing Your Mind?* (New York: Harmony (1997) 128.
2. Author's Note: Those in control sometimes set up workarounds to regain control. The 13th Amendment ended the legal control slave owners exercised over those who had been legally deemed to be their property, but that did not address root causes. As a result, various forms of extralegal control arose that allowed segregation to be imposed and the lives of Black Americans continued to often be controlled.
3. Martin Luther King, Jr., "Pilgrimage to nonviolence," *The Christian Century*, April 13, 1960, accessed Oct. 7, 2022, https://www.christiancentury.org/article/pilgrimage-nonviolence.
4. Natasha Lennard, "Baltimore didn't go from peace to violence. The violence was there all along," *Splinter News*, April 28, 2015, accessed May 4, 2023, https://splinternews.com/baltimore-didnt-go-from-peace-to-violence-the-violence-1793847417.
5. Author's note: This is an example of rules being written for the benefit of the rule makers—those in control.
6. Bruce A. Dixon, "Lawless President Obama Chides Baltimore 'Criminals And Thugs,' Ignores Savagery Of Baltimore Police," *Black Agenda Report*, Apr. 29, 2015,

accessed May 4, 2023, http://www.blackagendareport.com/nonviolence-and-hypocrisy.
7. Peter Wagner and Wendy Sawyer, "Mass Incarceration: The Whole Pie 2020," *Prison Policy Initiative*, March 24, 2020, accessed May 4, 2023, https://www.prisonpolicy.org/reports/pie2020.html.
8. Greene, "Repeat performance: is restorative justice another good reform gone bad?," *Contemporary Justice Review: Issues in Criminal, Social, and Restorative Justice, see* footnote 8.
9. King, Martin Luther, Jr. "Pilgrimage to Nonviolence," *The Christian Century*, April 13, 1960, accessed Oct. 7, 2022, https://www.christiancentury.org/article/pilgrimage-nonviolence.

ARC 3: COMMUNICATION

1. *Merriam-Webster Dictionary*, s.v. "deception (*n.*)," accessed May 19, 2020, https://www.merriam-webster.com/dictionary/deception.
2. "Half of rape victims drop out of cases even after suspect is identified," *The Guardian*, Nov. 10, 2019, accessed May 7, 2021, https://www.theguardian.com/society/2019/nov/10/half-of-victims-drop-out-of-cases-even-after-suspect-is-identified.
3. Code of Virginia, § 20-107.1, "Court may decree as to maintenance and support of spouses," accessed May 5, 2023, https://law.lis.virginia.gov/vacode/title20/chapter6/section20-107.1/.
4. From the training program for incarcerated men and women, "Unitive Prison Culture Change," © 2023 by Unitive Prison Innovations, LLC.

ARC 4: ASSESSMENT

1. Luke 6:42 (TLB), "How can you think of saying to him, 'Brother, let me help you get rid of that speck in your eye,' when you can't see past the board in yours? Hypocrite! First get rid of the board, and then perhaps you can see well enough to deal with his speck!"
2. "Facts About the Death Penalty," *Death Penalty Information Center*, updated: March 24, 2021, accessed May 6, 2021, http://www.deathpenaltyinfo.org/FactSheet.pdf.
3. Pauline H. Tesler, "Goodbye Homo Economicus: Cognitive Dissonance, Brain Science, and Highly Effective Collaborative Practice," *Hofstra Law Review*, Volume 38, Issue 2, Article 7, 2009, 635-684, accessed May 18, 2020, http://scholarlycommons.law.hofstra.edu/cgi/viewcontent.cgi?article=1785&context=hlr.

ARC 6: STRENGTH

1. Rosa Flores and Rose Marie Arce, "Why are lawyers killing themselves?" *CNN*, January 20, 2014, accessed Jan. 1, 2023. https://www.cnn.com/2014/01/19/us/lawyer-suicides/index.html?iref=allsearch.
2. Flores and Arce, "Why are lawyers killing themselves?"
3. *Ibid.*

4. Virginia Code § 19.2-163. "Compensation of court-appointed counsel," accessed May 5, 2023, https://law.lis.virginia.gov/vacode/title19.2/chapter10/section19.2-163/.
5. Virginia Code § 1-200. "The common law. The common law of England, insofar as it is not repugnant to the principles of the Bill of Rights and Constitution of this Commonwealth, shall continue in full force within the same, and be the rule of decision, except as altered by the General Assembly." Accessed May 5, 2023, https://law.lis.virginia.gov/vacode/title1/chapter2.1/section1-200/.
6. Reva B. Siegel, "'The Rule of Love': Wife Beating as Prerogative and Privacy," *Yale Law Journal*, Vol.105, 2117, 2147-48 (1996) (discussing the English common law origins of the husband's right), cited in Jonathan L. Hafetz , "A Man's House is His Castle," *William & Mary Journal of Race, Gender, and Social Justice*, Issue 2, *William & Mary Journal of Women and the Law*, Volume 8, 190, Feb., 2002.
7. Siegel, "'The Rule of Love': Wife Beating as Prerogative and Privacy," 188.
8. Paul A. Lombardo, "Turning Back the Clock on Sexual Abuse of Children: Amending Virginia's Statute of Limitations," *Dev. Mental Health L.*, July-Dec. 1992, 21-22.
9. *Ibid., see also* Elizabeth Pleck, "Criminal Approaches to Family Violence, 1640-1980, in *Family Violence*, Vol.19, 29-30 (Michael Tonry & Norval Morris eds., 1989) (noting that "[n]o laws against family violence were passed from the time of the Pilgrim statute against wife beating in 1672 until a law against wife beating was enacted in Tennessee in 1850"; explaining that "[t]he general lack of interest in family violence can be attributed to the growing distrust of government interference in the family, the increasing respect for domestic privacy, and the waning zeal for state enforcement of private morality."
10. *See* Virginia Code § 8.01-220.1 "Defense of interspousal immunity abolished as to certain causes of action arising on or after July 1, 1981," accessed May 5, 2023, https://law.lis.virginia.gov/vacode/title8.01/chapter3/section8.01-220.1/. As late as 1997, however, the Virginia Supreme Court upheld such immunity in cases of unemancipated children, except in cases of intentional, willful or malicious torts, such as murdering one's child. *See* Pavlick v. Pavlick, 491 S.E.2d 602 (1997).
11. Lombardo, "Turning Back the Clock on Sexual Abuse of Children: Amending Virginia's Statute of Limitations," 41.
12. Constitution of Virginia - Article IV. Legislature, Section 14. "The General Assembly's power to define the accrual date for a civil action based on an intentional tort committed by a natural person against a person who, at the time of the intentional tort, was a minor shall include the power to provide for the retroactive application of a change in the accrual date. No natural person shall have a constitutionally protected property right to bar a cause of action based on intentional torts as described herein on the ground that a change in the accrual date for the action has been applied retroactively or that a statute of limitations or statute of repose has expired." Accessed May 18, 2023, https://law.lis.virginia.gov/constitution/article4/section14/.
13. *See* Jean Gebser, *The Ever Present Origin*, trans. Noel Barstad with Algis Mickunas, (Athens, Ohio: Ohio University Press, 1985).
14. Marty Schirn, "What Did Baha'u'llah Teach?" *Bahai Teachings*, Oct 22, 2020, accessed Jan. 10, 2023, https://bahaiteachings.org/what-did-bahaullah-teach/.

ARC 7: GUIDING MORAL PRINCIPLE

1. Howard Zehr, "Doing Justice, Healing Trauma: The Role of Restorative Justice in Peacebuilding," *Peace Prints: South Asian Journal of Peacebuilding*, Vol. 1, No. 1 (Spring 2008), 10, accessed May 5, 2023, http://www.academia.edu/2335779/Doing_Justice_Healing_Trauma_The_Role_of_Restorative_Justice_in_Peacebuilding.
2. Christina Caron, "Spanking Is Ineffective and Harmful to Children, Pediatricians' Group Says," *New York Times*, Nov 5, 2018, accessed May 5, 2023, https://www nytimes.com/2018/11/05/health/spanking-harmful-study-pediatricians.html?emc= edit_nn_20181105&nl=morning-briefing&nlid=4863895920181105&te=1.
3. Judy Klemesrud, "A New Idea in Discipline: Spanking," New York Times, Oct. 25, 1970, pg. 45, accessed May 5, 2023, https://timesmachine.nytimes.com/timesmachine/1970/10/26/86385916. html?pageNumber=45.
4. Caron, "Spanking Is Ineffective and Harmful to Children, Pediatricians' Group Says."
5. *Ibid.*
6. Author's note: Some argue that the results of the Stanford Experiment were because the experiment design was flawed—the way it was set up promoted the abuse. Perhaps, but such abuse also occurs in poorly run prisons and other environments that are hierarchical, judgmental and punitive when such abuse is condoned.
7. More information about the Stanford Experiment is available online at http://www.prisonexp.org/.
8. Author's note: I suggest that we need a new Stanford Experiment, one that looks at what happens when people who have a criminal record are put in a unitive system. I predict that this experiment would show that, in a unitive culture, the best would be brought out in most of the subjects being studied, despite their past, because Unitive Justice tends to encourage the positive side of human nature.
9. "Secrets of History: The C.I.A. in Iran," *New York Times*, (archived, undated) accessed May 19, 2023, https://partners.nytimes.com/library/world/mideast/041600iran-coup-timeline.html.
10. *Wikipedia*, s.v. "Alleged Saudi role in September 11 attacks,", accessed May 18, 2020, https://en.wikipedia.org/wiki/Alleged_Saudi_role_in_September_11_attacks. Two of the other attackers were citizens of the United Arab Emirates, one was Egyptian and one was Lebanese.
11. "Prince Sultan Airbase," *Global Security*, accessed May 18, 2020. http://www.globalsecurity.org/military/facility/prince-sultan.htm. (No longer available.)
12. Richard Sisk, "US Troops Are Likely Headed to This Saudi Air Base," Military News, Sept. 24, 2019, accessed May 5, 2023, https://www.military.com/daily-news/2019/09/24/us-troops-are-likely-headed-saudi-air-base.html.
13. Neta C. Crawford, "Human Cost of the Post-9/11 Wars: Lethality and the Need for Transparency – November, 2018," *Watson Institute of International and Public Affairs, Brown University*, 1, accessed May 5, 2023, https://watson.brown.edu/costsofwar/files/cow/imce/papers/2018/Human%20Costs%2C%20Nov%208%202018%20CoW.pdf.
14. Crawford, "Human Cost of the Post-9/11 Wars: Lethality and the Need for Transparency – November, 2018," 5.

15. Neta C. Crawford, "The U.S. Budgetary Costs of the Post-9/11 Wars - Sept. 1, 2021," *Brown University* and *Boston University*, 1, accessed May 5, 2023, https://watson.brown.edu/costsofwar/files/cow/imce/papers/2021/Costs%20of%20War_U.S.%20Budgetary%20Costs%20of%20Post-9%2011%20Wars_9.1.21.pdf.
16. Author's note: At the time the cited article was published, Maria J. Stephan was Director of Educational Initiatives at the International Center on Nonviolent Conflict. Erica Chenoweth was Assistant Professor of Government at Wesleyan University and a Postdoctoral Fellow at the Belfer Center for Science and International Affairs in the John F. Kennedy School of Government at Harvard University.
17. Maria J. Stephan and Erica Chenoweth, "Why Civil Resistance Works: The Strategic Logic of Nonviolent Conflict," *International Security*, Vol. 33, No. 1 (Summer 2008): 7–8, accessed May 5, 2023, https://www.belfercenter.org/sites/default/files/legacy/files/IS3301_pp007-044_Stephan_Chenoweth.pdf.
18. Stephan and Chenoweth, "Why Civil Resistance Works: The Strategic Logic of Nonviolent Conflict," 8-9.
19. *Ibid.*, 9.
20. *Wikipedia*, s.v. "West Nickel Mines School shooting," accessed May 19, 2020. https://en.wikipedia.org/wiki/West_Nickel_Mines_School_shooting.
21. Diana Butler Bass, "What if the Amish were in charge of the war on terror?" *Sojourners*, Oct. 11, 2006, accessed May 5, 2023, https://sojo.net/articles/what-if-amish-were-charge-war-terror.
22. "Mother of gunman who killed five Amish girls in 2006 cares for survivor of son's massacre," *Associated Press*, Dec. 9, 2013, accessed May 5, 2023, http://www.nydailynews.com/news/national/mother-amish-killer-cares-survivor-son-massacre-article-1.1542337.
23. *Ibid.*
24. Elahe Izadi, "The powerful words of forgiveness delivered to Dylann Roof by victims' relatives," *Washington Post*, June 19, 2015, accessed May 5, 2023, https://www.washingtonpost.com/news/post-nation/wp/2015/06/19/hate-wont-win-the-powerful-words-delivered-to-dylann-roof-by-victims-relatives/?utm_term=.26b0ea46dde7.
25. Nikita Stewart and Richard Pérez-Peña, "In Charleston, Raw Emotion at Hearing for Suspect in Church Shooting," *New York Times*, June 19, 2015, accessed May 5, 2023, http://www.nytimes.com/2015/06/20/us/charleston-shooting-dylann-storm-roof.html?_r=0.
26. Justin Worlan, "This Is Why South Carolina Raised the Confederate Flag in the First Place," *Time*, June 22, 2015, accessed May 23, 2023, https://time.com/
27. 3930464/south-carolina-confederate-flag-1962.
28. Matthew 5:39.

ARC 8: BENEFIT

1. *See* David Bohm, *Wholeness and the Implicate Order* (New York: Routledge, 1980).
2. *AZ Quotes*, "Without the human community, one single human being cannot survive," accessed May 29, 2023, https://www.azquotes.com/quote/680004.
3. Christie, "Conflicts as Property," 4-5.

4. Michel Foucault, *Discipline and Punishment: The Birth of the Prison*, trans. Alan Sheridan, (New York: Vintage Books, 1977) 272.
5. Lawrence S. Krieger and Kennon M. Sheldon, "What Makes Lawyers Happy? A Data-Driven Prescription to Redefine Professional Success," *George Washington Law Review*, Vol. 83 (2015) 554, accessed May 5, 2023, http://ir.law.fsu.edu/articles/94.
6. Krieger and Sheldon, "What Makes Lawyers Happy? A Data-Driven Prescription to Redefine Professional Success," 615.
7. *Ibid.*, 607.
8. *Ibid.*, 554.
9. *Ibid.*, 615.
10. *Ibid.*, 596.
11. *Ibid.*, 597-598.

ARC 9: SOCIAL FRAMEWORK

1. Author's note: For example, if you search "corruption in Congress" on the Internet, you are led to a multitude of news reports and studies, and Congress is just one part of a very large system.
2. Author's note: There are examples of a majority of our legislators, aspiring to serve the common good, passing laws that make corruption illegal, only to have judges, whom in most states are not elected, strike down those laws on one ground or another. See Citizens United v. Federal Election Commission, 558 U.S. 310 (2010), a U.S. Supreme Court decision that struck down as unconstitutional a federal law prohibiting corporations and unions from making large expenditures in connection with federal elections, giving them significant influence among legislators.
3. *Wikipedia* s.v. "Crew Resource Management," accessed May 19, 2020, https://en.wikipedia.org/wiki/Crew_resource_management.
4. "AGCS Aviation Safety Study: A review of 60 years of improvement in aviation safety," *Allianz Global Corporate & Specialty* (AGCS) (2014), 36, accessed May 19, 2020, https://www.agcs.allianz.com/content/dam/onemarketing/agcs/agcs/reports/AGCS-Global-Aviation-Safety-2014-report.pdf.
5. Alan Diehl, "Crew Resource Management...It's Not Just for Fliers Anymore." *Flying Safety*, *Allianz Global Corporate & Specialty* (AGCS) Vol. 50, no. 6, pp. 8-11, *USAF Safety Agency* (June, 1994).
6. *Wikipedia*, s.v. "Crew Resource Management," accessed May 5, 2023, https://en.wikipedia.org/wiki/Crew_resource_management.
7. "About TeamSTEPPS," *Agency for Healthcare Research and Quality*, accessed May 5, 2023, https://www.ahrq.gov/teamstepps/about-teamstepps/index.html.
8. John 13:34 (KJV).
9. Matthew 5:44, Luke 6:27 (KJV).
10. Rita Geno, "The Meaning of Namaste," Yoga Journal, Nov 12, 2018, accessed May 5, 2023, http://www.yogajournal.com/article/beginners/the-meaning-of-quot-namaste-quot/.
11. Email from Ahva Lenay describing what was shared in a group (August 16, 2017) (on file with author).
12. "Ranters" is a generic term for various maverick self-proclaimed messiahs, prophets and preachers who emerged in England in the late 1640s to mid-1650s. "The

Ranters," *BCW Project*, accessed May 19, 2020. http://bcw-project.org/church-and-state/sects-and-factions/ranters.

ARC 10: SAFETY

1. *Merriam-Webster Dictionary*.
2. "Scapegoats, the Bible, and Criminal Justice: Interacting with Rene Girard," *Mennonite Central Committee, New Perspectives on Crime and Justice*, February 1993, Issue no. 13, 41.
3. Daniel Goleman, *Social Intelligence: The New Science of Human Relationships*, (NY, NY, Bantam Books, 2006) 4.
4. Daniel Goleman, *Social Intelligence*, 5.
5. *The Spiritual Roots of Restorative Justice*, edited by Mihael L. Hadley, (Albany, NY: State University of New York, 2001) 68.
6. *Mennonite Central Committee*, endnote 2 above.
7. See Jean Gebser, *The Ever Present Origin*, trans. Noel Barstad with Algis Mickunas, (Athens, Ohio: Ohio University Press, 1985).
8. Author of *Discovering Agreement: Contracts That Turn Conflict Into Creativity* (American Bar Association, 2016). More information at www.discoveringagreement.com.
9. Peter Gabel, "The Bioenergetics of Authoritarianism", *Tikkun*, May 15, 2020, accessed May 6, 2023, http://www.tikkun.org/the-bioenergetics-of-authoritarianism.

ARC 11: GOAL

1. Gabel, "The Bioenergetics of Authoritarianism," 5-6
2. *Ibid.*, 6.
3. Margaret Wheatley, "Bringing Schools Back to Life: Schools as Living Systems", in *Creating Successful School Systems: Voices from the University, the Field, and the Community*, 3, edited by Francis Duffy and Jack D. Dale, (Norwood, MA.: Christopher-Gordon Publishers, 1999). Wheatley's article is also available at http://www.margaretwheatley.com/articles/lifetoschools.html.
4. Wheatley, "Bringing Schools Back to Life: Schools as Living Systems," 2.
5. See Tracey Pyscher and Brian D. Lozenski, "Throwaway Youth: The Sociocultural Location of Resistance to Schooling," *Equity & Excellence in Education*, (October 2014) 533, DOI: 10.1080/10665684.2014.958964, accessed May 6, 2023, https://www.researchgate.net/publication/268529252_Throwaway_Youth_The_Sociocultural_Location_of_Resistance_to_Schooling.
6. See "Test, Punish and Push Out: How 'Zero Tolerance' and High-Stakes Testing Funnel Youth into the School-To-Prison Pipeline," *Advancement Project*, (March 2010 Revised), accessed May 6, 2023, https://www.justice4all.org/wp-content/uploads/2016/04/Test-Punish-and-Push-Out-How-Zero-Tolerance-and-High-Stakes-Testing-Funnel-Youth-Into-the-School-to-Prison-Pipline.pdf.
7. Author's note: In Dominic Barter's Restorative Circle, he calls stage two "self-responsibility."

ARC 12: FOCUS

1. *Dictionary*, s.v. "context (*n.*)," accessed May 6, 2023, https://www.google.com/search?rls=as&client=gmail&q=definition%20of%20context%20&authuser=0.
2. Author's personal notes from Dominic Barter's training.
3. This limited focus is addressed by Kathleen Nolan, "Critical Social Theory and the Study of Urban School Discipline," in *Theory and Educational Research: Toward Critical Social Explanation*, edited by Jean Anyon, (New York, N.Y.: Routledge, 2009), 27-48.
4. Google Dictionary defines externality as "a side effect or consequence of an industrial or commercial activity that affects other parties without this being reflected in the cost of the goods or services involved." An example is a mining operation that pollutes the water supply by dumping the waste tailings into the water source (lake, river), then it has no responsibility for the negative impact on the health of those who drink the polluted water.
5. Alan Dettlaff, Kristen Weber, Maya Pendleton, Bill Bettencourt and Leonard Burton, "What It Means to Abolish Child Welfare As We Know It," *The Imprint*, Oct. 14, 2020, accessed June 18, 2021, https://imprintnews.org/race/what-means-abolish-child-welfare/48257.
6. *Wikiquote*, s.v. "Ronald Reagan," in Reagan's speech at the Republican National Convention, Platform Committee Meeting, Miami, Florida, July 31, 1968, accessed May 18, 2020. https://en.wikiquote.org/wiki/Ronald_Reagan.
7. Phillip Bivens and Bobby Ray Dixon, "When the Innocent Plead Guilty," *The Innocence Project*, Jan. 26, 2009, accessed May 6, 2023, https://www.innocenceproject.org/when-the-innocent-plead-guilty/. This article introduces 31 individuals who pled guilty to crimes they didn't commit—usually seeking to avoid the potential for a long sentence (or a death sentence). They served a combined total of more than 150 years in prison before they were exonerated.
8. *See* Pyscher and Lozenski, "Throwaway Youth: The Sociocultural Location of Resistance to Schooling," 533.

ARC 13: ANIMATION

1. "Synergistics," *Buckminster Fuller Institute*, accessed May 6, 2023, https://www.bfi.org/about-fuller/big-ideas/synergetics.
2. Owen Bowcott and Caelainn Barr, "Half of rape victims drop out of cases even after suspect is identified," *The Guardian*, Nov. 10, 2019, accessed May 23, 2021, https://www.theguardian.com/society/2019/nov/10/half-of-victims-drop-out-of-cases-even-after-suspect-is-identified.
3. Lincoln Caplan, "Rhetoric & Law: The double life of Richard Posner, America's most contentious legal reformer," *Harvard Magazine*, Jan-Feb. 2016, 55.
4. Caplan, "Rhetoric & Law: The double life of Richard Posner, America's most contentious legal reformer," 50.
5. The Sixth Amendment requires the "assistance of counsel" for the accused "in all criminal prosecutions."

ARC 14: ENERGY/SPIRIT

1. John 4:18 (NCV).
2. Bruce Lipton, *The Biology of Belief* (Santa Rosa, CA.: Mountain of Love/Elite Books, 2005), 151-154.
3. Bruce Lipton, *The Biology of Belief.*
4. German Lopez, "Ukraine's Warning," *New York Times*, March 27, 2020, updated March 28, 2022, accessed May 6, 2023, https://www.nytimes.com/2022/03/27/briefing/ukraines-russia-global-peace.html.
5. T. N. Hanh, *Being Peace* (Berkeley: Parallax Press, 1987) 62, quoted in *Toward a Socially Responsible Psychology for a Global Era.* edited by E. Mustakova-Possardt, M. Lyubansky, M. Basseches, & J. Oxenberg, (New York: Springer, 2014), Chapter 7, *Toward a Psychology of Nonviolence*, by Harry Murray, Mikhail Lyubansky, Kit Miller and Lilyana Ortega, pg. 154.
6. Author's note: I gratefully acknowledge Dominic Barter's Restorative Circles teachings as the primary source of our Unitive Justice Circle process; I am grateful for his teaching and work. His circle process aligns with many sources from which I learned on my journey of understanding Justice as Love; it gave me a means to replicate the experiential learning that is so important to understanding the transformation from punitive to Unitive Justice. For more information on Barter's process visit https://www.restorativecircles.org/.
7. Bruce Perry and Oprah Winfrey, *What Happened to You? Conversations on Trauma, Resilience, and Healing,* (Flatiron Books, 2021), 142.
8. Kerri O'Brien, "Bill extending Virginia's statute of limitations for child sexual abuse could soon go to Northam's desk," *ABC 8 News*, January 23, 2020, rev. February 19, 2020, accessed May 6, 2023, https://www.wric.com/news/politics/capitol-connection/proposed-bill-would-extend-virginias-statute-of-limitations-for-child-sex-abuse/.
9. A term used by Dominic Barter in an email, Nov. 1, 2017 (on file with the author).
10. John Lash, "Embracing the Feedback of Conflicts," *Juvenile Justice Information Exchange*, Sept. 13, 2013, accessed May 6, 2023, http://jjie.org/2013/09/13/op-ed-embracing-the-feedback-of-conflicts/105347/.
11. These quotes and additional outcomes achieved using the circle process are reported in peer-reviewed research by Lilyana Ortega, available in her article, *Outcomes of a Restorative Circles Program in a High School*, available at ResearchGate.net, https://www.researchgate.net/publication/301717483_Outcomes_of_a_Restorative_Circles_Program_in_a_High_School_Setting.

CHAPTER TEN

1. Molly Soeby, personal notes from Dr. Bruce Perry's lecture at NDSU Spring Professional Development Conference, Fargo, N.D. (2002). On file with Ms. Soeby.
2. Perry and Szalavitz, *The Boy Who Was Raised as a Dog: and other stories from a child psychiatrist's notebook; what traumatized children can teach us about loss, love and healing*, 18.
3. Bruce Perry and Oprah Winfrey, What Happened to You? Conversations on Trauma, Resilience, and Healing (New York: Flatiron Books, 2021), 26.
4. Perry and Winfrey, *What Happened to You? Conversations on Trauma, Resilience, and Healing*, 130-132.

5. Perry and Szalavitz, *The Boy Who Was Raised as a Dog: and other stories from a child psychiatrist's notebook; what traumatized children can teach us about loss, love and healing*, 50-52.
6. *Ibid.*, 364, 367.
7. *Ibid.*, 364.
8. There are now many resources to help us better understand trauma. An informative video that explains more about Adverse Childhood Experiences, called "How Childhood Trauma Affects Health Across a Lifetime," by Nadine Burke Harris is available on YouTube.com at https://www.youtube.com/watch?v=95ovIJ3dsNk (16 min.). You may take the ACE quiz and determine your own ACE score at https://www.npr.org/sections/health-shots/2015/03/02/387007941/take-the-ace-quiz-and-learn-what-it-does-and-doesnt-mean.
9. Margaret M.C. Thomas, Daniel P. Miller, Taryn W. Morrissey, "Food Insecurity and Child Health," American Academy of Pediatrics, October 1, 2019, accessed May 20, 2023, https://publications.aap.org/pediatrics/article/144/4/e20190397/38475/Food-Insecurity-and-Child-Health?autologincheck=redirected.
10. Jill Anderson, "The Effect of Spanking on the Brain: Spanking found to impact children's brain response, leading to lasting consequences," *Harvard Graduate School of Education*, April 13, 2021, accessed June 12, 2021, https://www.gse.harvard.edu/news/uk/21/04/effect-spanking-brainhttps://www.gse.harvard.edu/news/uk/21/04/effect-spanking-brain. Anderson is reporting on new research by Jorge Cuartas, David G. Weissman, Margaret A. Sheridan, Liliana Lengua, Katie A. McLaughlin, "Corporal Punishment and Elevated Neural Response to Threat in Children," *Society for Research in Child Development*, Apr. 9, 2021, https://srcd.onlinelibrary.wiley.com/doi/abs/10.1111/cdev.13565.
11. "Seven Early Experiences with Potential Benefits in Adulthood," *Psychologytoday.com*, Sept. 09, 2019, accessed May 18, 2023, https://www.psychologytoday.com/us/blog/the-athletes-way/201909/seven-early-experiences-potential-benefits-in-adult hood.
12. "8 Research-Based Reasons I Rose-Tint Some Childhood Memories." *Psychologytoday.com*, Sep 11, 2019, accessed May 18, 2023, https://www.psychologytoday.com/us/blog/the-athletes-way/201909/8-research-based-reasons-i-rose-tint-some-child hood-memories.
13. *Ibid.*
14. *Ibid.*
15. *Ibid.*
16. Perry and Szalavitz, *The Boy Who Was Raised as a Dog: and other stories from a child psychiatrist's notebook; what traumatized children can teach us about loss, love and healing*, 260.
17. *Ibid.*, 273.
18. *Ibid.*, 274.
19. *Ibid.*, 267.
20. This description of Dr. Perry's work is based on an article by Molly Soeby, "UJ Circle Processes Work – And Now We Know Why," that she wrote for the training manual used in the UJEd Whole School Program offered by the Alliance for Unitive Justice, July, 2022.

CHAPTER ELEVEN

1. Bruce Petersen, "Spiritual Evolution and the Law," *Tikkun*, July 3, 2015, accessed May 20, 2023, http://www.tikkun.org/nextgen/spiritual-evolution-and-the-law.
2. Wikipedia, s.v. "Loving-kindness," a version accessed on March 13, 2018. https://en.wikipedia.org/wiki/Loving-kindness. It was last edited on 23 August 2018 and no longer includes the list in this format. The author made minor edits to the original list.
3. Gillian Brockell, "A Black preacher, a White sheriff and the punch in the face that put Selma on the map," Washington Post, February 21, 2021, last visited Aug. 15, 2023. https://www.washingtonpost.com/history/2021/02/21/ct-vivian-selma-punch-sheriff/.
4. *See* C.T. Vivian's posthumous memoir, "It's in the Action: Memories of a Nonviolent Warrior," co-written with Steve Fiffer, (NewSouth Books, 2021).
5. Gillian Brockell, "A Black preacher. . ."
6. *Ibid.*
7. *Ibid.*
8. Engel v. Vitale, 370 U.S. 421 (1962).
9. Kennedy v. Bremerton School District, 597 U.S. ____ (2022).
10. Pete Williams, "Supreme Court rules for former coach in public school prayer case," *NBCnews.com*, June 27, 2022, accessed Dec. 27, 2022, https://www.nbcnews.com/politics/supreme-court/supreme-court-rules-coach-public-school-prayer-case-rcna31662.
11. Williams, "Supreme Court rules for former coach in public school prayer case."
12. A good video on this subject is "School Suspensions are an Adult Behavior" by Rosemarie Allen, available on YouTube.com at https://www.youtube.com/watch?v=f8nkcRMZKV4 (13 min.).
13. Author's note: UPCC is owned by Unitive Prison Solutions LLC, and is not part of AUJ, but it is based on Unitive Justice principles.
14. J. A. Faris, Professor, "African Dispute Resolution: Reclaiming the Commons for a Culture of Harmony," Address at the Lawyers as Peacemakers and Healers: Cutting Edge Law Conference at the Phoenix School of Law (Feb. 23, 2013).
15. Natti Ronel and Ety Elisha, "Positive Criminology: Theory, Research, and Practice," *Oxford Research Encyclopedia of Criminology*, online publication date: Feb 2020. DOI: 10.1093/acrefore/9780190264079.013.554.
16. *I.e.*, against the idea that inmates are inherently bad people so they cannot change.
17. Ronel and Elisha, "Positive Criminology: Theory, Research, and Practice."
18. Chamberlen and Carvalho, "Feeling the Absence of Justice: Notes on our pathological reliance on punitive justice," 17.
19. Ronald Benjamin, "Support Political Parties that Embrace Unitive Consciousness," *Aliran*, Oct. 20, 2022, accessed Oct. 30, 2022, https://aliran.com/web-specials/support-political-parties-that-embrace-unitive-consciousness.
20. Abigail Censky, "Heavily Armed Protesters Gather Again At Michigan Capitol To Decry Stay-At-Home Order," National Public Radio, May 14, 2020, accessed June 18, 20221, https://www.npr.org/2020/05/14/855918852/heavily-armed-protesters-gather-again-at-michigans-capitol-denouncing-home-order.

21. Chauncey Alcorn, "Gun stocks soared as a pro-Trump mob invaded the US Capitol Hill," *CNN Business*, Jan. 7, 2021, accessed June 18, 2021, https://www.cnn.com/2021/01/07/business/gun-stocks-capitol-rioters/index.html.
22. Jen Christensen, "Homicide is a leading cause of death in kids, and rates are rising, study finds," *CNN*, Dec. 19, 2022, accessed April 16, 2023, https://www.cnn.com/2022/12/19/health/homicide-child-death/index.html.
23. Martin Luther King, Jr., "The American Dream."
24. Perry and Szalavitz, *The Boy Who Was Raised as a Dog: and other stories from a child psychiatrist's notebook; what traumatized children can teach us about loss, love and healing*, 364.
25. Luke 23:34 (KJV).
26. Katherine Rose, "The Truth Behind Einstein's Letter on the 'Universal Force' of Love," Huffpost, Dec. 6, 2017, accessed Oct. 24, 2023, https://www.huffpost.com/entry/the-truth-behind-einsteins-letter-on-the-universal-force-of-love_b_7949032.